PADDY MACHIAVELLI

How to Get Ahead in Irish Politics

JOHN DRENNAN ～

Gill & Macmillan

Gill & Macmillan
Hume Avenue, Park West, Dublin 12
www.gillmacmillanbooks.ie

© John Drennan 2014
978 07171 5810 2

Typography design by Make Communication
Print origination by Síofra Murphy
Printed and bound by CPI Group (UK) Ltd, CR0 4YY

This book is typeset in Minion 12.5/15 pt.

The paper used in this book comes from the wood pulp of
managed forests. For every tree felled, at least one tree is
planted, thereby renewing natural resources.

A CIP catalogue record for this book is available from the
British Library.

5 4 3 2 1

CONTENTS

About the Author

John Drennan is a *Sunday Independent* political columnist, occasional broadcast pundit and the author of two books on Irish political life, *Cute Hoors and Pious Protestors* (2011) and *Standing by the Republic: 50 Dáil Debates that Shaped the Republic* (2012).

Praise for John Drennan

'There is a fierce intelligence and fierce independence at work here. No one escapes his gimlet eye, and he brings to the whole bizarre ecosystem of the Dáil a unique perspective: that of the insider who remains resolutely outside.'

Brendan O'Connor, *The Sunday Independent*

'John Drennan has a David Attenborough-like fascination with the unique traits and curious customs of pond life, though his creatures dwell in Leinster House. His storytelling style is stage Irish, and like a culchie Cicero, he laces his brilliance with bile. It is the politics of Paddy and in the tradition of Hall's Pictorial Weekly via Craggy Island.'

Gerard Howlin, *The Sunday Times*

'If Paddy really wants to know the story, generally he asks Drennan first.'

Lise Hand, *Irish Independent*

'Drennan is one of the best pundits in Ireland. He has an understanding of politics that is both instinctive and intellectual.'

Pat Leahy, *The Sunday Business Post*

'[Drennan] reads the political game like the sort of bookie who always leaves Cheltenham with a full satchel.'

Ivan Yates, *Newstalk*

ACKNOWLEDGMENTS

Thanks must first go to the dedicated, hardworking Gill & Macmillan staff who have put up with all of my tantrums and, in particular, my ever-patient editors, Fergal Tobin, Conor Nagle, Deirdre Rennison Kunz and Teresa Daly.

I would also thank the knowledge imparted, often against my will, about the ways of the world from the late Aengus Fanning and Anne and Eoghan Harris whose work constantly reminds us of the importance of journalism in a world that is strangely anxious to denigrate the profession.

Those colleagues who have been supportive are too many to mention and are also thanked but I reserve a special mention for Jason O'Toole.

And of course finally thanks to those who are close to me; in particular Tim Drennan, Micheál Drennan, Alice, Ciara and Caroline.

INTRODUCING OUR TALE

As princes cannot help being hated by someone, they ought, in the first place, to avoid being hated by every one …

It might appear strange that a 16th-century Italian political philosopher would provide us with the roadmap for the acquisition of political power in Ireland. In fact, the ongoing relevance of Niccolò Machiavelli's advice to politicians is not surprising, for *The Prince* is a study of human nature, and human nature does not change too much, whether we are referring to the Irish or our Italian Mediterranean cousins. The template set by both of these polities means that examining the qualities needed to become an Irish Prince runs the danger of evolving into a reductive 'celebration' of the politics of cynical amorality. But, whilst Irish politics and politicians would make such a task easy, that would be facile. It would also go against the precedent of *The Prince*, for whilst his reputation may have been set by Shakespeare's reference to that 'crooked Machiavelli', our theorist was a puritan idealist who believed in the republican virtues.

The passing of the centuries means that some differences exist between post-Renaissance Italy and our world. But they are qualitative differences mostly, for when it comes to the relationship between states, war has been replaced by economics, whilst in an Irish context at least, Machiavelli's warnings about mercenaries are today more applicable to top mandarins. And, just as Machiavelli concluded his outwardly amoral text with an emotional plea for someone to rescue the failed political system he lived in, now, sadly, we, some five centuries later, find ourselves in a similar broken polity waiting for a similar miracle.

In looking at the journey that our central character, Paddy Machiavelli, must make if he is to become a 'Dear Leader', our text explores the role of the ageless political virtues of dissimulation, empathy with the citizenry and the keen art of choosing the correct political scapegoat. We ask, Can the Irish Prince ever really be independent, or is it his role to eternally embrace the hot-water bottle of orthodoxy? Is it really true that our Aspirant Prince has no alternative beyond recognising that, as we are a peasant state, the best thing is to adopt pragmatic virtues?

Paddy Machiavelli also explores whether a fatal attraction exists between our political elite and the vices of the citizenry. Machiavelli may have noted that the best the Prince can do is to avoid being hated by all the citizens. We intend to ask if the desire of the modern Paddy Mac to be loved by everyone is why Ireland appears caught in an appalling loop where the citizens are fated to eternally repeat the cruel denouement suffered by the wistful habitués of *Animal Farm.*

PART ONE:
NOT SO NEW BEGINNINGS

Chapter 1 ❧

THE CHILD IS FATHER TO THE MAN — LEARNING TO TAKE THE LOW ROAD TO LOW OFFICE

… for men change their rulers willingly, hoping to better themselves … wherein they are deceived, because they afterwards find by experience they have gone from bad to worse.

On Paddy Mac's moment of perfection • the addiction of the sport • Rousseau's noble savage emerges from the womb • the joining of parties • be not a student prince • a CV fit for a crown • some peasants from the council to see you, dear • Ming, the ideal councillor • gimmicks • the great triumph of roundaboutery • silly photographs and Dún Laoghaire bath houses

When it is over and he is no longer the Prince, Paddy Machiavelli can always be consoled by the memory of that single moment of perfection. It is that all-too-brief state of joy after the last vote is counted and the last box sealed, where all that he has schemed and dreamed about lies before him, like a virgin bride. In that transcendent time, even the bonhomie of his media 'friends' appears genuine. And it may actually be, for in a Republic, the selection of a new Taoiseach is a moment of rebirth similar to when a royal family secures a new male heir. On that day, we embrace hope, if only for a moment, as our hero stumbles from the Plato's Cave of the cabinet talking about 'politics before people', our status as 'a fortunate country' or how 'Paddy likes to know the story'.

Of course, in the aftermath of the cheering the questions will begin:

Who are you?

How did you get here?

And why on earth do you want to be here anyway?

This book aims at the very least to explain to current and future Paddy Machiavellis how little miracles such as these come to pass.

If Paddy Machiavelli does want to end up in this enchanted place, the first piece of advice we will give may appear simple. But, in one regard it is the hardest of all, for if he is to ever become the Dear Leader, he must admit, if only to himself, that he is addicted to the sport of Irish politics. In time, we will teach our Aspirant Prince about the capabilities, vices and virtues required in order to become a Dear Leader, but the first step Paddy Mac must take is to admit that being a future Prince is his sole desire. Paddy Machiavelli may feel uneasy about making such a confession, for truth — be it speaking, knowing or being suspected of knowing it — is a dangerous variable in the world of Irish politics. But, our wise Aspirant Prince should always ensure that they know everything about their true selves. This may not always be an easy process, as David Norris discovered in such a torrid fashion in the Presidential election of 2011. However, if Paddy Machiavelli repeats the great error of poor Norris, and turns away from the reality of his life, he is like the general who does not know the strengths and weaknesses of his own army. Such men may occasionally win battles, but it is all down to luck, and luck is not a friend that you need if you are to be the Irish Dear Leader.

Paddy Machiavelli may also be reluctant to confess, since, normally, when addicts confront their demons, it is the stark prelude to abandoning what they most desire. The good news here is that, since politics is not yet illegal, confessing to his secret lust has no such consequences. Instead, admitting to the addiction is a form of release, for Paddy Machiavelli will be a happier creature when he reveals to himself that the core of his existence is politics. It is only when he admits that politics, like alcohol or drugs or a vocation, really is more important than friendship, family or possibly even money, that he can fully commit to that which he desires most. This, of course, should not occur in public. Instead, when speaking to the outside world Paddy Mac should make it clear that he can take or leave his political career. The reason for this is that once you are that thing called a politician, some are suspicious of your motives if you want something too much, whilst others will simply desire to hurt you as recompense for their own empty lives. But, in the secret chambers of his heart, our Aspirant Prince should be open about what he desires, if only so that he may understand the sacrifices that must be made.

When it comes to the impulses that generate this divine spark, no one can say if our Aspirant Prince's entry into politics is informed by nature or nurture. In general, though, the evidence tends towards the latter. The self-made man or woman can become Taoiseach in Ireland, but even someone as talented as Haughey had to marry into a dynasty in order to establish himself on the road to power. Paddy Mac will also find that the desire to become the Irish Prince, whether you are a commoner or a dynast, emerges early in life. This means it is generally infused with the warm, sepia tint of nostalgia that accompanies all childhood memories. He — and it is important to note that when it comes to describing our aspirant ruler we use the male gender, for a woman has never been Taoiseach — is generally aged about eight or nine. It is an impressionable age where, like Rousseau's noble savage, the template is still malleable. But, at that point, some commotion or drama will catch Paddy Mac's attention and enchant him. In simpler times, the source of that first innocent wonder would have been a torch-lit procession where flickering shadows cast by burning sods of turf hinted at the strange 'wink and nod' narrative of political life. Or perhaps the thirst began that day he realised his father, the local TD, was in some way special. Such a mix of nostalgic enchantment for an idealised past is embodied in the persona of Brian Cowen, in whose political career can be read an attempt to reconstitute the damage done to his complex psyche by the death of a loved father by recreating that life. Intriguingly, despite our status as a young country, Mr Cowen's predecessor, the supposedly youthful Bertie Ahern, and his grandfatherly successor, Mr Kenny, were both formed by a similar school of politics. There are lessons there for our friend Paddy Mac about how the top tier of Irish politics is more often than not an old man's game, which he would be wise to pick up early. Whatever the source, once the incubus of desire has glided in, Paddy Mac no longer resides with the ordinary race of men. Instead, like the lost knight in 'La Belle Dame Sans Merci' he is in thrall to the 'faery's child' of politics. And no amount of warning from 'pale kings' about how all Dear Leaders — be they Haughey, Albert or Bruton — end up 'alone and palely loitering' will chill his desire.

Before he gets to that place, Paddy Mac must, if he is not born into FF or FG, consider which party he will join. In taking such a decision he must understand that to become Taoiseach he has a choice of two. Once that is realised, happily, the choice is simplified further by the absence of any real ideological difference between Fianna Gael and Fine Fáil. However, should Paddy Mac decide not to leap into the alluvial mud created by the two great FG and FF rivers, then the road will be impossibly steep. If, for example, our Aspirant Prince has Labour-style tendencies, the first question he must ask is, could, through some freak of nature, someone from Labour ever be Taoiseach? The sad fate of those 'Gilmore for Taoiseach' posters flapping around on the pavements like fish stranded on a beach, after being frantically torn down from telegraph polls by Labour candidates trying to save their seats, should give Paddy Mac his answer.

So, given this is not an option, which of the two parties should he join? Given they are Coalition partners, crude logic would dictate that those possessing a Labour soul join Fine Gael. However, whilst FG will always be compatible partners for those troubled ones who have indulged in some youthful fooling around with the PDs or even the Greens, they are a toxic partner for anyone with a Labour hue. Paddy Mac should not be too hard on FG over their instinctive 'Upstairs, Downstairs' attitude to Labour, for the Blueshirts cannot refrain from behaving in the way that they do. It is, in a real way, the political equivalent of the sibling dilemma where the elder brother cannot disguise the belief he knows so much more about the world than his younger sibling, and then wonders why his domineering ways provoke such adolescent tempests. And, sadly, as is often the case when FG tries to overcompensate by treating Labour with exaggerated cautious respect, the patronising attitude just makes things worse.

This means that if Paddy Machiavelli comes from a left-wing background, he should join FF. It will help that, like FG before 2011, the currently decommissioned soldiers of destiny are always grateful for a bit of talent to take the bare look off things. In selecting between this duo, if he has a choice, our Aspirant Prince should realise that there is more space for the self-made man in FF, as the careers of Charles Haughey, Jack Lynch, Albert and Bertie show. Outside of noting that FF is going through one of those unique episodes where they are in a humble, apologetic mode, those who are of the left should consider one other critical factor. Unlike Labour, which often appears to be far more comfortable dealing with those who would reform the working classes — as distinct from dealing with the actual working class themselves — FF is instinctively closer to the working man. If, by contrast, Paddy Mac is on the right of the political spectrum, he should confine his attentions to Fine Gael. It would be wise, however, for him to be circumspect about revealing such tendencies, for, in their secret souls, Fine Gael is as unnerved by ideologues as Fianna Fáil. Fine Gael just manages to hide it a little better. The best thing our ideologue can do, therefore, is to let FG get used to him first and then come out of the closet.

Conventional theory holds that for those who are not the children of dynasts a career in student politics offers a route to the Dáil. Certainly, becoming a student prince will get you attention. But, is attention what you want or need? Student politics may offer Paddy Mac a useful apprenticeship in the important arts of dissimulation and the crueller realities of human nature, but in terms of usefulness, the best that will be achieved is that it may teach our Aspirant Prince about his utter unimportance in the greater scheme of things. Sadly, since a high-profile career in student politics is characterised by high levels of self-importance, and a capacity to talk at great length and quite noisily about everything, without actually knowing anything, this happens rarely. In time, Paddy Machiavelli will learn that such tendencies will not rule him out of high ministerial office or even the leadership of the Labour Party. But, he will need more than these unfortunate traits if he is to some day be seen swinging on the top of the political tree.

That is not to say Paddy Machiavelli should eschew the life of student politics, for a statement of modest intent can do little harm. But, Paddy Mac should target key posts such as Entertainment Officer, where he can learn the key arts of looking after people, finding cheap beer, doing favours, partying and cultivating friends. These, he will find, are more useful than making speeches on a lorry parked outside the Dáil beside indifferent bearded ICTU trade unionists and opposition politicians who secretly despise him. Far better instead, and it is rarely that we will say this, that he follows the path of Biffo in cultivating the Students' Union Bar and a reputation for being an unthreatening character and great lad all round. And it could indeed be argued that, the nature of the Irish psyche being what it is, the Aspirant Prince would be better off joining a winning Sigerson Cup team than engaging in campaigns to bring Fair Trade coffee into public life.

In building his political profile, our Aspirant Prince must attend carefully to his CV. In particular, a degree must be secured, for life is no longer quite as simple as it was in those halcyon days when Paddy Machiavelli essentially inherited a small farm, the village pub, the grocer's shop, the undertaker's, and, finally, in his late 40s to early 50s, marriage and his father's immaculately preserved seat. In truth, such a career would not be the worst apprenticeship in political life, for it is hardly accidental that our tougher, more courageous politicians secured their apprenticeships in the rough and tumble of the cattle and dog-food trades. But we are a more enlightened state now, one that even, apparently, has its own 'smart' economy.

Paddy Mac should not, however, secure a business degree. A degree of the arts variety may be as useful as one of those 17th-century Grand Tours that our aristocrats used to indulge in. But, if he is truly addicted, Paddy Mac should recognise that a business degree takes too much effort, which distracts the Aspirant Prince from those important alcohol-consuming, network-building skills he should perfect in college. And, more critically still, such a degree makes the voters skittish, for the electorate at best tolerate the notion that politicians might be more intelligent than their good selves. There are other important reasons why Paddy Machiavelli should attempt to avoid as many connections as possible with business. Irish businessmen, or some of them at least, believe in a world of order, logic, planning and enthusiasm, and this really is not at all how Irish politics — and, in particular, the civil service that Paddy Machiavelli will someday theoretically run — actually operates. This dissonance means that the businessman in politics swiftly becomes fretful. Unfortunately, this is confused with arrogance, for Irish voters prefer harmless, nice-but-dim chaps. Therefore, they will always rate those who desire to regulate employment above those who want to create it.

For similar reasons, it is not wise for Paddy Machiavelli to go into academia. The classic example of the unsuitability of the intellectual for a career in Irish politics is Alan Dukes, who, it is alleged, once informed a less-than-awed audience: 'I am pure logic.' Unfortunately, Mr Dukes discovered to his subsequent cost that the Irish electorate do not really like logic at all, and they certainly do not like it in their political leaders. It also did not help that on becoming leader of Fine Gael, Mr Dukes appeared to go slightly mad. But, in its own way, it should be said that this was an entirely logical response to becoming the leader of Fine Gael. Some will argue that Garret FitzGerald provides Paddy Machiavelli with a template for the successful public intellectual. However, in opposition, Dr FitzGerald was more of a national grand-uncle, whilst it also helped his cause that the country was being run by an avaricious egotist who appeared to be intent on running the state over a fiscal cliff, in order to assuage his political and financial needs. And, once Garret became Taoiseach and attempted to remake the country in his intellectual image, the electorate could not wait to defenestrate poor Garret and return to the not-so-tender embrace of the avaricious egotist.

One other critical factor in Paddy Mac's career choice is securing a job that provides our man with a lot of excess time. Being a teacher, for example, is a good choice, for whether his interest lies in politics or building or training hurling teams — and the difference between the three is often a matter of degree — teaching is the job for our man Paddy. Outside of the time factor, it helps that, like politics, teaching is not too challenging intellectually. Instead it develops far more critical skills necessary for political success, such as a capacity to talk for hours on end.

Alas, Paddy Machiavelli will, as part of his apprenticeship, have to spend some time in local government. When it comes to this trade, the attitude of the electorate, let alone the higher echelons of society, is captured in the moment when the wife of a Fine Gael frontbench grandee, Gerard Sweetman, opened the door to a group of local councillors and trilled, 'Some peasants are here to see you, Gerard.' But, ultimately, outside of blood, the real route to power is provided by the humble council seat. The council may be somewhat despised by the political glitterati of the media, but it is the school for scandal that will guide Paddy Mac on to the low road to low office. He will sometimes dream of evading the political equivalent of national service, but it is rare indeed that a successful candidate will take the easy route of being ushered into the constituency by a smiling Dear Leader. Indeed, it is significant that those who are most often parachuted into constituencies are high-flying lawyers, academics and businessmen. Were such creatures more aware of the political world, their suspicions about their potential to actually win a seat would be aroused by the delight with which their candidacy is met by the experienced local TD. Instead, buoyed by a yet unblemished ego, they are not at all troubled by reality until the day of the count, when our barrister candidate quietly departs after the fourth count with a grand total of 1,500 first preferences.

So what sort of a councillor should our Aspirant Prince endeavour to be? The first and most critical lesson Paddy Machiavelli should learn is that he must create an appearance of utter guilelessness. His ambition is to cut the throat of one of the constituency TDs, but, whilst they will obviously suspect this, having taken the same route themselves, for now Paddy Mac must adopt the persona of a humble local representative who is genuinely fascinated by the Tidy Towns Committee, the great issue of the hanging basket and how it might look at you, the chamber of commerce, young people and their troubles and, perhaps most critically of all, the roundabout. It may be tough for our Aspirant Prince to put on his cloth cap and discard his interests in the European Union stance on democratic legitimacy, but Paddy Mac, now that he has joined the land of the Lilliputians, has no choice but to fret about the ban on smoking in children's playgrounds, or dog dirt on the pavement. These he will endow with a small degree of dignity by calling them 'the people's issues'.

A great list of enemies, including primarily the council whose interests you theoretically serve, must be compiled. These include rates, since Paddy Machiavelli is inevitably *for* enterprise. It is something of a small problem that he is also opposed to all the cutbacks in services that might be necessitated by the cuts in income he is proposing. Paddy, though, need not worry too much about any cognitive dissonances, since he will learn quite early in the game that logic is generally an orphan in Irish politics. In this case, happily any illogicality is resolved by ensuring that Paddy Mac's chief opponents will be the County Manager and the great race of bureaucrats who constantly thwart all his proposals for reforms because they have to actually run the place. This small fact does not of course matter, for one of the great skills that Paddy Machiavelli must nurture is the art of creating scapegoats for the public to rail against. Paddy Mac must also, amidst this festschrift of negativity, find the occasional thing to be for. And, put at its simplest, he must be for 'the people', whoever they may be.

Luke 'Ming' Flanagan is, in many respects, the prototype of the ideal councillor. The great genius of 'Ming' is that his elevated narcissism facilitated the investiture of every act he took with a level of high dignity. Mr Flanagan was also wise enough to use his councillor's salary as some political variant of the farmer's dole. Ancestral notions of snobbery mean that the electorate will never elect a man on the dole to the Dáil. But, if he is a gainfully employed (or elected) 'community activist', then he is a different kind of creature entirely. Just as training youth soccer teams saw Mick Wallace carried shoulder high into the Dáil, Ming's attempts to scrape the doings of Roscommon's feral dogs from children's playgrounds — while making sure everyone heard tell of these selfless acts of hygiene — was as good a way of getting into Leinster House as all that fuss about ideology. Indeed, it might even be a better way, for no one is ever going to feel threatened by a man wearing a hemp jumper and brandishing a pooper scooper. This secular clericalism even led to a fool's pardon being given to the cannabis smoking, where Ming evolved from being the Roscommon equivalent of Scarface to a grand fellow who enjoyed a quirky little foible on the lines of the liking of some old ladies for Buckfast Tonic Wine. It also helped immeasurably that Ming had a unique talent for the Irish art of scapegoating.

Outside of the politics of safety first and of whataboutery — as in, what about my constituents, what about the big salaries the bureaucrats are getting and what about all the huge projects the next constituency is getting — if one was to define the essence of what it takes to be a successful county councillor, it might be described as being a case of learning to love the roundabout. For some, this might appear to be a prosaic sort of thing. The councillor, though, must perceive the construction of the roundabout or the cycle lane as an act of love. Egypt has its pyramids and the Sphinx, but the aspirant councillor must aim somewhat lower. And, of course, the joy of the roundabout is that it too is part of the great orthodoxy of health and safety, which is the latter-day equivalent of being sound on the national question. Paddy Machiavelli will swiftly learn that if he can wrap the mantle of health and safety around him, he will soon be perceived to be a doer who is at home with the concerns of the citizen. Better still, he will be poised to tap into the great well of scarcely suppressed hysteria that guides public life in Ireland. In time, for example, he may follow up his roundabout triumph with a fatwa on dogs running on beaches. Ultimately, he might even reach the heights of the great apotheosis of the horse nappies in Killarney, where the unfortunate horses of the town now wear nappies to appease the delicate nostrils of the great bureaucrat panjandrums who actually run councils.

Outside of wrapping the nurse's uniform of health and safety around his persona, our councillor must also develop a capacity to enjoy being photographed doing silly things. Acquiring a reputation for being photogenic is also of critical importance for Paddy Machiavelli, who must learn that to be loved by the camera is more critical than anything else in modern politics. This is particularly the case if you are a female candidate, for the Dear Leader of your party loves nothing more than to be snapped beside a set of youthful women whose names he can never remember. For Paddy Mac, being photogenic proves that he is a 'good sport' and 'a threat to no man, beast or woman'.

Paddy Mac should, though, also be careful about the silly photographs. Being snapped beside scantily clad models is no longer popular, as there is a little too much of the hubris of the Celtic Tiger attached to it. Instead, our man should endeavour to be captured engaging in sporting activities. Bog snorkelling, for some strange reason, appears to be quite attractive, as does anything involving running, sweating, cycling or other variants of pain. Such activities are important, given that they tend to involve the loss of weight, and politics is, alas, a trade that is not available to those who look as though they need a spell in a fat club. In this regard, our wise Aspirant Prince should also associate himself with activities such as organic gardening, for now that citizens are no longer interested in ideology, religion or poetry, their sole remaining obsession is food. Of course, in this new age of hyper-morality, he should be associated with healthy food, as distinct from the kind that requires slaughtering or mechanised production. It is an act of spiritualism to be photographed beside organic courgettes, organic trees, organic greenery and organic smiling children, as distinct from unhealthy things, such as cigarettes, cakes and ale. Instead, in a variant of that post-World War II era where Oliver J Flanagan used to cycle around Laois with 'here comes Oliver J' on the front and 'there goes Oliver J' on the back, the most valuable canvassing item an aspirant urban TD could invest in is a bicycle. Sadly, he will then have to learn how to ride it, but if Boris Johnson can do it then all things are possible.

Though our advice to the conventional party man is to eschew excesses of controversy, it is also important that Paddy Mac acquires some form of gimmick to help him stand apart from the herd. One of the better examples of this particular strategy was the decision by the Fine Gael TD Brendan Griffin, in Election 2011, to volubly promise the electorate of Kerry that he would quite happily give half his salary back to the taxpayer, if elected. In fairness, Mr Griffin did very publicly keep that promise. However, he also hired his wife as a secretarial assistant and his cousin Tommy Griffin as a PA, at the expense of the taxpayer. But, who reads the fine print in such affairs? And anyway Brendan is now sweetly ensconced in the Dáil at the expense of his less than happy FG running mate, Tom Sheahan.

Ultimately, the iron discipline that Paddy Machiavelli must apply to himself is to think both small and local. Nothing epitomises the importance of this more than the curious triumph of Richard Boyd Barrett, whose primary objective is to bring the capitalist system to its knees. Oddly enough, the electorate of Dún Laoghaire were less than enthused by such grand designs. Instead, the arrival of Boyd Barrett to the Dáil was fuelled by the more prosaic issue of the Dún Laoghaire bath house. It was a bit of a step from masterminding the downfall of world capitalism to the 'restoration of the Victorian heritage' of the seafront. Indeed, one might even have thought that Boyd Barrett would wish to erase all traces of our imperial past. But, when 5,000 votes are marching to save a swimming pool, an Aspirant Prince must respond to the spontaneous revolution of the South Dublin petite bourgeoisie. And, in a South Dublin ward, Paddy Machiavelli, or in this case Paddy the Trotskyite, must learn that, when it comes to the sort of issues that win elections, derelict bath houses are streets ahead of the fall of capitalism.

Chapter 2 ∿

CULTIVATE YOUNG COLLEAGUES TO SUBVERT THEIR AMBITIONS

Because this is to be asserted in general of men, that they are ungrateful, fickle, false, cowardly, covetous …

Beginnings • cultivating friends; meeting the 'lads' • the sad tale of wandering Aodhán • courtly intrigue and the Dáil bar • welcome to the slim club • 'cappuccino kids' • dealing with the 'ladies' • love and marriage (to an Irish girl, please) • and the hiring of family members

So, the great moment has finally arrived. Paddy Machiavelli has either been the beneficiary of a landslide, his constituency rival has died or he has done a Bertie in Drumcondra-style execution of the *ancien régime*. Whatever the reason, through some little miracle Paddy Machiavelli has, at the count, experienced for the first time the opium of being hoisted onto heaving shoulders. He has had a lick of that elixir called political success and there is no way back for him now.

The moment Paddy Mac walks through the gates of Leinster House resembles that equivocal moment of unblemished perfection in *The Picture of Dorian Gray*, where the paint has just dried on the canvas. Paddy Mac knows nothing yet of his ancestor's cautious warning about the fickle nature of men. Or, if he does, then for one day at least, he should allow himself to escape from such realities. Instead, all is brightness and joy, right down to the shiny new suit bought in Marks & Spencer, for it is not good for Paddy Machiavelli to appear too flashy by arriving in the stripes of Louis Copeland.

It is important that Paddy Mac realises that this rule applies to more than suits, for, like a cute new curate in his first parish, our Aspirant Prince must avoid flamboyance in all things. But, on the first day, this is particularly critical because the arrival of TDs can define their reputation for a decade. This reality is evidenced by the horrified reaction of the austere Jack Lynch to the first incarnation of Pádraig Flynn. In a classic example of how a grand entry can set your image in stone — or this occasion Flynnstone — when it came to this most unique of Jack's many 'accidents' in 1977, an incredulous Lynch attracted by the 'particular hullabaloo as a man in a white suit and polka-dot shirt was shouldered to the front door' of the Dáil asked, 'Who in the name of God is that?' The tone of the question did not suggest that Lynch was planning to promote the Mayo special one any time soon.

White suits are not fashionable at the best of times, but Paddy Machiavelli would be wise to be circumspect in more matters than his appearance. In a place where even party colleagues can be bitter enemies, depending on circumstances, his first priority should be the cultivation of allies. Political friends are the rarest and most disposable of creatures, but, no matter what Paddy Machiavelli might think, they are a necessity. A politician who has no friends is being honest about his ambitions. But, such a stance fails to comprehend the reality of the boarding-school mentality in Leinster House. This ethos of Tom Brown's schooldays crossed with the world view of Sir Desmond Glazebrook in 'Yes Minister', who correctly believed that the apex of fiscal theory was that 'chaps always look after other chaps', means that the Leinster House 'chaps' are not at ease with 'chaps' who are not happy to be part of the herd. The political sole trader is tolerated. But, they are known and are regarded with a fierce suspicion by a hierarchy who didn't get to where they are today by favouring lone wolves.

Though he must make friends in Leinster House, it is also terribly important that our Aspirant Prince retains a little spike of ice in his soul, for if our man is to get on in the world, he must be prepared to betray them at a moment's notice. Paddy Mac might, in his first few months, think it terribly cynical that he should be prepared to wound even his closest friends. The history of Leinster House shows, however, that he will generally at some point have to shank a dear 'colleague'. Richard 'the lesser' Bruton, Enda's long-term wingman on brainy things, was the one who attempted to snatch the chalice from Enda's lips right at the point of power. And when it came to the last months of Haughey, those who finished him off with bleats of 'Ah, Boss, sure maybe you've suffered enough' were the old Country and Western gang of Pee Flynn, Albert Reynolds and Seán Doherty — the wild men who had borne him with such triumph all the dead years ago. Lest you feel sympathy for Haughey, he too had perpetrated the cruellest of betrayals on Brian Lenihan. The then Tánaiste might have been Haughey's friend from the 1960s, but when faced with the prospect of losing a final desultory year on the less-than-merry-go-round of politics, Mr Haughey still sacked Lenihan right in the middle of the latter's run for the Presidency, after Dessie O'Malley had put on the well-worn PD black cap.

Such necessities must not deter our Aspirant Prince from his critical initial task of becoming 'one of the lads'. Should he need encouragement in this regard, one of the most poignant case studies in the dangers of separating from the herd is provided by the Labour TD Aodhán Ó Ríordáin. When he arrived in the Dáil, our exile from 'The West Wing' (for, truly, this is Aodhán's and new Labour's spiritual home) appeared to possess all the qualities required for success. Aodhán is pro-choice, but discreetly so, unless he is being taped. He is viscerally against Fianna Fáil. He is for the working class in a distant, paternalistic sort of way that sighs at their unreconstructed attitudes on matters such as the purchasing of the *Daily Sun*; he is also passionately for the Sancerre-sipping, RTÉ-loving Soviet of Sandymount. In those first days after he was elected, Aodhán was the special child of the Dear Leader Eamon Gilmore, who barely tolerated those old-fashioned rural TDs who are needed to make up the sort of numbers that gets you the extra seat in cabinet for the Sandymount set.

The attitude of the Labour mandarins to the latter was epitomised by the dismissive characterisation of a group of the more truculent Troglodytes as being 'the sort of fellows who still eat hairy bacon every day for dinner'. Aodhán is, by contrast, more of a child of the new age of sushi. Unlike 'the hairy bacon gang', Aodhán is dapper, but in an austere sort of way. He used to have a blog — and he has his little Twitter account — and, inevitably, he was a public sector worker. And unlike those chubby, working class-style, full breakfast-eating, pint-guzzling, querulous union leaders who are such an embarrassment, in the young Mr Ó Ríordáin was the shining example of the public sector worker 'higher ethic' that Mr Gilmore was so fond of.

Predictably, given his profession as a primary school teacher, Aodhán was accompanied everywhere he went with the sort of grizzling cloud of cantankerous moral seriousness we had not seen in Leinster House since the great age of Fergus Finlay. It was a persona that sparked unease in many quarters, but whatever about the rest of us, Labour tends to like that sort of thing. To be fair, Paddy Mac should note that Aodhán was not opposed to laughter. It was just that, rather like alcohol, Labour's new young man about town believed it should be endured in manly moderation. Aodhán could not be at the laughter for more serious reasons, because he was openly ambitious for office, and quick as you can, please. You might be surprised that this ambition did not damage Aodhán with his bosses. However, political hierarchies tend to like thrusting young TDS, so long as they are not too threatening, because they create the impression of vigour and dynamism within the party. Their thirst for the catnip of publicity, where attention is often confused with achievement, means that they can make for a more useful cat's paw than their wiser, less ambitious colleagues when Sean O'Rourke or Pat Kenny is looking for some innocent to murder.

Aodhán's ambitions did, however, lead to serious problems lower down the food chain. There is no harm in politicians acquiring the sweet, gentle and modest characteristics of our ministers when they actually become one. But, if you do so without having the job, and more important still, the power that comes with it, you are a hollow man. And, once your own discover this and start to mock you by calling you 'Minister' behind your back, then you are in serious trouble. The problem with Aodhán and the Labour 'lads' was that Ó Ríordáin forgot there were a lot of other fairly ambitious new fellows wandering around on a similar point on the political pay scale. And though they still smiled at him, the Labour 'lads' — and ladies too — did not appreciate Aodhán's kindly decision to become their spiritual leader without bothering with mere formalities such as an election.

Unfortunately, this meant that when Aodhán found himself engaged in a risible series of political controversies over issues as varied as his views on Monaghan homophobes, or the proposal by one of his constituency organisations that senior public servants be screened to ensure that they do not show 'inappropriate deference' to the Catholic Church, there was no friend waiting to help. This absence undoubtedly played a role in the unravelling of Ó Ríordáin's political profile. Were the 'lads' on board, someone would have taken Ó Ríordáin aside when the bright new TD suddenly began to evolve into a more refined version of Luke 'Ming' Flanagan. Instead, there were no helping hands to guide Aodhán away from trouble when he began to display unnerving symptoms of the common, but generally suppressed, political gene of self-piteous belief that the world, and in particular the media, were against him.

Actually, the truth was that both were indifferent. It would be a lie to say that watching political kittens drown isn't fun, but we actually want politicians to succeed. However, when a politician starts to lecture the media on its vices and its indolence, then, like the sleeping dog that has been kicked, it will turn on him. Sadly, the various scrapes that Aodhán landed in didn't merely alienate his backbench colleagues, or a media pack that has more things to be doing with itself than massaging the feelings of an eternally hurt backbench TD. Once he became a difficulty, a leadership who had enough problems of its own to be dealing with disappeared, and Aodhán was literally left to fend for himself. Now, as Aodhán wanders lonely as a cloud (of the grey variety) through Leinster House, he looks every bit the one-term TD. It's a cruel old world, for outside of suffering from an excess of egotism, he has not done anything terribly wrong. The bitter truth, though, is that in the scale of the Leinster House ocean, poor Aodhán is a grain of sand. And the only grain of sand that is smaller or more disposable than a Labour TD who has no political friends is a lost future Labour leader.

As part of his campaign to become — or, more accurately, to 'resemble' — one of the 'lads', Paddy Machiavelli must also swiftly master the curious geography of Leinster House. New entrants may dream of chats in ministerial offices or wandering through the gilded splendour of the Department of the Taoiseach, but the humble TD will be a long time waiting to sport and play in such an Elysian place. Instead, this is reserved for the cabinet, ministerial spin doctors and the occasional journalistic pet. Paddy Machiavelli should therefore set his sights lower and realise that the Dáil bar is a far more critical public arena. A great many myths have built up over the bar which, in the peasantry's imagination, consists of a palace of Berlusconi-style excess where half-naked showgirls, dressed in togas, feed grapes to the reclining forms of portly FG TDs.

Sadly, apart from the tubby state of our TDs, the reality approximates more closely a well-appointed Midlands hotel bar with a declining passing trade. That said, the most dangerous myth to which any Aspirant Prince runs the risk of falling victim is that which declares the Dáil bar's political influence at an end. Although the triumph of this not-so-brave new world, of pious and loudly moral politicians, means the power held by the retainers of the Dáil bar is not what it once was, each party still contains a sufficiency of that group called 'the bar lobby'. Paddy Machiavelli must therefore cast a wide and fertile net within that group while remaining mindful of the importance of not spending too much time in the Dáil bar. Politics may once have been a hazy and pleasant land — where you could while away afternoons watching the racing channel with future Taoiseach Biffo whilst your current Taoiseach Bertie was under fire in the Dáil chamber — but all that is over now. Indeed, it is believed that even the subscription to the racing channel has been cancelled, so all the poor lads can watch now is Oireachtas debates, which probably goes a long way towards explaining the bar's deserted status.

But, whilst we are living in an age of modesty in a political scene which certainly has a great deal to be modest about, the experiences of Noel Dempsey and Dermot Ahern indicate that Paddy Mac, if he wants to secure the love of his colleagues, should not be a permanent Puritan either. Ahern and Dempsey might have been occasionally efficient ministers who, on occasion, fooled themselves and others into believing they were blue-skies thinkers. However, the way in which this duo treated the prospect of talking to fellow TDs in the bar, or of being in a bar at all — as though it were some variant of the white man's burden — went a long way towards explaining the peals of laughter that greeted their occasional forays into 'leadership positions'.

When it comes to the Dáil bar, there are other rules that Paddy Machiavelli must follow. In particular, it is important to become inebriated on about six occasions a year. Otherwise you will attract suspicion that you are some sort of Micheál Martin *manqué* who dines on fruit for breakfast, and those who constitute 'the lads' do not like what they would define as the civil servant-style drinker whose idea of excess is two pints of Murphy's stout after 11pm on a Sunday. So, unless you occasionally disgrace yourself, the suspicion will swiftly arise that you are only there on sufferance as part of a great plan to pretend to be one of 'the lads'. That said, Paddy Machiavelli must equally always be sure to retain some degree of secret sobriety. A drunken man is a fool who will spill his secret soul, but the Dáil bar is not the place for such largesse. It is a harsh enough discipline, certainly within an Irish context, to expect a man to stay at least secretly sober for 30 years, but, if you are the Aspirant Prince this sacrifice must be made. The best example of this technique is provided by Enda Kenny. Our Taoiseach may have carefully maintained a Jack the Lad sort of a roistering playboy image. But, when observed at close quarters, it became clear that unlike Mr Cowen who would attack pints like the Assyrian wolf, Mr Kenny was a priestly sort of a drinker who always kept his wits closely enough about him.

Excess on the pints front, though often tempting, should be avoided for more reasons than the danger that you might end up dragging a female fellow TD onto your lap in the full glare of the TV cameras during a 3am debate on abortion. Ruairí Quinn may once famously have bewailed the fact that the Irish voters would never elect a bald Taoiseach. But, the voters' distaste is not confined to hairless politicians, for they will never elect a fat one either. Some will argue the premiership of Brian Cowen contradicts this claim, but the voters had very little to do with that particular experiment, and they ended it as soon as they could. Before Paddy Mac thinks it is unfair that he cannot have sausages every morning, he should note that there is nothing uniquely modern about the flab issue, for imagery has defined the fate of politicians since the dawn of kingship. And, be it fair or not, what the Aspirant Prince must recognise is that this is the age of television, where the fickle voter will not be convinced by the man struggling to close the top button of his shirt. Fat is equated with an absence of discipline and a sloppiness of character, and whilst we may mock Micheál with the leaves of lettuce for breakfast, or Enda in the shiny cycling shorts, the Aspirant Prince must embrace the concept of the slim club and steel himself for a lifetime of abstinence from the cooked Irish breakfast.

Though it may come as a shock, Paddy Machiavelli will soon learn that when it comes to the making of allies with the lower orders, there is more to life in Leinster House than the Dáil bar. A different template for our new *ingénue*, in terms of the securing of friends, is that FG phenomenon known as the 'cappuccino kids' where between 10 and 20 of the party's TDs engage in the subversive activity of meeting regularly to discuss ways in which the country may be reformed. Paddy Mac should note that FG's occasional susceptibility to ideological notions means that this will always be more of an FG than an FF phenomenon. In fact, one of that party's main problems sometimes is that it has suffered from an excess of thinkers.

Sadly, intellectually preoccupied backbenchers secure a chilly response on a cross-party basis from all Dear Leaders. And this is certainly the case with the latest variant, if only because, for once, that cute old warhorse Enda Kenny did not quite know what to do with his free-thinking TDs. Were the 'cappuccinos' simply aligned to the defeated forces in the failed FG *coup d'état* of 2010, the Taoiseach would know where he stood. But Enda faced a problem, in that the kids were not part of any identifiable group. They were instead slightly idealistic non-conformists who simply wanted the country to be run in a better, fairer way. Unsurprisingly, given that nothing in his political life had prepared Enda for the phenomenon of ideological ministers, let alone thinking backbenchers, the current Dear Leader was unhappy.

The Taoiseach's mood was not at all improved when recently it was revealed that the 'kids' are not perturbed by the Dear Leader's fret. One wise observer accurately summarised their curious relationship by noting the problem is that 'the new TDs feel they owe Enda nothing. In fact, some openly mock him and actually enjoy being in trouble.' Significantly, and it is something our Aspirant Prince should file away for future reference, the absence of any patronage means the Taoiseach could not even break the spines of his frolicsome young cubs with vague promises of political preferment. Paddy Machiavelli should also note that a Tudor-style fox like Enda is right to fear the cappuccinos. It may be very well to say, 'Leave the kids alone', but the not unreasonable nagging doubt that an Enda has, given the cappuccinos' intrinsic nature, is that at some future tumult — like Stanley in the Battle of Bosworth that did for Richard III — the cappuccinos could be the force that, after waiting in the wings during the initial stages, make the decisive intervention. Enda will have to deal with his problems in his own way. The lesson, however, that Paddy Machiavelli must take from all this is that in terms of securing a retinue within Leinster House, the Falstaffian way of being one of 'the lads' is no longer enough. Instead, if he wishes to secure the respect of his colleagues, he must infiltrate that strange new breed of free-thinking backbencher who believes that politics and the electorate must be respected.

Outside of finding out where the bar is, one of the other critical things our man Paddy Mac must accomplish is how to deal with the ladies. The template for the Irish politician's attitude to 'female' issues generally consists of a cross between Sir Humphrey, who called every woman 'Dear Lady' with varying levels of distaste, and Father Ted, who was utterly terrified by any woman who did not conform to the 'lovely girl' stereotype. This core belief means that if our Aspirant Prince is to separate himself in a subtle manner from the rest of the bison, he must secure the reputation of having respect for the ladies. This is a difficult enough old game, for the problem with women is that if you attempt to fake sincerity they are far too guileful for your own good. Paddy Machiavelli will note that one of the more poignant examples of this flaw is Pat Rabbitte, who is technically quite 'progressive' on all these issues. The problem, however, is that deep in his heart Pat is as much of a lads' man as any FF backbencher. Or rather he is a lads' man in a terribly posh Law Library way. But, though Pat's weakness is rather more refined, no matter how he tries the genie will always at some point — such as when he compared Michael McDowell to a menopausal woman — leap out of the lamp and tip the women a big wink.

It is a difficult task to appear intuitively sympathetic to the cause of women, and another who tries, but fails, is Enda Kenny. The Taoiseach is always anxious, sometimes desperately so, to be photographed in the company of attractive young women. But, in his secret soul, Enda, when it comes to assertive women, is a closet Father Trendy. Ironically, the one politician who managed that intuitive connection was Bertie Ahern. The former Taoiseach's great achievement was to stimulate the female pity gene, which is no easy thing for anyone, let alone a politician, to achieve. That is not to say our man Paddy should go around dabbing soup stains on his shirt, keeping his tie at half-mast and ensuring that his shirt-tails hang out beneath an ill-fitting anorak. But should he develop the capacity to stimulate that deep-hidden Mammy gene, which even the most modern of Irish women retain, Paddy Mac will have taken a significant step indeed.

As part of this process, Paddy Mac, whether he likes it or not, will have to get married. We may be the progressive society and all the rest, but no one is comfortable with a long-term bachelor TD. This is not even a matter of sexual orientation. The cruel truth of the matter is that voters like stolidity, and there is nothing quite as stolid as a man who is married … to a woman, preferably. And marriage is not that bad a thing anyway, for once they are reasonably pretty, like most men, one woman is the same as another. As part of his ongoing plan to be seen to be respectful to women in his private life, it is important that Paddy Machiavelli marries that strange thing called a 'career woman'. This shows that he respects women as being equals. Of course, in marrying a 'career woman' Paddy Machiavelli should not engage in anything too excessive. A teacher, nurse or any of the caring professions is more than sufficient; for you do not want to end up being attached, as was the case with poor Michael McDowell, to someone who is seen as being more intelligent than you. No one, you see, respects a politician whose spouse has a mind of her own. Marrying a nice member of the caring professions is also to be encouraged, for it implies that you might be a bit of a carer yourself. And, given the nature of pay and conditions in the 'caring' professions, it is easier to persuade them to return to the bosom of the family home when, Paddy Machiavelli's respect for career women having been displayed, convenience dictates that she look after the children.

The final, critical domestic issue that our Aspirant Prince must resolve is the tricky question of reform. If he is on his first visit to Leinster House, Paddy Mac will generally have been elected on some sort of 'reform' ticket — even if the 'reform' we are talking about is the desire to get his incumbent party colleague out. Once Paddy Machiavelli is there, though, if he is to be fully free he must cast the shackles of reform away as swiftly as he can. Nothing epitomises this necessity more than the critical issue of creating his retinue, for though we are left only with the backwash of the great era of Bertie Ahern, even the last scrapings of that pork barrel mean you can hire staff. In this regard, the Aspirant Prince will, if he has any sense, always hire family members to conduct his constituency affairs, for no one else will have the knowledge and the requisite thoughtless enthusiasm. Sadly, Paddy Mac is not a free agent here because the great curse of ethics stretches into the kind little acts of graft that make the life of a politician worthwhile. Of course, if he unthinkingly embraces this queer ethics thing, then it is entirely his own fault if he falls under the hooves and horns of a runaway moral fury. Here, the fate of the FG TD Brendan Griffin offers our Aspirant Prince a useful case study in the dangers posed by virtue. We have noted earlier how Mr Griffin got into some trouble when, after an election where he had promised to only take half his salary, our man appeared to employ a substantial number of his family connections in the service of the state. The subsequent denouement should teach the Aspirant Prince that excess in all things, but particularly ethics, is bad for his health. People quite happily believe that, like themselves, all politicians are covetous sole traders who look after their own interests. So, Paddy Mac will only irritate and unnerve people if he makes a big fuss about how he will behave in a better way than those they previously elected to office. From that point onwards, unlike the fellow who slips in winking, nodding and smirking, they — and in particular Paddy's Mac's colleagues — are looking out for him, so that they can celebrate when poor Paddy is inevitably dragged down to the level where they believe he resides.

However, the denouement of the Griffin saga should teach the Aspirant Prince another critical lesson. There may have been a terrible ruckus — like the other dozen controversies involving FG carefully looking after their own — but after a week, Joe Duffy's circus died a gentle grumbling sort of death. Our Aspirant Prince should learn from this that in times of crisis nothing beats the patented Bertie technique of lying terribly still and saying nothing, on the grounds that if you don't move, trouble will swiftly get bored and find someone far more interesting than you.

Chapter 3 ～

WATCH OUT FOR THOSE 'LEFT-WING POLITICAL QUEERS' FROM TRINITY. WHY A REPUTATION FOR LOFTY THOUGHTS SHOULD BE AVOIDED

It much assists a prince to set unusual examples in internal affairs ... one that would be talked about.

On the art of politics • a theatrical game • the artful dodger of Drumcondra • left-wing Trinity queers • Hamlet's clown • Richard 'the lesser' Bruton • first find your intellectuals • on being authentic • the importance of character and the art of the surrendered ego

Time flies in Leinster House when you are so busy in internal party committees, external committees, chairing committees, legislating, questioning, attending the constituency clinic, the hospital clinic, defending the government, attacking the government, drinking, equivocating, electioneering, jeering, emoting, opposing and talking to such an extent it is almost impossible to think, thank God. Strangely, such a flux of activity means a decade can pass and it feels as if you are still on your first day. But you arc not. For a dccadc has indccd passcd, and you arc still in the same position.

There is, however, much to learn yet if Paddy Mac is to succeed in the tricky task of acquiring the sort of profile that can help carry him to the Taoiseach's office. One critical thing our Aspirant

Prince must embrace is the role of art in high politics. Before Paddy Machiavelli gets nervous, we are referring to art as in the learning of a profession, rather than writing poetry or painting or suchlike. He can, of course, go a long way in Irish politics without treating it as a form of art. Talent (rarely), hard work (occasionally), or the sort of hard neck more commonly seen in a timeshare salesman may bring Paddy Mac as far as the cabinet table. But, unless he brings some form of artistry to his public discourse, when it comes to the great prize, he will be like a pony trying to jump an eight-foot fence and win the Puissance.

When Paddy Mac nervously considers the issue of art in politics, the discipline he should particularly study is the relationship between theatre and politics. This may be seen as being dated in an age of scientific polling and focus-group research, but what the modern 'Mad Men' of the dark art of spin often fail to realise is that the most ruthless politicians have always recognised the importance of creating a sense of drama around their harmless activities. Brutal pragmatists like not-so-cute old Phil Hogan will hawk and snort at such 'notions'. But, Paddy Machiavelli should note that the politicians who do not generate a narrative about their private selves that is of interest to their voters will be mere ciphers. Intriguingly, our two closest cultural neighbours fully recognise the importance of theatre, for whilst America is a republic, the office of the President is steeped in the sort of iconography that renders it a sacred space. In England, outside of the wily manner in which politicians such as Tony Blair crafted a narrative of simple freshness and youth, the theatre of kingship indicates how sometimes invisible power binds with the tightest string.

If Paddy Mac is looking for a mentor on how theatre is a stepping-stone to power in politics, our man could do worse than to examine the career of Éamon de Valera. His ascetic image may look somewhat dated today, but de Valera's ascension to the status of a quasi-religious icon, whose image was generally sited between JFK and the Sacred Heart in the then cosy homesteads of Ireland, meant that for the voters he was seen more as a demigod than a mere politician. The sainted one may, in the course of a long and fruitfully remunerated political career of half a century, have also snaffled control of Ireland's then largest media group, the *Irish Press*. However, his public image almost to the very end was one of pious asceticism. In examining Dev, our Aspirant Prince should not be discouraged from using 'the long fellow' as a template by the mockery of the infamous *soi-disant* 'comely maidens' speech, for, ironically, the ongoing criticism of the Lincoln-style evocation of that 'Ireland that we dreamed of' is a testament to the long shadow that this caster of political spells created.

The speech also indicates the importance of art in politics. De Valera, even in the 1950s, was open to the accusation that Ireland was absolutely not a land of 'cosy homesteads, whose fields and villages would be joyous with the sounds of industry, with the romping of sturdy children, the contest of athletic youths and the laughter of happy maidens.' Instead, the reality was one of emigration, enforced chastity, poor housing, a dysfunctional economy and children who coughed, rather than romped. Even the poets and scholars who de Valera celebrated for their ability to inspire 'successive generations of patriotic men' to 'give their lives to win religious and political liberty' were either on the censor's blacklist or in exile. However, by virtue of slipping in the caveat that the Ireland of romping children was the one 'we dreamed of', rather than the one that actually existed, in one bound our hero was free. Dev knew instinctively that one of the great arts of politics is to create expectations and then convince the voters that you are the Messiah who can lead them there. In this case, by defining the desires of an uncertain people for this tranquil Arcadia, de Valera became the politician who embodied and understood the needs of the citizenry, who then continually elected him in the hope that this Moses might some day lead them to the Promised Land he talked so poetically about.

De Valera's capacity for political theatre and the making of myths was also facilitated by the greatest practitioner of that art, Winston Churchill. This occurred when, in a rare slip, after World War II had ended, the British PM warned that such had been Britain's peril in 1940 that had it not been for the 'loyalty and friendship of Northern Ireland we should have been forced to come to close quarters with

Mr de Valera or perish for ever from the earth.' De Valera's response was one of the finest positive examples of how politicians can shape a narrative that the citizens of the state can take pride in. The then Taoiseach commended the British PM for 'resisting his temptation' for 'Mr Churchill, instead of adding another horrid chapter to the already bloodstained record of the relations between England and this country, has advanced the cause of international morality.' But after recognising that 'Mr Churchill is proud of Britain's stand alone, after France had fallen and before America entered the War', de Valera slipped the political knife in, asking if the victor could 'not find in his heart the generosity to acknowledge that there is a small nation that stood alone not for one year or two, but for several hundred years against aggression; that endured spoliations, famines, massacres in endless succession; that was clubbed many times into insensibility, but that each time on returning consciousness took up the fight anew.' Without firing a single shot, in other words, Dev put it up to the Great British Empire. For a post-colonial people, that provided a serious boost to the psyche.

We are not saying to Paddy Mac, who can take things literally, that he should go around the countryside making speeches about comely maidens. Our man, though, should realise that a far grander school of politics exists than that practised in the Dáil chambers, RTÉ studios and meetings about focus-group studies. This is that variant of politics crafted in silent thought where the politician steps away from the flux and chaos of the news schedule and attempts to define and articulate the needs of his society. More should try it.

Of course de Valera is not the sole template for the role of art and theatre in politics. Paddy Mac might note our ongoing post-colonial psyche meant that when a considerably plumper chief, in terms of the trimmings at least, arrived, Mr Haughey's status as the fat chieftain chimed with a certain national mood. This was not just a matter of impressing the simple peasantry of the 1960s, for though we might publicly condemn him now, intriguingly, the tale of our Celtic Tiger reveals that we took the first chance we got to replicate the lifestyle and spending habits of Mr Haughey in spades. Mr Haughey, who projected an aura of grandiosity, also recognised that, when it comes to the art of politics at least, the most potent narratives tend to hinge on the most minor details. Nothing epitomised this more than the occasion where, after sacking Martin O'Donoghue, a key enemy, from the cabinet, the then Taoiseach couriered a 'gift' of two ducks of the deceased variety with the message 'shot at dawn on my estate' to O'Donoghue. The message was not quite as clear as the horse's head in *The Godfather*, but it was a fairly close-run thing.

When it comes to the political X factor, however, Paddy Machiavelli should note that the wily de Valera's closest latter-day acolyte was Bertie Ahern. The Bertie was, to put it mildly, a radically different creature from the Episcopal Mr de Valera. But, the ward boss's *comme ci, comme ça* ordinary-man persona disguised an utter cunning in how he presented himself to the public that would have impressed a Hollywood star. Intriguingly, the Artful Dodger of Drumcondra reinvented himself most effectively in 2007. During his first two campaigns, Bertie had run with the grain via his invented 'Jack the Lad' persona. In 2007, though, the wind was in Mr Ahern's teeth. But, as a fragile Taoiseach strained to disentangle himself from the web being spun around him by the Mahon Tribunal, and as, like a butterfly, he ensnared himself more deeply, suddenly an international statesman emerged new born from the rather dusty chrysalis. The makeover transformed our hero to such an extent that Mr Ahern grabbed the last political benefits of a decade-old Good Friday Agreement, draped himself in the respectable iconography of addresses to the UK Parliament in Westminster, and engaged in a historic meeting with Ian Paisley to bury the three-centuries-old hatchet over the Battle of the Boyne. After that, and testimonials from Blair and Clinton, it almost appeared vulgar to mention such petty issues as a bit of loose change in the safe.

Paddy Machiavelli should also learn that sometimes politicians have a far more knowing understanding of the art of theatre than outward appearances suggest. Our Aspirant Prince will note that whilst Seán Lemass cultivated a gruff, artless public persona, his understanding of the power of imagery, as displayed by his concerns over the rise of RTÉ, was far more sophisticated than people thought.

Lemass adopted a brusque public profile, because he instinctively realised that the citizens had endured enough of specious orators outlining mazy dreams as they died for Ireland on a serialised basis. They instead simply wanted to be convinced that a professional was in charge of the shop.

Art and theatre may play a critical role in politics, but Paddy Mac should be careful not to be too obviously associated with such concepts. Rather, he should temper these interests with a canny recognition of the great suspicion that Irish politicians and the public have about original thinkers. In this regard, our political project should take his cue from the ageless wisdom of the little-known FF justice minister Micheál Ó Móráin, who famously warned the people of Ireland to avoid 'left-wing political queers from Trinity and Telefís Éireann'. The former Fine Gael Taoiseach, Liam Cosgrave, more gently summarised the instinctive suspicion of the plain people towards intellectuals when, responding to Mr Haughey's first budget speech and its reference to 'Art and Culture', he noted Haughey had obviously been told 'you had better say something about culture. It sounds well even if you do not mean to do anything about it. A reference to culture is always impressive.'

In fairness, the career of Mr Haughey was not at all damaged — even amongst the common citizenry — by his status of a patron of the arts, despite the fact that much of this appeared to consist of lavish portraits of the Napoleonic One sitting astride some puzzled horse. The voters, even today, like their leaders to have a bit of a touch of the gentry, and whilst some might mock the distance travelled between Mr Haughey's musings about the Medicis and the political boon companions he kept, a Renaissance Prince should be able to glide easily between both worlds. It is better therefore that Paddy Mac might, at least, try to get along with the Irish intellectual. Our Aspirant Prince, in casting a benevolent eye across the world of culture, does not actually need to understand it. Indeed it would be very unwise if he tried, for when it comes to the poems and the books, Paddy Mac is far too busy being busy to have time to think. Our man should, though, in terms of creating a reputation for being engaged in the arts, indulge in the occasional book review for *The Irish Times*, since this can always be done by an intern. Outside of that he should embrace the view that culture is essentially a good thing, so long as it lifts the spirit of the nation, does not cost the taxpayer anything, does not create unhappiness and is not hierarchical or inaccessible. The latter troika in particular are the constituents of real art and Paddy Mac doesn't want to be getting mixed up in that territory!

However, even when playing footsie with the intellectuals, Paddy Mac should always bear in mind the wise advice of Mr Ó Móráin. Of course, despite the best attempts of the voters, the occasional intellectual has fluttered on frail wings into that web of hairy spiders that constitutes the Irish political system, but it rarely ends well. The most profound example of this phenomenon is the now almost completely forgotten FG don, John Kelly. For many in his era he was the Hamlet-style philosopher-prince of Irish politics. In his time of greatness, Kelly's analysis of how the Irish state had confined its ambitions to behaving 'like a crew of maintenance engineers, just keeping a lot of old British structures and plant ticking over' summarised the great failure of Irish governance in a sentence. Kelly's critique of Bertie Ahern's Brer Rabbit-style 'keep the nose down and keep out of trouble' philosophy — after the ward boss was caught telling a group of women councillors that to succeed you had to 'sell your soul, keep your balance, keep well in with everybody, say hello to your local TDs and councillors even if you hate them, and you might get nominated at your local convention' — was not just entertaining. There was also something prophetic in the FG don's observation that Ahern's warning that the women must 'take the middle ground. You may hate your TDs but you must do what is required. We all have to swallow humble pie and I have been doing it for years. But if you keep at it — this unremitting diet of humble pie — you can break through' had not been plucked out of the air. Kelly, possibly even before Bertie, had divined that the ward boss was Haughey's special child and inevitable successor.

Given that opposites attract, Kelly, inevitably, had a special relationship with Haughey. Few other politicians could have summarised Charlie Haughey's equivocation on the first divorce referendum as representing a case of Haughey being 'caught between his hillbillies and *Hot Press*' to such an extent that he had become 'the absentee warlord' of the Dáil. Kelly's capacity for rhetoric and the broad sweep of his vision made for a stark contrast with the self-confessed politics of Bertie, which consisted of turning up at the local supermarket to flirt with the women and to joke about football with the men. Paddy Machiavelli, though, would do well before he gets tempted by diversions like thinking deeply about society or human nature to consider the fate of this iconoclastic thinker. Kelly might have been believed by many to be the cleverest man in a FG party that was not short of fellows who believed they were special. But, perhaps precisely because he thought too deeply and was too radical, Kelly's ministerial career was a circumspect one.

Ironically, when he suddenly left politics, his own were the least enthusiastic of the mourners. From as far back as the 1970s, in *Ambiguous Republic* Diarmaid Ferriter reveals that the deep absence of love amongst Kelly's own colleagues was epitomised by one tart observation that 'Senator Kelly, particularly, is deeply resented. He is forever talking about doing something but then disappears back to the university in the middle of a meeting.' It is doubtful that the eternally embattled FG leader Alan Dukes was any more appreciative when, in 1989, John Kelly sent him a letter suggesting that FG should disband, with the constituent parts of the party going to FF and Labour as per their political preferences. Mr Dukes, whose then preference was personal and political survival, ignored the missive. Ultimately, it was Michael D Higgins who most acutely divined Kelly's woes via the observation that being an intellectual in Irish politics was 'worse than being sexually perverse' — not that the latter was too popular in the 1970s either. Michael D was undoubtedly referring to himself (in terms of being an intellectual, we stress!), but the last public intellectual to hold a seat in Dublin South experienced similar difficulties. Of course Kelly's observations on Irish politics and the Irish character are as relevant and as fresh now as they were 30 years ago, but the sad problem is that Paddy the voter is as indifferent to the story now as he was then. And in some respects, far from being a Hamlet, Kelly's legacy was far better defined by Hamlet's observations to the skull of his favourite clown, Yorick, of 'where be your gibes now, your gambols, your songs, your flashes of merriment that were wont to set the table on a roar?'

A far more prosaic example of the danger of associating with public intellectuals, or of being one of those intellectuals yourself, is provided by Richard Bruton. The failure of 'the lesser' Bruton does not merely provide Paddy Machiavelli with the classic example of how intelligence and application are never quite sufficient if you are to seize the top job. Our backbench TD should also learn from Richard of the dangers posed to your own career by these fellows. No shortage of fine and brave TDs followed Richard into enemy fire when the last of the FG intellectuals was shanghaied into saving us from Enda. But whilst, like all aristocrats, Richard was saved from the consequences of his actions and allowed to skip back into cabinet, the foot soldiers saw their political careers being razed.

There are more modern reasons why Paddy Mac should be at a minimum suspicious of involving our intellectual class in the base conduct of politics. Nothing justifies this disdain more than the collapse of the great party that all the intellectuals and Eamon Dunphy were going to create just before Election 2011. Sadly, after much talk of the 'why I ought to' variety by public thinkers such as Fintan O'Toole, the whole thing folded up rather inelegantly when the political class declared the election somewhat earlier than expected. The bleats from our academics about the damn inconvenience of having to go to war ahead of any designated schedule did occasion some mirth amongst the collective peasantry of the media and the political classes.

Afterwards, showing a level of charity that is not normally a prime characteristic of his analysis of political affairs, O'Toole noted of the attempts to find 20 candidates of some kind of substance 'that for too many people, and it's not that anybody chickened out but they just — at that moment — said, "I can't be sure I can do this on Monday".' Some observers did note rather sardonically of the academics' discomfiture that if these fellows were so clever, why was it, given the ongoing imploding state of Biffo's government, that the announcement of an election a month ahead of schedule came as such a shock to all of them? And whilst Fintan O'Toole and David McWilliams might have decided that the 'only thing worse than not doing this would be to do it badly', it was hardly a decision informed by the sort of radical spirit that characterises all great revolutions.

Academics are all well and good, but there are other more prosaic qualities that our Aspirant Prince should attempt to cultivate, such as the virtue of being 'authentic'. One interesting example of the complexity of this underrated trait is Enda Kenny's 'special relationship' with America. It has been suggested that Mr Kenny's capacity to sound like John F Kennedy is pastiche dressed up in rhetoric. Certainly, when Enda starts on with the 'we are one people, ancient and new, on a journey, a single journey of continuous transformation' the average Irish citizen starts to blink. The plain people understand that 'the Yanks' like that stuff about how 'philosophers say our horizons are not fixed but travel with us as we go' but it is all a bit rich for poor Paddy the voter's liver. And in fairness, given the comparative track record of Irish and American politicians, who could blame the plain people for squinting suspiciously when Enda talks about creating 'dreams and imaginings, strength and belief passed silently and unobtrusively from mother to daughter and father to son over the millennia.' But, could it be the case that Mr Kenny, far from being a mere ventriloquist, is actually an authentic American politician who is lost in his own country? They may be a tough audience, but our American friends love it when Enda starts into the 'my old grandpa was a lighthousekeeper' routine, for Mr Kenny is connecting to the idealistic American mentality. Sadly, for Mr Kenny at least, the Irish peasant mindset is more puritanical.

The issue of authenticity may, however, cut to the core of the apparent contradiction between Mr Kenny's low popularity ratings and the apparent tolerance that Paddy the voter has for his ongoing leadership. The citizens may not be excessively taken with Dear Leader Enda's American waffle. But, whilst the relationship with the voters is chilly, Kenny is accepted as being a legitimate Taoiseach. The reason for this, and the cardinal virtue of authenticity, is that the voters sense that Enda knows his own mind. This means that whilst the voters do not warm to Mr Kenny, they know he is a leader and that, ultimately, is the person they want behind the boss's desk.

Outside of the importance of authenticity, when it comes to the formation of his political mind Paddy Machiavelli should also note that, rather like Gaelic football, in politics that first cousin of authenticity, character, is a far more valuable commodity than the mistrusted art of skill. One classic example of how skill — or in this case a facile sort of intelligence — is overrated in politics is Mr Alan Shatter. He may have been the sort of Truman Capote-style genius who could draft three legislative bills before breakfast. But, whilst Mr Shatter was undoubtedly a pedigree horse, in that he was mercurial, temperamental and fast, the successful Irish politician is more of a shire horse who is built for durability, not speed. Theirs is the life of pulling the permanent plough, where the cheering and the excitement of Derby Day is an unknown experience.

For all his self-proclaimed intelligence, character or temperament was the Achilles' heel of Mr Shatter, for his persona was too tart for his own good. Paddy Mac will admit that acidity can be refreshing, in a bracing sort of way, when it comes to the 'all the lads in the same bed together' ethos of Leinster House. The problem, however, with Mr Shatter was that, like the overly effete courtier, he took too much pleasure from being venomous. He was the small boy who could not see a passing political butterfly without wishing to pull its wings. However, whilst this may entertain us, he made way too many political enemies for either his or his colleagues' good health.

Character, of course, is also the first cousin of judgment, and the career of this petulant courtier was an ongoing thesis in misjudgment, where every issue, be it constitutional referenda, his relationship with the Garda Representative Association (GRA) or even being stopped by a Garda checkpoint, appeared to evolve into a contest of hysterics. It should be noted that a capacity for hysteria is no harm at all in the opposition benches, and heaven knows it has certainly been a defining characteristic of the GRA. But the grown-up world of ministerial politics requires something more substantial.

This means that whilst Mr Shatter was entertaining in a superficial sort of fashion, as the former minister's unhappy ending proved, he was not something that Paddy Machiavelli should seek to emulate. Instead, he should realise that Mr Shatter's tartness was that of the bewigged courtly fop who, outside of swaying too easily with every breeze in court, when battle arrives, far from drawing his sword, will end up being pulled squealing out of the broom cupboard.

It is, when it comes to the character issue, useful to compare Mr Shatter with Séamus Brennan's lesson in the virtues of the surrendered ego. Mr Brennan may have been somewhat more bumptious in his youth, when he danced around in his underpants with Frank Dunlop celebrating FF's victory in 1977. Over time, hard experiences taught Brennan the virtues of having a more modest disposition. Nothing epitomised the virtue of such a persona more than the response of Brennan when, during his spell as Chief Whip, he was overlooked by Bertie in a reshuffle. Given that looking after Jackie Healy-Rae — and three other Independents whose votes were needed in order to keep Bertie's minority government in power — was more difficult than being Minister for Finance during a recession, others might have thrown a strop and stormed into the Taoiseach's office. Instead, when Bertie, who didn't like Brennan's slightly independent spirit, claimed that Séamus was too valuable to be moved, Brennan's mock despair at the sly nature of the compliment secured the laughter and the sympathy of all sections of the House. It was a wise move, for Bertie's anxiety to be as popular in the Dáil as he was in the country meant that Brennan was promoted at the first opportunity.

Paddy Machiavelli could learn a great deal from Brennan's ability to accept the political limitations he had to deal with. Of course, like all politicians, Séamus had a healthy ego. But, his capacity to surrender that ego to the needs of a Taoiseach or a party was a rare blossom in a house where the slightest display of humility, or of some sense that you realise you might actually be mortal, is as rare in Leinster House as a humble PD. The scarcity of such qualities means that if Paddy Machiavelli cultivates them, he will inspire warmth and a certain respect from his colleagues. And those truly are rare emotions in Leinster House.

Chapter 4 ∿

TELL THE PEOPLE WHAT THEY WANT AS OFTEN AS THEY WANT TO HEAR IT

Never let any Government imagine that it can choose perfectly safe courses; rather let it expect to have to take very doubtful ones …

Building trust • turnips and knowing your place • tell the people what they want to hear • why you must not be interesting • defining your persona in the chamber • the art of the question • please don't be a maverick • how to behave in party meetings: the committee • taking on big government • meeting ministers and being a moral boy

So, now that he is snugly in Leinster House with his friends the 'lads', the next grand issue our friend Paddy Machiavelli must embrace is how he is to make his way in the public sphere of politics. The most important art in that regard that our Aspirant Prince must cultivate is the capacity to secure and maintain the trust of the citizens. Since Paddy is still a mere backbencher, it is unlikely that he will be challenging the voters on complex issues for some time. But, it is no harm to start as he means to go on. The core value when it comes to the critical art of securing the trust of the electorate is that he must never show the voter his true face. This means that Paddy Mac must, even in defeat, never challenge the belief of the voter that they are the most sophisticated electorate in western Europe. Such a position must incorporate a mighty leap of faith, given the roll-call of who has preceded him, but rigorous honesty is not the game he is at. One simple example of what we are referring to is that Paddy Mac may of course refer to the voters as 'punters' when he is within the safety of the inner circle of the 'lads', but in the moral outside world, the most appropriate phraseology consists of words such as *citizens*, *taxpayers* or, if he is feeling particularly obsequious, *citizen taxpayers*. They are also, by the way, all hard-pressed. Happily, should he abase himself and his views sufficiently, he will then secure the respect of the citizens.

Paddy Machiavelli must also swiftly embrace the principle that there is no more loved and trusted politician than the man who knows his place. He can engage in a great deal of mischief if he is seen to be safe, but we will for the moment keep quiet about that. Instead, when it comes to promotion, Paddy Machiavelli should note that aged Taoisigh, when they want to make gestures about promoting the youthful, are always far keener to appoint the good TD who does not want to be difficult. What is of even more importance is that the electorate also like politicians who are not a threat. There are those who dream of radicalism and that there somewhere lies, hidden in Ireland, an as-of-yet undetected army of revolutionary Janissaries. This disguises the fact that, outside of that little fracas in 1916, we are an utterly conservative electorate who, if given the chance, would still be voting for the Irish Parliamentary Party.

When it comes to knowing his place, Paddy Machiavelli must also recognise that he is less important than an astonishing variety of social groups. It is to be expected that he must walk behind Taoisigh, ministers, junior ministers and senior civil service mandarins. But that, alas, is only the start of it. He is also, you see, less important than committee chairpersons, deputy committee chairpersons, councillors, the local chamber of commerce, journalists, press officers, focus groups, ministerial advisors, advocates, bloggers, the Muppet Show that is Politics.ie, academics, intellectuals, primary schoolteachers, businessmen and citizens in general. Indeed, about the only poor creature he is more important than is a senator.

If Paddy Machiavelli is looking for the perfect template for knowing his place, he could do far worse than observe that species of TD known as the FG 'turnip'. This phrase came into being during the final heave for the FG party leadership in 2010. One side consisted of the young Chevalier FG Whig aristocrats who were reforming, independent-minded individuals. The other was populated predominantly by rural deputies, nearly all of whom were male, and all of whom were characterised by a deep suspicion of inquiry. This meant that anything carrying the taint of radicalism or originality was certainly greeted with great suspicion by a group whose defining watchword was loyalty. What these TDs, who were dismissively referred to as 'turnips' by the FG aristocrats, were loyal to — apart from the leader known as 'the boss' and the party — was unclear, and why they were loyal to the leader and the party was even more unclear. The only certain thing surrounding the poor 'turnip' was that, when it came to matters of conscience, the spine is an unnecessary bone that only confuses things. However, their capacity to gather together in the centre of the political field during thunderstorms, to bleat with one voice, was unparalleled, and when it came to FG's War of the Buttons it was the 'turnips' who ended up dining at the winner's table.

The triumph of the 'turnips' should also teach Paddy Mac that one other key aspect of building trust with the electorate is to tell the voters what they want to hear as often as possible, for that is what the 'turnips' most certainly do. And they would be right, because telling people what they want to hear is how Paddy Mac gets elected. When it comes to this critical art, it would be helpful if the voter were kind enough to tell Paddy Mac what it is they want him to say. But that, alas, is not Paddy the voter's way. The problem he must face is that Paddy the voter has — on contrasting issues and sometimes on the same issue — the memory of an elephant and of a goldfish. Paddy the voter is, depending on circumstances, a dreamer, a peasant and a psychopath. Sometimes, as Enda Kenny half correctly divined, he wants to know the story. But, Enda only managed to reach the first step of the long ladder of Paddy the voter's characteristics. Had he reached the second rung of that heart of darkness, he would know that the last thing Paddy the voter wants to hear is the actual story. He instead wants to be soothed by a nice story. It is a template that our Aspirant Prince would be wise to follow.

One of the most critical traits that new TDs must also avoid — if they are to secure the reputation of being sound — is to be too interesting. In theory, being of interest should be a good thing. But this inevitably creates sensations of deep unease amidst Dear Leaders. If our Aspirant Prince is looking for a role model that might summarise the danger of being interesting, he might look no further than the so far uniquely colourful career of the former Labour TD Colm Keaveney. Not since a white-suited Pee Flynn levitated into Leinster House has quite so exotic a political blackbird entered the precincts of the Dáil. Even within a Labour Party which throws up backbench turbulent priests in the manner that FG and FF cultivate the 'turnip', Mr Keaveney was special. In particular, uniquely amongst his peers, Keaveney embraced the concerns of middle Ireland in a manner that slightly terrified a Labour Party that prefers to keeps Ireland's 'coping classes' in the same pen of right-wing ignoramuses as the American Republican Party and the US pro-gun lobby.

Keaveney's archaic use of language and uneasy but strangely confident public persona, which meant that, unlike his leader, Colm would be noticed everywhere he went, was redolent of Charles Haughey. Mr Gilmore's acolytes were right in fearing that this would not be the only similarity, for politically at least, he shared similar dreams and desires. Significantly, like Haughey, Mr Keaveney was the loved child of the Labour Party members, for Colm empathised and sympathised with their concerns, whereas an increasingly distant leadership simply fulminated at them. Paddy Machiavelli will note, however, that being interesting inevitably brings the enmity of the leadership, for the interesting politician is the original cuckoo in the leader's nest. In Mr Keaveney's case, this was intensified by the appalling scenario where, in the election for the party Chairman's post, Mr Keaveney beat the leader's man to the job. This created no shortage of unhappiness, for whilst a

Labour Dear Leader can choose his ministers and apparatchiks, the Party Chairman is the creature of the members. The problem, though, for Colm was that if you talk in an interesting fashion you must act in an equally fascinating way. So it was that Mr Keaveney talked himself into a whole lot of trouble on the budget and then did that which the Dear Leader most desired: he left the party on a point of principle. In the aftermath of the departure, even as Colm basked in the transient love of the Labour rank and file, the response of the Labour hierarchy was chilly. Already he had acquired the nickname of Vicky Pollard, the comedic 'Little Britain' character who began every soliloquy with the catch phrase of 'yeah, but no, but yeah'. Rather like Aodhán Ó Ríordáin, Colm may still believe that hope exists, for when he left, there were hugs from some backbench TDs. The reality of things meant that these hugs, even before he joined FF, were swiftly followed by harsh words, for the herd, you see, always gathers back together. The jig was up, for in leaving the flock Keaveney became a black sheep. And whilst, like Keaveney, the black sheep intrigues far more than the rest, the reality is that even if the black sheep is reaccepted into the flock, it will never lead it.

Though Paddy Mac should be cognisant of the dangers that accompany originality, he must equally avoid the danger of becoming a cipher. In avoiding this particular trap, Paddy Mac should be circumspect in his response to claims that his behaviour in the Dáil chamber is an irrelevance. It is certainly true that, for the most part, if you want to keep something a secret then this is the best location to disclose it. But, like other cases of conventional wisdom, the analysis is not entirely correct. All politics is a stage and the Dáil, in tandem with parliamentary party meetings, is one of the critical areas where you can define your political persona. Indeed, merely by engaging in the odd act of speaking in the chamber you will send out the first strange intimations that you have a personality. In doing so, Paddy Mac must not make the terrible mistake of engaging in complex philosophical debates or closely technical arguments whilst a minister sleeps gently below him. Nor should he fret over parliamentary questions or the amount of time he spends speaking, for since *Magill* and the *Sunday Tribune* folded, no one counts up that stuff anymore. And the fate of those two publications suggests few did at the best of times.

Instead, the only two public forums that are of value are Leaders' Questions and the Order of Business. Paddy Machiavelli will note that the occasionally perky nature of exchanges that occur on such occasions is captured by a list of banned insults that includes *brat, buffoon, chancer, communist, corner boy, gurrier, coward, fascist, guttersnipe, hypocrite, rat, scumbag, scurrilous* and *yahoo*. Paddy Machiavelli must, however, be careful, for whilst in the past the voters, who lived in a quiet country, were partial to this sort of 'Hall's Pictorial Weekly' stuff, these days they ring into the Ceann Comhairle's office to complain since, oddly enough, they do not associate smirking, grinning and yahooing with good governance. Our Aspirant Prince will secure attention if he joins the clucking clique of FG backbenchers who raise a din every time an opposition TD — and in particular Gerry Adams — dares to in any way put the slightest of blemishes on the perfect halo of the Dear Leader, Enda. But, whilst they inspire laughter amongst their own, it does not secure the respect of the House, or of ministers, who only wish for the Order of Business to be over so that they can return to their usual activities of being adored.

If Paddy Mac is looking for a classic example of how the new arrival in Leinster House secures the attention of the citizens, this is provided by the Labour Senator John Whelan who, two and a half hours after he signed in to the Seanad, declared that the institution he had just been elected to was as 'dead as a dodo' and full of 'blather, back-slapping and hot air'. Mr Whelan has since then spent a very great deal of his time defending the very institution he wanted to abolish. But, whilst the denouement was somewhat incongruous, we will not criticise too much, for the main objective was achieved. Whelan had succeeded in creating a stir and had impacted upon the subconscious of the political classes.

If he is seeking to secure the attention, or better still respect of the citizens, Paddy Machiavelli might also observe the curiosity where, given the amount of accusations they engage in, so few politicians appear to know what a question is. They give opinions, they engage in bouts of shouting and rhetoric, they accuse and applaud each other. However, the one thing they appear to be incapable of doing is asking a straight question. Everything must have an introduction, an explanation, an accusation and some context before we get to the question, if indeed it is ever reached. So, if Paddy Machiavelli wants to stand out in the Dáil, it would help enormously if he actually simply asked a question. Everyone from the Ceann Comhairle to the attendant media and distressed visitors watching the chaotic proceedings from the gallery will be dizzy with gratitude. And Paddy Mac will assuredly stand out from the crowd.

When it comes to the art of securing attention, Paddy Mac must, however, avoid the dangerous trap of becoming a maverick. It is important to note that whilst they are often treated like fools, our maverick is not an idiot. The fool, such as James 'Bonkers' Bannon, can be safely patronised, but a maverick generally has a past involving some level of promise. The other defining feature of mavericks is that they also have a bad tendency to speak truthfully. Our classic maverick is, of course, FG's John Deasy, who was once genuinely seen to represent the future of Fine Gael. The problem with Deasy, though, was that Fine Gael's young prince was not capable of dealing with the sly courtiers' world of the palace of Enda, where the Dear Leader's ideas, even when they did not exist, were always genuinely the best. Deasy wished to lead a revolution in governance. Sadly, straight talking and telling voters the truth, though commendably honest, is far too self-indulgent a pursuit to be in any way accepted by connoisseurs of princely power. Deasy's exile was initiated after a frolic in the Dáil bar over the smoking ban. But, rather like the departure of Lucinda and the Fine Gael rebels, this was a mere Aunt Sally that disguised far more fundamental differences between those courtiers who could pass a lie detector test whilst praising a naked emperor and those who are too honest to thrive in the Dáil satrapy of happy flatterers. We will note, in passing, that Deasy comes from a noble line of mavericks, a group that has included Fine Gael's

John Kelly, Brian Lenihan Senior and Junior, Charlie McCreevy and, of course, the doyen of FF 'mavericks', Conor Lenihan, whose final parting shot in Irish political life was a duel of hysterics with Vincent Browne. All, though, with the happy, accidental exception of McCreevy, were damned by sneering phrases from fellows in dark bars, winking slyly as they smirked about how 'our man is fierce clever but …'

When it comes to Paddy Machiavelli's ongoing career development, our man needs to also recognise the power of the parliamentary party meeting. It is particularly important that Paddy Mac should act as though this is occurring in the full glare of TV cameras. Theoretically, such meetings are exercises in mutual trust where political issues are discussed under a confessional form of seal. But, if Paddy Mac does not tell hovering journalists what he, and more important still, others say at these affairs, he can be certain that his own contribution, if any, will be reported upon by those who have less kindly feelings towards him. This cruel reality was epitomised by an encounter when Brian Cowen's party whip, John Curran, as part of yet another disastrous attempt to engage with the press, engaged in a series of post-parliamentary party briefings with the media centred on the theme of how well everyone was getting on. Seeing as FF by this stage resembled piranhas in a pool that has been cut off from the river, it was a less than convincing stance. On one occasion, however, the circumlocutions involved in maintaining this pretence became too much for the harassed Curran. On spotting a smirking hack, the whip asked if he had any questions for the briefing, only to receive the sardonic response of: 'Ah no, I'll ask the other TDs what really happened later on.'

Once its status as a mirror to the world is recognised, the parliamentary party can be of great use to our Aspirant Prince. If it is, for example, to his benefit to be seen as someone who wants to exile all Travellers to Spike Island, and if he wishes, without being too obvious, for this to be the source of public controversy, the parliamentary party meeting is the place to speak out bravely. Within seconds, out it will go to the world, courtesy of Paddy Mac's loyal colleagues, after which he can enter the subsequent public fray, modestly claiming that he had never wished to be involved in such a controversy and had merely made the suggestion in a discursive way. And, of course, he has been misquoted, for Paddy Mac (wink) is actually a friend of the Traveller (nod) and their special ways (double nod).

It is critical to follow a number of other rules when it comes to parliamentary party meetings. If you think the Taoiseach or his ministers will be grateful should you ask probing questions, you are a Peter Mathews. The first is a job for the opposition, whereas finding solutions is a task for the civil service. Long speeches on the state of the country are frowned upon, for the 'lads' are on their midweek break from the family, and are anxious to get to the pub, or, as is more likely to be the case these days, the gym. But if Paddy Mac simply sits in stolid silence, then he will swiftly be relegated to the intellectual wastelands of the 'turnip' wing of the party. What he must do, if he is to secure some passing identity amongst the party hierarchy, is to become involved in the occasional backbench revolt. The ideal precedent for this was the FF revolt against Charlie McCreevy's tax individualisation policies, which was so serious it was authorised by Bertie and facilitated by the Fianna Fáil Press Office.

It is, of course, better if the revolt is about a 'local issue'. In such circumstances, sympathy will be high, for Paddy Mac is being driven by political self-interest. In short, he is not mad. The leadership will instead know that his motives are to protect the basic values of the party, which are to win and retain as many Dáil seats as possible. If Paddy Mac cannot find a constituency issue to kick up about, he still has plenty of cover for trouble, since the first rule of coalition appears to consist of the abandonment of the majority of both parties' pre-election commitments. It is critical, though, that if he goes to war, for example over the abandonment of his party's entire tax strategy, the fault for any unhappiness lies not with the Dear Leader or his ministerial acolytes. Rather, it lies in the excessive kindliness of the Dear Leader, who is allowing his domineering coalition partners to ride roughshod over the values of the party.

Paddy Mac would be surprised at how effective such a claim can be, for FF used to make it regularly about the Greens.

In acting independently, Paddy Mac should note that one revolt every six months is enough to garner the attention of the leadership and Paddy's colleagues. He is enough of a nuisance to be promoted, but not such a nuisance that they might want to have him expelled. It is important, though, not to indulge excessively, for if he is too good at being a modest thorn in the cabinet's side, as John McGuinness found to his cost, he will be called before the Taoiseach and the Minister for Finance and be berated for his cheek in fulfilling his duty to represent the taxpayer.

Paddy Mac should also be careful not to ignore the underrated world of the Dáil committee. It is the most mocked of institutions, but if he plays the game carefully, he will get attention and, at this point in his career, this must be his priority. In making his mark, Paddy Mac should be careful to avoid acquiring too taxing a committee. Our Aspirant Prince might, for example, think it would be grand to be appointed to investigate something like a banking crisis. He should, however, keep in mind the chilling experience of one of our more enthusiastic younger politicians when a wise old mandarin explained the consequences of engaging in such great work for the nation. Our young TD started to retreat from that particular front once he was told that it would mean he would have to abandon the constituency for two years. His mood was not improved as the happy mandarin, who was not at all anxious to be embroiled in a banking inquiry, expounded on the vast number of files our aspirant Eliot Ness would have to examine each week whilst his party colleague was making hay in the constituency, the early hour of the morning when he would start his day's work, and the lateness of the hour when he would finish. The amount of gratitude he could expect was not exactly munificent, for, oddly enough, the plain people do not like to be told they are corrupt. And if Paddy Machiavelli is inclined to disregard such advice, he should recall that the gratitude Jim Mitchell received from the voters for chairing the DIRT inquiry was the loss of his seat.

The good news for Paddy Mac is that there is no need to be engaged in major inquiries to secure a positive reputation in matters such as 'taking on big government'. The even better news is that it is not difficult to acquire such a reputation, for all that is required in this regard is to shout a lot at civil servants. Paddy Machiavelli must therefore find a committee where very little work secures a large amount of publicity. Anything involving the Departments of Finance, Environment, Enterprise, Transport, the Marine, or semi-state companies, will provide Paddy Mac with no shortage of opportunities.

Committees are also vital training grounds for the critical art of leaking, because Paddy Mac's most valuable work is not done in public, where he is competing for space with his 'colleagues'. Instead, the best route to attention is to leak a report just before it is to be published. Having done this, Paddy Mac's next task at the private meeting of the committee is to vocally condemn the leak. And having done that, he must ensure that his condemnation of such irresponsible behaviour should be leaked to the press, so as to complete the job.

Our Aspirant Prince must learn one other critical lesson. When a member of the cabinet deigns to acknowledge Paddy Mac's existence, our man's mood at all times must be one of 'fantastic'. He might think when the minister solicitously asks, 'How is it on the ground?' that he wants a full rundown on the difficulties that the citizens, and Paddy Mac as their representative, are facing. So, when he is spoken to by the minister, he shouldn't complain. The minister does not want to know about Paddy Mac's woes, for the whole point of being a minister is to escape from such petty concerns. He instead wishes to be praised and desired. The meeting is all about him, not about our Aspirant Prince. The occasional bleat may secure a fool's pardon, but should our man wish to continue on in this vein, the minister will grimace politely and move swiftly on. Forever.

Our Aspirant Prince must also, amidst all this positioning, sedulously maintain what chefs might call a light drizzle of respectability. It all represents somewhat of a change from previous colourful eras of political rough trading. However, the age of Haughey, 'Rambo' Burke, Albert Reynolds and Ray MacSharry appears to be definitively over. Many think this is a good thing, but would the banks, when they came trotting in looking for a bailout, have got their way so easily had they been faced by a Haughey or, for that matter, a Liam Lawlor? It is a point that Paddy Mac should bear in mind before he submits to the dead age of ethics where, like FG's Regina Doherty and Simon Harris, he must either be constantly appalled or prepared to be appalled at the drop of a mixed metaphor from the party Press Office.

Following in the invisible footsteps of Simon and Regina is, alas, only the start of Paddy Mac's apprenticeship into the bleak world view of our triumphant pious protestors. Ultimately, the template he must assiduously follow is that of Simon Coveney. Our Minister for Agriculture may not in over two decades in politics have made a single original statement. Yet, despite this none too minor lacuna, Mr Coveney has arrived at the strange position where he is now the chilly favourite to succeed Enda Kenny as the party's leader.

If Enda secured his position by virtue of a rare level of stamina and a happy shrewdness, Mr Coveney appears to be a contender precisely because of his permanent air of high aristocratic seriousness in a party that has a similar relationship to piety as the pussycat has to catnip. Some are suspicious that Simon's innocent facade disguises a hidden ruthlessness. It was, after all, Coveney's tweet about Biffo's morning-after-the-night-before condition that pulled the final curtain down on the dying FF Green Coalition. Nothing epitomised this particular capacity more than the failed *coup d'état* of the innocents, where he agonised publicly on both sides of the fence. Indeed, he agonised so effectively that at one point imagined 'friends of Simon' suggested that Coveney should be a compromise candidate who would end all that vulgar fighting between Enda and Richard. Sadly, the absence of real friends was epitomised by one comment after the debacle when a defeated conspirator, seeing Simon dining in the Dáil canteen, snarled: 'Look at him enjoying his strawberries and cream. If I could get a poison-tipped umbrella, I'd soon take the pleasure out of that.' Though Mr Coveney was the subject of some mockery, our Aspirant Prince should note that there was reason behind the dipping of a careful toe into that lake of sharks, for once you have been associated with the edges of a leadership contest, and survived, in Irish politics at least you will generally be in the centre of the next one.

PART TWO:

DEFINING YOUR POLITICAL IDENTITY

Chapter 5

EMPTY VESSELS APPEASING VESTED INTERESTS; THE IMPORTANCE OF PROVING WHY, ONCE YOU BECOME A MINISTER, YOU ARE THE RIGHT MAN FOR THE JOB

And it ought to be remembered that there is nothing more difficult to take in hand, more perilous to conduct, or more uncertain in its success, than to take the lead in the introduction of a new order of things. Because the innovator has for enemies all those who have done well under the old conditions and lukewarm defenders in those who may do well under the new.

On avoiding becoming a minister too early • the first step • do avoid being difficult • the featherless state hen • on Departments that are of worth • as a minister it is important to be sound • the apotheosis of 'careful now' • a cautionary tale • learning to love the enemy • the cleverest mandarins in the world and the futility of resignations

It might seem strange to suggest that our Aspirant Prince should be glad not to secure office too quickly in his career. However, early triumphs are rarely appreciated by colleagues, whose votes will be needed during some leadership crisis in the distant future. Paddy Mac's cabinet colleagues instead will be eternally wondering just how they may quench his rising tide of good fortune. Still, whilst patience is all well and good, it is always pleasant when, after a decade, a modestly smiling Taoiseach approaches, visibly delighted with his own kindness in offering Paddy Machiavelli the opportunity to be that political spittoon otherwise known as a junior minister. Finally, and this is genuinely important, his wife can call him a minister at the local golf club soirées.

Of course, Paddy Mac will, if he still has the brains he was born with, realise that the worst thing a junior minister can believe is that he is of any importance whatsoever. In general, junior ministers are appointed out of fear that you might become a cantankerous backbencher or pity because you have been a backbencher for a long time or because they want to shaft someone else, or they simply fancy a change. But you are never made a junior minister with the expectation that one might actually change anything. Still, whatever the reasoning is, Paddy Mac has a chance now. He might be so unimportant that he does not even get his own press officer, but he is on the pitch. Better still, he will find out that he and his junior ministry resemble those swans that mate for life, for once Paddy Mac is a mini-minister, nothing outside of personal or national bankruptcy will see him being sacked.

Once Paddy Mac realises that his sole task as a junior minister is to advance his career to a place where he has some power in the future, he will be happy. Some may still hanker for acts of zealousness, but realists will swiftly understand that, when you are ushered into your temporary office in the Department's broom cupboard, you are not in a place where greatness can thrive. Instead, the careers of those junior ministers who actually attempt to engage in reform generally end in tears. Nothing epitomises this more than the fate of John McGuinness, whose attempts to generate some level of efficiencies in Enterprise and Employment were put in a black sack and drowned like a litter of unwanted puppies by his senior minister, Mary Coughlan. Mr McGuinness's inability to realise that the good junior minister should avoid being difficult confirmed his status as one of those political lepers known as the 'maverick'.

There had already been troubles with McGuinness during the reign of Bertie. The attempt by the black swan from Kilkenny to take his role on the Public Accounts Committee (PAC) seriously had been the catalyst for a meeting with Biffo and Bertie, where McGuinness entered the room expecting to be praised for his efforts. Instead, as Bertie watched with silent, sorrowful eyes, Biffo set the tone with an agitated bark of 'what the f**k are you at?' Apparently, the subsequent exchanges did not get any warmer. Paddy Mac should also note that one of the key objectives behind the 'surprise' appointment of McGuinness to a Department nominally controlled by Mr Cowen's key ally, Mary Coughlan, was to soften the bark of Mr McGuinness, so that Mr Cowen would not have to bark at McGuinness any more.

Sadly, the failure of that experiment was signalled in the unlikely surroundings of the annual conference of the Beverage Council of Ireland where the junior minister tore into a public sector whose defining ethos of a 'lack of accountability, the lack of professionalism and the virtual impossibility of being sacked is destructive, steals individuality, encourages arrogance, forces compliance to a culture and drains enthusiasm'. The *crème de la crème*, however, occurred when McGuinness recalled how during his time at the PAC he had watched 'a procession of representatives of boards and bodies peering into a series of financial black holes, completely unable to explain the mystery of it all, but content that no one would lose his job over it'. McGuinness's comparison of such figures to 'featherless, but still plump, state hens, puzzled by what had happened when they tangled with swift, suave commercial foxes' sealed his fate as the Unforgiven One. Biffo despatched him from the ministry as swiftly as he could. A few years later, whilst under the regime of the 'democratic revolutionaries' of FG and Labour, the chairman of the PAC found himself dealing with controversies over the quality of the toilet paper that had been used in his ministerial office in 2007. It was, of course, entirely felicitous that so much information was so freely available about McGuinness just as a knife fight started about who would chair our banking inquiry. Other less charitable souls, alas, simply noted that mandarins, like the elephant, never forget.

McGuinness has often been dismissed as a contrarian by his political and mandarin foes. Yet, in a recent newspaper article Dr Maurice Hayes, the former Northern Ireland Ombudsman, asked, 'What has happened to the service I was proud to work in for most of my career, and to the fine people I worked with in the public service that it should now be reviled as unfit for purpose and exposed to derision and ridicule?' Hayes noted that it had not been 'so long ago since that archetype of the ideal public servant, TK Whitaker, was selected in a poll as the Irishman of the century — epitomising the values of honesty and impartiality, respect for the law, respect for persons, diligence, responsiveness and accountability'. Now, Hayes warned, a public service whose morale 'has been shattered by mindless criticism on the one hand and blind self-interest on the other' cannot even act as 'a brake on autocracy'. Unlike McGuinness, Hayes was not derided. But, he was ignored.

The sort of junior minister who tries to change things is an aggravation, but the worst of the junior ministers, in the eyes of their masters, are those who go around Leinster House wailing about the pains of their status as a singing eunuch. Unfortunately, in a house where most of the habitués have a great deal to do, even if most of it is useless, such complaints will not engender too much sympathy from the peasant classes. More seriously still, Paddy Mac will note that the discontented junior minister swiftly attracts the enmity of the senior minister who knows well that a discontented subordinate is someone who aims to do to you what Oedipus did to his father.

The most recent example of the dangerously difficult junior minister was Róisín Shortall. It was difficult to see how a happy marriage could ever have occurred between the austere Róisín and Dr Reilly. They instead soon bore a far closer resemblance to Jackie Gleason's infamous quarrelling 'Honeymooners'. Sadly, it all became too much for Róisín, who broke the cardinal junior ministerial rules of never think and never resign. After Róisín's departure there was a bit of a flurry and some over-excited comparisons to Noël Browne and Dessie O'Malley's decision to stand by the Republic … by abstaining in a Dáil vote. But, the essential truth of the matter is that Róisín was a nuisance, Róisín revolted, Róisín is gone, Róisín's replacement is settling in very nicely, and whilst Róisín could very well have been right, Róisín won't be coming back any time soon. Oh, and by the way, the good ole boys ain't losing a wink of sleep over that particular 'loss'.

Paddy Mac should not, however, abandon hope, for more by accident than design, some Departments are of worth, even to the junior minister. Great indeed is the joy of the mini-minister who lands the Office of Public Works, for many are the grants that are there to be allocated. And though the grants are small, you can plant a mighty forest of happy backbenchers with a few grand here and there for playgrounds for kiddies. Another junior ministry of great use is one that keeps you close to the Dear Leader you plan to replace some happy day: the role of Chief Whip fits that description nicely. Such a responsible task offers the benefit of 'special time' to be spent together where, on happy moments, the Dear Leader unwinds, you empathise with his woes and everything said by the unappreciated Dear Leader is stored for future reference.

The good news for Paddy Machiavelli is that once you have secured a junior ministry, rather like the public sector and seniority, no great talent beyond resilience is required in order to become a minister, for if you are there long enough, they will promote you, if only out of embarrassment. When the call does finally come, you are of course grateful, again, to serve anywhere. Having made that somewhat obvious point, the next steps should be informed by the sort of reputation our Aspirant Prince wants to build. Happily, if he wishes to be known as the great reformer, there is no shortage of dysfunctional Departments. In fact, if anything, we have a surplus of them. Paddy Mac should note in this regard that the great virtue in securing a Department of duds is that you are, first of all, a victim. Ironically, in this regard, Health is far from being the worst ministry. It is instead like being appointed to be the new captain of the *Titanic* after the iceberg has hit, the crew has already abandoned ship, and the passengers are asking why the music has stopped. The rest of the trip is not going to be a success, but you can hardly do any worse than the fellow who drove the thing into the iceberg.

It is, of course, far more likely that Paddy Mac is probably going to get one of what we might term the Little Ministries. Should that occur, before Paddy Mac goes crying to the media, he should note that many outwardly unattractive ministries offer unexpected opportunities. Enda Kenny in Trade and Tourism was somewhat mockingly dubbed the Minister for Fun. There is, however, a lot to be said for encouraging politicians to let a little light into the country. And in the case of Mr Kenny, his up to then non-existent reputation was at least burnished by his ability to bring the Tour de France to Dublin and his capacity to sit in a chair at the World Trade talks. His Little Ministry served to provide, as we now see, good enough training for his role as Taoiseach. Furthermore, as his earlier career shows, once you have secured the title of minister you are one of the selected few Knights Templar who can contend for the leadership.

On being appointed, 'friends' will tell Paddy Mac to tread carefully. But is this a routinely wise course to take? Some innocents, or malcontents, will recall that in better, but more 'simple' times, politicians such as Donogh O'Malley grabbed troubled Departments by the scruff of the neck, ignored cautious finance ministers like 'honest' Jack Lynch, singed the beard of the revolutionary icon Seán Lemass and simply reformed the place. In a confessional, fearful state, O'Malley was the original black swan. But, it could be argued that his role is a testament to the courageous political genius of Lemass, for O'Malley was unique in one other regard. He was that rare example of a maverick who was carefully cultivated by Lemass to be let loose upon the sacred sheep that had corralled any sense of change with their collective bleats. Unlike his predecessor Noël Browne, O'Malley's capacity to do this was facilitated by his status as a maverick who carried the far bigger clout of Fianna Fáil, as distinct from Clann na Poblachta.

It perhaps says something about the rarity of an O'Malley that almost five decades after his tenure in Education he is still an Irish icon. And some would say it is a testament to the capacity of our governing elite to winkle out such pebbles that O'Malley represented the last triumph of the political maverick until the very different Charlie McCreevy arrived in Finance three decades later.

Sadly, the absence of romance in Irish politics means it is far likelier that Paddy Machiavelli, once he becomes a Little Minister, will spend his initial years confirming his carefully cultivated status as an empty vessel who poses a threat to no man. It may seem somewhat without ambition, but his priority as a minister will be to acquire the reputation of being 'sound'. In fairness, our Aspirant Prince may not have much of a choice in this matter, for this generally is what the Dear Leader wants. During the era of Bertie Ahern, for example, many a minister was sacked or appointed purely on the basis of their capacity to 'keep de unions happy'. It was hardly a blueprint for radical innovation but few of the appointees objected.

Mr Ahern was not unique in this regard, for when it comes to how Paddy Mac must operate, he will find no better map than the great triumph of the ethos of 'careful now' under our radical, reforming Rainbow *manqué* of Grumpy Old Men. If Paddy Mac is a bit nonplussed, the ethic of 'careful now' is derived from those parents of a first-born child who respond to its every move with anxious clucks of 'careful now'. Eventually, the most cautious of parents realise that if the child is to thrive, or at least live a normal life, the nursing strings must be snipped. This, alas, however, rarely happens in Irish politics, where clucks of 'careful now' can follow ministers right into their sunset years.

Although it has always been strong, the 'careful now' principle has reached its apotheosis under the present government. This has surprised some, for originally the mood of the returned refugees from the Rainbow was one of 'in great haste'. A Taoiseach who genuinely modelled himself on Michael Collins told us that he intended to be the leader of a wartime-style government. Under this dispensation, even the relatively ancient status of the Grumpy Old Men was sold as a benefit. The whispered message was that whilst they may, for two decades, have been sauntering around Leinster House with all the verve of overly well-nourished pedigree dogs taking their ease in a summer meadow, this meant that they were actually in a state of peak fitness for the job.

Such, however, is the strength of conservatism in Irish politics that, like the desert orchid which flowers for an hour every century, dropping the enchanted ways of radicalism was the only thing that was done in great haste. This administration might have genuinely wanted to be infused by a radical temper. However, the fightback of the petit bourgeois spirit meant that the template of the government increasingly resembled a latter-day version of 'Upstairs, Downstairs', where the butcher, baker, bank manager and clerk knew their place. And, perhaps not so surprisingly, the longer the Grumpy Old Men settled into their ministerial easy chairs, the less it actually appeared to be the case that they felt they had nothing to lose. This fightback of the 'careful now' principle meant that, within weeks, those who dared to question Croke Park, that dying final tendril of social partnership, were warned to be 'careful now'. The ferocious Mrs Merkel was now the friend of Eamon and Enda, and there would be no 'irresponsible' wars over banking debt. Anyone who dared to suggest that we need a purge of the banks received the same warning of 'careful now'. Annex the Bank of Ireland's flagship offices on College Green, the setting for Grattan's Parliament, as a form of reparations? Careful now, we don't want to trespass upon the independence of the banks. End upwardly mobile rents? Careful now, the Constitution says we can't. And as for cutting welfare benefits for the richest pensioners in Europe, well that's definitely a case of 'careful now'.

Intriguingly, though it is a tempting seductress, Paddy Mac might also consider that whilst the politics of 'careful now' represents the easy choice, appeasement does not facilitate happiness. Instead, the more the Desiderata of Inertia wrapped itself around our Grumpy Old Men, the bitterer they become. Caution may be the watchword of Irish politics, but often this political emphysema does not bring long-term ease.

In looking at the speed with which the virus of 'careful now' can strike, it might appear strange to suggest that a small retirement soirée for a retired public servant was an epochal moment in the life of a government. But, in retrospect, the going-away do that our bright new Coalition provided for Dermot McCarthy, Bertie's top mandarin and the author of so many of our current fortunes, was such a moment. It was a strange enough event, given all that previous talk about how the axe would be taken to all those who had led us through the rose garden of the boom and into the current thorns. Happily, all that was swiftly forgotten, as, in the wake of the soirée, a graphic account informed us that 'an A-list political line-up of guests' had attended our mandarin's departure. In a signal of how we were all suddenly friends, Mr Gilmore had jocosely said the only two things that would keep the Taoiseach away from the gathering were a European Council meeting or a Connacht football final. Then, after the customary speeches, the 200 partygoers were treated to an extravagant spread of Italian food in the Italian Room of the building which, we were told, was all paid for by Mr McCarthy. The claim was not entirely correct, for it was the poor taxpayer who was stumping up for the bill via Mr McCarthy's lavish pension. Still, one thing was clear. Amidst the sumptuous dining, after the fret and flux of the early days, the mandarins were back in town, if indeed they had ever left it. The speedy return of the triumphant mandarin is something therefore that Paddy Mac should remember before he trots into his new offices with too much of a radical strut.

The preceding sequence of events should lead Paddy Mac to another critical epiphany. Politicians are always obsessed by other politicians and the media. But, in fact, like Churchill, who was always more concerned about those 'supporting' him from behind than his political enemies in front, political opponents are the least of Paddy Machiavelli's troubles. Instead, now that he has secured power, Paddy Mac must prioritise how he is to deal with those strange and dangerous figures known as the public sector mandarins. Up to now, the relationship has been a simple and untroubled one, where our Aspirant Prince has been the people's advocate. If he has been in opposition, this means that he has wanted to axe the pay and conditions of the very same group of feline gentlemen who are now smiling at Paddy the Minister. Of course, be it as a government TD or as an aspirant minister, Paddy has spent his time attempting to seduce small favours from the self-same mandarins. Now, suddenly, like a colonial satrap who has usurped the lawful king, he finds himself to be the master.

The good news is that when Paddy the Minister skips in the door wearing his new Louis Copeland suit, the new man's plans for great reforms are met with a level of enthusiastic approbation which would lead one to wonder why the need for reform exists in the first place. One example of how on the initial days everyone does get on so well is the new great tradition where the mandarins will wryly present our Minister with a box set of 'Yes Minister' DVDs. Everyone will laugh and claim that of course this is not the way it works here. But, in a classic example of the old three-card trick, this is precisely how it works, for if our Aspirant Prince is looking to locate his real place in the hierarchy, he must ask one simple question. In the outside world, when something goes wrong in the workplace, it is the most junior staff member, rather than the board of directors, what get the blame. So, if the ministers are really in charge, how is it then that it is as entrenched as the Mount Rushmore sculptures that if anything ever goes wrong in the Department, it is the minister who ends up in the ducking stool?

The astonishing thing is that our ministers, who are normally more precious than the seven wise virgins about anything to do with their reputation, acquiesce so easily with such a process. Doing so represents an implicit admission that, when it comes to the Department, Paddy Machiavelli is not the master in his own house. And if you are not that, how can you reform it? Should Paddy Mac want to understand how this occurs, he should note that one of the features of the post-colonial society is the sacred cow. In our case, this originally was the Church, though that did not end too well. There was the law and the judiciary, though this, in the wake of the pay and pensions debacle, did not end happily either. The poor old political system, rather like the media, was never at the races.

In contrast one of the most cunning triumphs of the mandarin class is their creation of the belief that mandarins always serve the public interest, rather than self-interest. Such a carefully cultivated aura of righteousness plays no small role in ensuring that Paddy Machiavelli trots into the Department carrying a secret cultural cringe. Paddy Mac is also hamstrung by another equally serious dilemma. One of the great misconceptions of Irish public life is that it is believed top civil servants are far more intelligent than the rest of human society. Once again, 'Yes Minister', with its Aesop's fables of the scheming Sir Humphrey and the gormless Jim Hacker, has much to answer for. In challenging this, it is important to note we are not saying that politicians are secretly clever. Instead, what we are actually suggesting to Paddy Mac is that he should remain keenly aware that often the great panjandrums of the Sir Humphreys are as witless as their 'masters'. There may, during the Whitaker era, have been public servants who drove the process of social and economic reform. But, at some indefinable point, this ethos of intellectual inquiry and public service was replaced by a brackish belief in careerist self-service. And whilst we are told that our civil servants are inspired generalists, the story of how we have been misgoverned suggests it might be more accurate to suggest that they resemble spoofers.

The problem for Paddy Machiavelli is that due to his natural deference, he cannot recognise that, to quote the original Machiavelli, often the modern mandarin resembles those 'mercenaries and auxiliaries' who 'are useless and dangerous and if one holds his state based on those arms he will stand neither firm nor safe; for they are disunited, ambitious and without discipline, unfaithful, valiant before friends, cowardly before enemies.'

There is a certain familiarity surrounding the further condemnations that 'in peace one is robbed by them' for the 'fact is they have no other attraction or reason for keeping the field than a trifle of a stipend which is not sufficient to make them willing to die for you.' Paddy Machiavelli may try to revolt against such a set of circumstances. But, when it comes to his mandarin masters, should the Aspirant Prince follow the 'very brave minister' style of precedents set by fellows such as Martin Cullen or John McGuinness, he may become the victim of an unfortunate series of 'accidents'. Rather, as part of the training for his main task of being an empty vessel serving invisible masters, our Aspirant Prince should instead learn to at least appear to love his mandarin masters. It might not be honest, but it will at least give Paddy Mac the chance to study his enemies before he makes any moves on them.

Though he will be tempted, the one thing that Paddy Mac must not do, should he meet resistance to a reforming agenda, is to resign. And if our man is even flirting with leaving over some 'moral issue', the best advice we can give is 'careful now'. Countries where politics is centred on ideology, as distinct from the tribe, may witness frequent resignations, but in Ireland the template for the ideological resignation was set in stone by Dr Noël Browne.

Our Aspirant Prince will note that resignations for such reasons were a comparative rarity up to this point. The Civil War had, understandably, quite eroded the national desire for such tempestuous actions. Dr Browne, however, overturned that particular rule as he took on a familiar troika of timorous politicians, over-mighty mandarins and hospital consultants. It was a fine, dramatic and very modern affair, with leaks to *The Irish Times* and then a speech to the Dáil that echoed through the ages. Once it was all over, the reality of things was, however, that the pedigree Blueshirts in the cabinet and the Law Library and, most importantly of all, the Irish Medical Association, had won a comprehensive triumph. There was something astonishingly modern in the warning by John A Costello that 'whatever about fighting the doctors, I am not going to fight the Bishops, and whatever about fighting the Bishops, I am not going to fight the doctors and the Bishops.' Some five decades later, a fellow called Bertie was to get three terms in the top job operating a very similar set of principles.

Amidst all the passion, it is worth recalling what happened to the good doctor in the succeeding decades. This incorporated less than radical options, such as the joining of, and exit from, de Valera's FF, and the even less radical decision to join, and his subsequent inevitable expulsion from, the Labour Party. Dr Browne's fate goes a long way towards explaining why the resignation concept did not take. There were quite a few sackings, mostly for endemic drunkenness and treason, but, as we anxiously scan the history pages of the 1960s, not a single name surfaces through the murk of the government benches. The resignation on moral issues is, unsurprisingly, not too evident in the 1970s either. Some will cite Dessie O'Malley and his decision to abstain by the Republic. But it is important for our Aspirant Prince to be aware that for all the fine and dandy talk about 'standing by the Republic' when the 'chips are down', less than five years later the chips came in, and Mr O'Malley was seen standing beside Mr Haughey, the enemy of the Republic, in the cabinet photograph, looking very pleased with himself. Even the government of Biffo the Unready, with its bailouts and that other treasure chest of disasters, witnessed no resignations, except for those exacted at political gunpoint. The ever-ethical Greens stayed through it all. Dermot Ahern and Noel Dempsey suffered indignities that would be endured by no other politician in any other state, and grumbled their way through to the golden trough of ministerial pensions that awaited them.

Paddy Machiavelli should note that the only resignation — or rather deliberately orchestrated sacking — that ever bore any fruit was that of Albert, and the only reason Albert departed was to be in a better position to catch the apple of power when it fell off Haughey's rotting tree. So, if Paddy Mac is to resign, it must be done with a short-term rather than a long-term plan in mind, for if he does not already know, our Aspirant Prince must always do his fighting on the pitch, rather than sulking in a ditch.

Chapter 6

THE JOY OF PATHOS; SELF-PITY IS THE STICK THAT SCRATCHES AN ELECTORAL ITCH

It makes him contemptible to be considered fickle, frivolous, effeminate, mean-spirited, irresolute, from all of which the prince should guard himself as from a rock.

On how you cannot be a vacuum • so what is this ideology thing? • an economic policy • the prince and enterprise • the banks • Celtic Tiger crouching • that problem called the North • crime • appropriate sentiments and catch phrases • good health • be not an angry man • Ming and the art of pathos • Bertie Narcissus and Mary Harney, Queen of Hearts

Whilst Paddy Machiavelli will get away with, and actually be commended for, being a vacuum most of the time, if he desires to be more than a Little Minister, he cannot be a vacuum all of the time. That has not stopped some politicians from believing this is a certain road to preferment. It is an easy trap to fall into, for all you want to do is oblige. But, if you abase yourself too much in the service of the Dear Leader and his acolytes, you are not yourself. Instead, Paddy Mac is a mere host who will accommodate all the desires of the parasite that will consume and consume until all that's left of the person is a husk. Sometimes, Paddy Mac will have no choice in the matter, but, before he gets too content with such a zombified position, he should realise that those who agree too easily to be the Dear Leader's cat's paw will be amiably despised by the Dear Leader they serve so faithfully.

Those Aspirant Princes who would sacrifice their self-respect in the service of the party — or, more accurately, in the service of their own ambition — would do well to realise that, like virginity, respect, once lost, cannot be regained. Even Gerry Collins, as cute an operator as you could find, never politically recovered from his teary-eyed plea to Albert to cease and desist when Reynolds made his first move on Haughey. The emotional appearance on national television was all the more surprising, for Collins was a fox who had survived in cabinet or the frontbench since 1970. The vicissitudes that had afflicted the party since that era meant it was no mean feat. Paddy Mac should, however, note that once fear and terror glide down a shivery spine, it snaps the tendons of the most acute sense of danger. So it was that a red-faced Collins appeared on RTÉ as Haughey's puppet blubbering about how Albert was 'going to wreck our party right down the centre … and burst up the government'. Were either claim credible, Collins might have got away with it. But the stance was so self-evidently risible, and the absence of backbone so public, that Collins became a national laughing stock. And, a year later, when Albert took the crown, Gerry became a backbench laughing stock.

One way our Aspirant Prince can avoid the label of being a vacuum is to acquire some form of an ideology. Paddy Mac should not worry, for so long as it's done quickly, it should not hurt at all. In defining his political identity, Paddy Machiavelli should not fret too much about whether he belongs to the right or the left. The truth is that Paddy Mac is actually stuck tighter in the muddled centre than a Siberian tiger splashing around a tar pit. And he should do everything in his power to stay there.

The first thing Paddy Mac must do is to articulate some sort of a personal economic policy. This means he will definitely stand out from a herd of politicians whose response to fiscal matters is generally informed by a mix of fear and chaste uncertainty. Though he will be chancing his arm, Paddy Machiavelli need not fret about being caught, for when it comes to sums, most of our media class and all our mandarins are in the same leaky ship of fools. Paddy Mac, if he is wise, should follow the precedent set by Mary Harney, where a few catch cries about the superiority of Boston over Berlin or light-touch regulation will secure him a high and honoured status.

When it comes to securing Paddy Mac's status as one of those rare politicians who are seen as being 'sympathetic to the enterprise society', it would help if he were to learn off a single transferable speech on such issues. One maestro of this particular art is Eamon Gilmore, who regularly used the issue of 'getting the job done' as a rhetorical crutch. Should Paddy Mac embrace the pragmatic virtue of 'getting the job done', he need not worry that anyone might ever ask or know what the job he wants to get done actually *is*. Indeed, some would argue that it is foolish and intrusive to complicate matters by actually defining what that job might be. It is instead sufficient to know, if asked, that our Aspirant Prince realises there is a job of work to be done, whatever and wherever that 'job of work' might be and that he is busy getting on with 'the job of work' that is required to do 'the job of work'. He is also intent on doing 'the job of work' quickly, of ensuring that everyone is aware of the importance and the scale of 'this job of work', of the difficulty involved in doing the 'job of work', due to the absence of low-hanging fruit, and the status of this 'job of work' as the best of a menu of bad options at a time where there are no easy solutions. That should clarify everything swiftly enough.

Paddy Mac should also at all times be for free enterprise and against handouts from the state, unless a grant is needed for the constituency, in which case the state and private enterprise are working hand in hand 'building enterprise-centred communities'. This stance of definitive vagueness is one that will carry our Aspirant Prince far in other areas such as the politically lucrative but dangerous territories of social protection. Here, our Aspirant Prince should be careful to be always for 'change' in social welfare rather than cutbacks. Change is a grand, vague word, whilst cutbacks can get you into trouble. Paddy Machiavelli will never be, therefore, for such vulgar brutalities as cutbacks in the basic social welfare rate or the rate for pensioners, or for cutbacks in free travel, free fuel, free TV, or for cutbacks for carers. It leaves a pretty thin menu, but if he is hoist upon a petard, Paddy Mac can push the boat out as far as being for 'targeted cutbacks', which should allow the merry dance of meaningless verbiage to continue without anyone being harmed.

Back in the strange world of being for enterprise, our Aspirant Prince may occasionally be asked what variant of enterprise he might be for. At equivocal moments such as this Paddy Mac should enthusiastically claim he is for smart technology, cloud computing and the knowledge economy, since the journalists won't know what he is talking about either. The future, he will declare, lies in smart green jobs, as distinct from dumb ones, presumably. There is, alas, one problem with all of these smart jobs, which is that a lot of Irishmen are not hardwired for the 'smart economy'. Our Aspirant Prince should, however, resolutely confine them to the refuse bin of more training, lest they take the shiny look off all the new Silicon Valleys residing in the Dreamland of the smart economy that Paddy Mac has created. No one, after all, ever got photographed for a newspaper because they officiated at the opening of a chicken farm. Our politician is, of course, also opposed to all the red tape he has legislated through on the nod. He will instead be anxious to be seen as a supporter of business icons like Michael O'Leary. However, whilst he will often ask why the Irish public service can't learn from Michael O'Leary, the not-so-secret truth is that he is somewhat frightened of O'Leary, who has quite the nasty tongue on him.

When it comes to the banks, Paddy Mac would be wise to be even more nervous. Like so many other things, our man's positioning in this regard fluctuates, depending on whether he is in opposition where he is the fearless enemy of the banks or in government where he must, regrettably, embrace the responsible course. In the case of responsibility, this is best translated as meaning that Paddy Mac intends, in government, to stay as far away from the banks as possible. Distressed mortgage holders may present us with a poignant spectacle, but if he skips gaily into the banks, he is like a tourist paddling in the Nile. The sun might beam on Paddy Mac's back for a while, but he is flirting with the sort of intellectual deep water where there is no shortage of furry crocodiles waiting to wrap their warm fangs around him and drag him down. Of course, one dare not say this in public. Instead, Paddy Mac must use the lexicon of digging deep, even as he backs away nervously from the terrible creature in the manner of the sort of postman who, when a flea-ridden mongrel sinks its teeth into his buttocks, coos, 'Good doggy', in the hope that the current level of pain will be as bad as things get.

The most cautious relationship of all that our politician must maintain is with our very dearly departed Celtic Tiger. This may be an easily slapped ragdoll, but our relationship with the now crouching tiger is somewhat more ambivalent than first appearances might suggest. Though Paddy the voter still nods his head obediently through all the sermons about his failings, like the dry alcoholic, Paddy the voter knows that he still has a taste for the excesses of the Tiger — the decking, the extensions, the holidays and the sense that if you went to the 'right' bank you could be a millionaire by lunchtime. If he is wise, our Aspirant Prince will, therefore, always cloak critiques of the Tiger with vague indications about how some things went well, whilst condemning 'excesses' which should be described as 'overly exuberant entrepreneurial spirits gone wrong'.

In calibrating his response to the Celtic Tiger, our Aspirant Prince should therefore be warned that Paddy the voter is becoming increasingly unimpressed with the queue of ongoing Celtic Tiger bashers. Paddy the voter suspects that whilst these enthusiasts are theoretically condemning the Tiger, they are actually slapping poor Paddy for having 'notions'. And, to be blunt, Paddy the voter does not need yet another left-wing Savonarola condemning him for his desire to ape the material lifestyles of those same six-figure-salary, cosily pensioned liberal sociology lecturers who are condemning him.

Though Paddy Machiavelli is engaged in the brave less-travelled road of cultivating, or rather borrowing, his very own ideas, our Aspirant Prince must keep his eye on the prize of never appearing to be too dangerous. He can't have people thinking he is one of those McDowells. Such a set of criteria means, oddly enough, that Enda is the perfect role model for our Aspirant Prince. Unlike rougher beasts such as Haughey, it is safe to treat him with contempt because he will not bite or leave in a huff. In fact, it is very difficult to get rid of him, for you can insult Enda all you want and, like the cat they could not kill, he will still be there, smiling affably as he remembers every word you said. In a world full of egocentrics Enda is liked because he creates the impression of being the original *tabula rasa* who always leaves a meeting with the perfect imprint of the last voice that imposed itself upon his presence. There is, of course, method behind the merriment, for in a land where ideology is treated like a porcupine, Enda has no views beyond the desire to win elections and, hopefully, to create a nicer world as a side effect. The former is, of course, something Mr Kenny has done in spades even while we mock him.

Paddy Mac must also, if he is to be respected, acquire the image of not being someone who collapses into a heap when confronted by what we shall term 'posh thoughts'. This means our man must acquire the appearance of having some expertise in areas such as foreign policy. In simpler, happier times, Irish foreign policy was confined to the somewhat inaccurate view that England's difficulty was always Ireland's opportunity. Then, for a time, things changed and Europe was Ireland's opportunity. These days we don't really know whether Europe is Ireland's difficulty or Ireland is Europe's difficulty. Nevertheless, Paddy Machiavelli must have a view on Europe if he is to be seen as a serious politician. This dilemma can be swiftly resolved once Paddy Mac learns that the art of 'knowing your place' is as popular with Paddy's European masters as it is with his domestic masters. Rather like our former British owners, the EU likes Paddy to play a limited number of carefully defined roles. He should, if possible, be entertaining and definitely hospitable. But when it comes to the causing of trouble, Paddy should be the quiet child in the class who would rather faint from hunger than annoy the teacher with any plaintive bleats. This is what others term being a good role model. Happily, it is a role that Paddy's colonial experience means he is perfectly placed to play.

As part of broadening his public profile, Paddy Mac must also learn something about that problem called 'the North'. The first thing he must do is learn to love it. He should even, for the purposes of broadening his cv, consider going on holidays there and be snapped enjoying himself, for the more civilised parts of Belfast are safe and quite enjoyable, so long as you can find a few English visitors to pass the time with. The North, however, is only your friend so long as it does not spill across the Border. Up there they can have all the rows they want about flags, identity and whether the moon is British or Irish. But, whilst Paddy Mac will patronise them with a gentle, supercilious smile, should they dare to come down here, he will take his stand with Retail Excellence in demanding that no parades should ever be allowed to endanger the Grafton Street Saturday shopping experience. In fairness, he would be right too, for he is wrestling with enough current problems without having a set of 17th-century squabbles landed on his desk.

Unlike the North, crime is something that definitely matters to the citizen. It will come as a surprise to Paddy Machiavelli but, even in opposition, he will have to be extremely careful on the crime front. Nothing epitomises this more than the ill-fated denouement of FF's love affair with Zero Tolerance. In fairness, Bertie was wise enough to ensure that Zero Tolerance never evolved beyond the half-life of being a slogan on a cab driver's door. Other more bullish characters were not so cautious, however, and tried to implement this Zero Tolerance thing. Such a position failed to understand that, like many other reforms, the plain people agreed with Zero Tolerance in theory, but definitely not in practice. In particular, the Gardaí were not even slightly supportive, wisely suspecting that enforcing it would create more work for them. But, in a reflection of how the state is set up, this would only have represented the first stage of the problem, for we would also have had to find a sufficiency of judges to sentence our discommoded criminal classes. That too, were it successful, would be a disaster, for prisons would have to be built to house those guilty of crimes. As with other matters, the attempted forced marriage between the ethos of that strange school of American legislator (who believes that if laws are passed they should be implemented) and Ireland's Mediterranean psyche collapsed in acrimony, discord and apprehension before this political changeling breathed its last after the Garda Blue Flu strike.

The lesson from Zero Tolerance that Paddy Mac must learn is that he is better off confining his analysis of policing in Ireland to the cultivation of appropriate sentiments. This means that should a hypothetical tribunal find that the entire force is corrupt, the proper response would be: 'The Gardaí are beating crime with limited resources, and a few (thousand) rotten apples should not be allowed damage perception of the force.' Some civil libertarian oddballs will, of course, claim that such obedience creates an underperforming police force that is contemptuous of its political masters. Paddy Mac, however, must treat this logic with the contempt that his Garda sources reserve for it.

Paddy Machiavelli must also be careful of any excessive association with the self-same civil libertarians. The susceptibility of Labour in particular to this vice is surprising, given that Labour's target audience would like to see criminals being locked up for the obvious reason that they are the biggest victims of their actions. However, the south Dublin liberals who define Labour 'values' believe it is their bounden duty to empathise with a set of criminals they will never meet. Sadly, the situation is further complicated by the great difficulty many of our Labour friends experience in differentiating between the criminal class and the working class. Our Labour opinion-formers may use kindness to criminals as a form of purgative for middle-class guilt. This, however, is not a trap Paddy Machiavelli should fall into unless he wants to be in a party that consistently wins 20 seats. He instead should consider FF's long and successful electoral history and, particularly while he is in opposition, constantly call for criminals to be banged up in prison cells that do not and will not ever exist. This is particularly important when Paddy Mac is in the fallow land of opposition, where each crime 'crisis' must be responded to with the delight of the dog who desires nothing more from life than to roll in fresh cow dung when he is released into a field. Presumably, like the dog, the opposition's objective when engaging in the political equivalent of this act is to disguise the rank scent of their own opportunism.

Rather like on the North, our Aspirant Prince might not want to have a policy on health. He will not, though, have the freedom of movement to escape from that particular territory. The situation is confused further by the reality that he must follow a different approach from that taken on crime. Paddy Mac, in opposition at least, wants to reform the justice system. In contrast, when it comes to the hydra of health, our Aspirant Prince should be opposed to reform in opposition and government. Of course, when he gets into government he should make a great fuss about 'delivery'. But, again, like the North or reform generally, he should shy as cautiously around that issue as a fox circling a cooked chicken hanging on a string from a tree. There is no great harm in having flurries of reform papers and consultation documents, and review and strategy papers. Indeed, the new minister may even sack a few boards, just to give the impression of having a ruthless streak. There is, however, one slight problem when it comes to reform, which is this: whether he is in opposition or in government, Paddy Mac must cherish the 'frontline staff'. These are the sacred cows of the health service, and just as George Washington apparently never told a lie, Paddy Mac will never have met a greedy hospital consultant or a bad nurse. So, if Paddy Mac touches their terms and conditions, there will be a terrible furore, until the Taoiseach eventually sidles over and says, 'Can we please leave the nurses alone?' Sadly, seeing as staff constitute 90 per cent of the HSE and you cannot touch their terms and conditions, this means that the reform agenda is somewhat circumscribed. Still, as minister, he can always aspire to reform, describe how beneficial reform will be, sketch out a vision of the wonderful health service that is coming, and leave the current one strictly alone.

Amidst all this fine thinking our Aspirant Prince should not neglect smaller but equally critical matters, such as acquiring a catch phrase to define his persona. One normally associates the catch phrase with a comedian or a light entertainer, but that shouldn't act in any way as a barrier to Paddy Mac. In fact, he might do well to study role models like Bruce Forsyth or Hector Ó hEochagáin, for in the wake of the success of our Italian friend, the comedian Beppe Grillo, nothing surely is impossible in this world. Some might even contend that cheery bellows of 'Hector here!' would surely meet the less than heavy demands of public discourse in the Republic. Our own maestro of that art was Bertie and his patented 'the hardy men working hard' unisex greeting for both men and women. The 'hardy men working hard' worked on more fronts than merely providing the then Taoiseach with a necessary crutch to facilitate the imitation of interest in the lives of the citizens. It also enhanced the mood of the approached layabouts who were being complimented for possessing virtues they actually did not have. It suggested that the Taoiseach was stupid, foolish or generous and these are qualities our electorate like to see in their politicians.

Catch phrases vary enormously, though, and some do not provide Paddy Machiavelli with happy precedents. John Bruton's catch phrase, for example, consisted of a braying laugh that could break a chandelier at a thousand yards. In contrast, with typical elegant minimalism Jack Lynch's catch phrase consisted of a pipe and a glass of Paddy. Like Mr Lynch, the current incumbent, Mr Kenny, does not exactly have a catch phrase. He instead has a sort of all-enveloping, American-style knuckle punch, whereby Enda will approach ministers and TDs, treat them to a playful punch, recall their names and request a 'status report' on whatever harmless duties they have been engaged in to fill the vacant time that can make the days appear to be so long. Apparently, some of the younger backbenchers find this to be an enormously exciting moment. Sadly, the Dear Leader did not fare so well when he approached a veteran TD and attempted the same trick. The TD returned the knuckle punch and said: 'Kenny, Taoiseach, status report.' An unimpressed Taoiseach departed without saying another word.

Of course, like the old midfield general in a soccer match, Paddy Mac must create an overall theme to cover all responses to the broad mass of issues he is obliged to address. For now, if he is to be compatible with the spirit of the age, the image Paddy Machiavelli must consistently project is one of modest concern. This doesn't mean the Aspirant Prince cannot be angry, for a politician without anger is like the cat without a tail who always finds it is missing something in the balance department. But, he must never be angry in an angry way. Rage is acceptable amongst those we do not treat seriously, such as trade union leaders who are anxious to maintain their six-figure salaries, or Joe Duffy. In contrast, the politician who is in a permanent rage leaves himself dangerously open to being stereotyped in the manner that FF draped Ruairí Quinn with an unprepossessing 'Mr Angry from Sandymount' persona. It also raises the possibility that our politician may be one of those revolutionary types, and whilst Paddy the voter may flirt with default, he is even more anxious to ensure that the money he has under the mattress will not be seized by the state and given to the poor. In short, Paddy is essentially a conservative pragmatist who uses the politics of Joe Duffyism as the psychic equivalent of a massage with a happy ending.

Surprisingly, given his vanilla persona, one of the important lessons in the dangers of anger for Paddy Mac is provided by Enda Kenny. The sheen was just beginning to come off the democratic revolution when our Dear Leader found himself in Athlone experiencing the sombre joys of a European referendum. So it was that when he was forced into meeting a more cantankerous than usual set of 'ordinary' citizens it was all the more critical that the Dear Leader maintain a tranquil persona. Instead, when confronted by an anti-household charges demonstrator who told the Dear Leader to 'take the bridge, go west and stay there', Mr Kenny snapped, 'You could do with a day's work, I'd say'. Were Enda a Haughey or a Biffo it might have been a run of the mill sort of fracas. But, for happy-go-lucky Enda, well, it was the equivalent of a surplice-wearing altar boy swearing at the parish priest to 'f**king hurry up. The pub is opening in five minutes.' In an age of mass unemployment, Enda's retort was also crass and insensitive. And, from that moment, a certain chill began to settle between the Taoiseach and an electorate who had just seen a bit of his secret snarling side. Enda has been cute enough to ensure that the event has not been repeated. But the stain is still there, for it is in the nature of man that one act of distemper rubs away the rubric woven by a thousand acts of kindness.

Our Aspirant Prince might think it odd, given all the work he has put into embracing the chastity belt of respectability, that Luke 'Ming' Flanagan is regarded as a far better role model for Paddy Mac than 'Angry' Enda. But beauty is found in strange places, and his most useful attribute — which Mr Flanagan shares with Bertie Ahern and Mary Harney — is the capacity to create a unique sense of pathos around him. The value of this art is that in Ireland the pity of the electorate is the absolution that washes away all sin. It might seem puzzling to us that a man on just under a hundred grand a year plus expenses, plus a leadership allowance, can define himself as one of the lost lambs of this earth. But, by doing so in a manner that would even impress Sinn Féin, Ming has become one of us. This position does have the unfortunate consequence that Ming is incapable of transforming or radicalising his electorate, since, by adopting the status of a victim, he, ironically, is instead part of the herd he aspires to lead. It is, however, a perfect tool for electoral successs and that, alas, appears to be good enough for Ming.

This quality of victimhood was evident from Ming's first day in Leinster House, when the Independent managed to weave his own life story into the somewhat less important story of who would be our next Taoiseach. At that time, it appeared to be a touching but hopefully isolated piece of rhetoric, as Ming wished Kenny 'the best of luck on behalf of my two children because if he has good luck and he does well, they will not have to take the boat or the aeroplane to London like 19 out of 20 members of my family and my wife's family.' Unfortunately, it swiftly became all too clear that Ming's status as a victim of forces that are so invisible most do not actually exist would be the defining motif of his Dáil career. The apogee in this regard was reached when, complaining about the 'abuse' he was receiving over his dress sense he said: 'The reality is I was born this way. I do not have a choice but to be the person I am. If I was born black or if I was born with one leg or whatever, would he have a right to have a go at me? No, he wouldn't.' Whilst Ming did not compare his right to enter the Dáil chamber dressed in an Oscar the Grouch

T-shirt to Nelson Mandela's battle against apartheid, it was a damn close-run thing. Paddy Mac, though, must note that those politicians who condemn Ming's politics of hysteria and victimhood miss the point. In other times, the politics of pathos would be disregarded. But, seeing as we live in the great age of political unreason that has elected such varying Frankensteins as Gerry Adams and Mick Wallace, Ming is perfectly attuned to the mindset of the citizenry. Mind you, whilst Paddy Mac can profitably study Ming, he should be circumspect in one regard. What Ming Flanagan does works for Ming, but no one is quite ready for a cannabis-smoking, jumper-wearing, tie-eschewing 'Dear Leader.'

The Aspirant Prince would also be wise to realise that the embrace of the politics of pathos is accompanied by one great danger. In doing so, you are surrendering your fortune to the forces of unreason. And just as the Irish mother's capacity for forgiveness is endless, our capacity for hatred can be boundless. Bertie Ahern certainly knows the truth of that: all the unequivocal love he inspired is now gone. The Aspirant Prince will note that there is something of the myth of Narcissus surrounding the betrayed electorate and the despised Taoiseach. Bertie may have been publicly pious and modest, but it was the Taoiseach's pride in his own perfection that diverted him from hearing the creaking in the false timbers he had used to shore up the Celtic Tiger. However, as is often the case with great betrayals, two parties were complicit, for the electorate too were unable to tear themselves away from the false reflection of ourselves that Bertie created. Ironically, this 'dancer and the dance' style of intimacy between Taoiseach and electorate meant that the shared break-up was all the more ferocious when the first ripples signalling future tsunamis appeared on the perfect pond that both had gazed so intently upon.

All the subsequent smashing of cups has disguised the real political potency of Bertie. But whilst the electorate may be experiencing memory troubles, Paddy Machiavelli should not forget that during Bertie's time of greatness, such was the fearful level of the enchantment, our focus was always on the wagging tail and the soulful eyes, rather than the political fleas that were hopping around on the Taoiseach's fur. Outside of success, which always helps, the protective shield that spared Bertie from the indignity of being treated as other men was his unique capacity for pathos. It was an art carefully cultivated from the start, with tales of a long-haired Bertie shambling around the disco, before the great art reached its astonishing apogee during the Bryan Dobson interview when Mr Ahern's adventures with Paddy the Plasterer et al. first began to bubble to the surface. Mr Ahern has previously noted that his favourite song is 'IIow Much Is That Doggy in the Window?' On that day, in a display that would have even enthralled that maestro of empathy, Bill Clinton, Bertie with the doe eyes and soulful look resembled the sort of dog in the window, with a little wag in his tail who fills all onlookers with the desire to cuddle it, no matter how much of a mess emerges from its nether regions. Like Clinton, it wasn't so much what Bertie said, but rather the woebegone Everyman persona that he invested the events with that won the day.

In an astonishing reflection of the times, the interview was a catalyst for an unofficial sympathy referendum where the Taoiseach routed the Grumpy Old Opposition to such an extent that he destroyed their nerve. In an indication that it was not solely the economy that had moved comprehensively from the territories of sanity, the debate on the Taoiseach's response segued into an astonishing dissertation on how Mr Ahern's defensive eyebrows had decommissioned his political critics. Amidst the solemn discussions about Bertie's 'passive aggressive' eyebrows and 'how they might waggle at you', nobody even whispered stop. The herd instinct had reached its peak and the only way after that for Bertie and the rest of us was to fall off the cliff together.

In truth, good as Bertie was, when it came to the capacity of inspiring pity amongst the electorate, the former ward boss was surpassed in this art by Mary Harney. It should be remembered that Ms Harney, during her initial years in opposition, defined her role in politics as a transformative reforming presence. As she left office, as bejewelled by pensions as the Queen of Sheba, the tale was somewhat different. She had played a central role in a government which had busted up a country, led a party to the edge and beyond of destruction and yet, somehow, Ms Harney escaped far more comprehensively than Bertie from the consequences of her actions. Intriguingly, despite Ms Harney's public profile as a political Florence Nightingale, the most revealing illustration of her private thoughts on politics was provided by her advice to the neophyte Green minister, John Gormley, that even the worst day in government was better than the best day in opposition. By the time he had finished 'partying' with Biffo and the boys, Mr Gormley might have had a few queries on the accuracy of that particular advice. But, Ms Harney was utterly genuine in her view.

However, such was her ability in the guileful art of pathos that few ever saw the careerist side of Harney. Instead, her mastery of the key art of pathos allowed 'poor' Mary to get away with a litany of escapades. Some were farcical, such as the holiday in a French villa owned by businessman Ulick McEvaddy, or getting the government jet to bring 'poor Mary' to Leitrim to open a new off-licence owned by a Progressive Democrat supporter. When it came to the many, many very long overseas trips and the great escapes, few could match Ms Harney's capacity for escapology after the furore over the hair-do in Florida. The genius of Harney was revealed when Leo Varadkar claimed the Tánaiste should resign over the affair. Though her powers were in decline, Ms Harney put on the patented sad face and tearful eyes, and a horrified media consensus rounded on Leo. In fairness, all of the public sector elite were enjoying the fine dining and the high living. But Mary, our self-proclaimed Queen of Hearts, was supposed to be opposed to such horrors. The fact that many still believe Ms Harney lived like an opposition style pious protestor whilst she was a Minister suggests 'poor Mary' really was, when it comes to pathos, the slyest fox of all.

Chapter 7 ~

ON THE POLITICS OF EMPATHY AND THE VIRTUE OF HATRED

… men judge generally more by the eye than by the hand because it belongs to everybody to see you, to few to come in touch with you.

On how 'honest' Jack invented empathy • a fatal flaw • Haughey embraces the peasant class • boybands and Bertie • the FG-Labour empathy-free zone • Enda's symposia with shopping trolleys • the flight of the Biffo • on learning from error • the art of the apology • Noonan's bluff • a Clinton tale • Micheál Martin chooses the apologetic way and no more Mr Altar Boy

Though he has now secured the high office of being a Little Minister for Something or Other, Paddy Mac cannot be fretting about ideology the whole time. Our Aspirant Prince should instead continue to refine his expertise in the softer political virtues, for these are the more popular ones. Intriguingly, empathy — and the concept of the Irish political leader being an ordinary decent citizen — is a relatively new political phenomenon. Éamon de Valera and Seán Lemass were revolutionary icons who retained an austere distance from the citizens. Fine Gael, far from embracing the virtues of empathy, was far happier to inform citizens of their appropriate lowly place in a country that, were God in His Heaven, would be governed by barristers, hospital consultants and cattle-fatteners from Meath. Then 'honest' Jack Lynch, the balloons and the T-shirts arrived, and Irish politics was never the same again. Under 'honest' Jack, in a measure of the times, his love of taking high tea in convents was the signifier of Lynch's status. And, indeed, if it were not for our slightly changed circumstances, we could see Micheál Martin sipping demure cups of tea and batting his eyelashes at radiant nuns whose cheeks have turned rosy with salacious thoughts.

If Paddy Machiavelli possesses a soul, he will be tempted to avoid the Gethsemane of empathy. But, before he steps down that road, he might consider the fate of the Greens and the PDs, who were equally ill at ease with the mere ordinary citizen. In the case of the PDs, this was epitomised by a famous description by Gene Kerrigan of Dessie O'Malley trying to mix with a group of builders during a general election. This involved an unfortunate sequence of events, beginning with Dessie first having to meet and talk to the workers and then, worse still, having to sit in a small hut with the lads eating a sandwich. Sadly, as poor Dessie grimaced amongst the Brennan's Bread and margarine, it was evident that, despite all the talk about the Republic, for Dessie, meeting fellows who ate a packed lunch in the middle of the day was something to be endured. Intriguingly, this unease was also shared by the Greens. In a sense, this was understandable, for the intrinsic Green vision of Paddy the voter was that he was a misogynist Neanderthal who clubbed the heads of seals for fun. With that in mind, perhaps the disappearance of both the PDs and the Greens is not quite such a surprise, for the political party that does not empathise with the broad mass of the people has reduced its support base to 10 per cent of the population.

If Paddy Mac is looking for role models, he might be surprised by the realisation that Mr Haughey was one of the better practitioners of the politics of empathy. Paddy Machiavelli will know that, privately, Mr Haughey had a preference for gentlemen of the millionaire class. This, however, did not damage his relationship with the voters, for most peasants aspire to be millionaires. In fact, it was generally the millionaires who were uneasy when the Little Prince trotted into the room patting a set of eternally empty pockets. Paddy Machiavelli should note that much of the public fascination with Haughey was informed by our man's capacity to put on a show at a time when all the citizenry had for diversion was an American soap opera called 'Dallas'. A harsher age, which knows the cost of everything and the value of nothing, is not in the mood to be tolerating the likes of Mr Haughey's Gatsby-style *folie de grandeur* now, and Paddy the voter may have a point too, for, as with all aristocrats, there was a price to pay and, as is generally the case with the upper orders, someone else picked up the tab. In fairness, despite the vast nature of Mr Haughey's delusions, the capacity of his ego meant that there was something incorruptible about him. However, it was the cover he gave to other fat chieftains that corrupted the Republic. Mr Haughey may have resided in a Yeats-style 'tower' but, like the Catholic middle men who did more damage to their own during the Famine, the real damage was done to the Republic by harsh men such as Ray Burke.

If, in the search for empathy, Jack Lynch favoured the convent, Bertie's method of connecting with the citizen via the boyband is of greater practical use to Paddy Mac, for the nuns are a little out of fashion. This might appear to represent a major change but, in truth, the difference is only one of degree. Paddy Mac should note that it is a measure of Mr Ahern's practical cunning that he invested himself in the iconography of the boyband, for what could be less threatening than the humble, ever-anxious-to-please, consumer-driven, derivative creations of Louis Walsh? The boyband was the equivalent of Mum's cooking and Barry's Tea, but, it was cloaked in a veneer of youthfulness that gave a sufficient edge to the safety-first person to make it interesting.

The attachment of Bertie to the boyband represented a perfect Celtic Tiger marriage in other respects. Ireland's contribution to culture up to that point had consisted of penniless poets and cantankerous novelists. Boybands, however, represented a new departure. They might have been safe, derivative, asexual, unoriginal and non-threatening, but that added to the perfection of the thing. As our boybands morphed into the musical equivalent of social partnership, superficially we had moved on a long way indeed from the Medici-style soap opera of the Haughey era. But, in a real way, we had also travelled no distance at all, for Mr Ahern's doings with boybands were of as much fascination to the citizenry as Mr Haughey's millennial fantasies.

It is hardly accidental that the utter incapacity of FG — or Labour for that matter — to build any degree of empathy with Paddy the voter ensured that once the plain people had decided 'it were de Valera what had been the real victim of the Civil War' they remained in opposition for most of the new Free State's existence. The FG template in this regard was created by James Dillon and Liam Cosgrave, who treated the ordinary citizen with the suspicion of a wealthy farmer watching a tramp sway up his driveway. Garret FitzGerald did provide the party with a brief change, courtesy of his clever marketing as the nation's Queen Mum, but after the Garret interlude we swiftly returned to the normal 'sleeping in separate beds' arrangement between the doleful plain people and the FG-Labour Brothers Grimm.

This made the great revolution in FG, led by Enda Kenny, all the more shocking. From the moment Enda became the FG Dear Leader he realised that, in order for FG to defeat FF, the Blueshirts would have to shadow all the techniques of their feared rivals. In one regard Kenny succeeded triumphantly, for it was under Enda that the *Lite* apogee of the politics of empathy occurred. Other FG leaders, such as John Bruton, dreamed of being recognised as public intellectuals at some point in their career. They liked being photographed beside books, lined in a pristine, untouched condition in mahogany cases. Books, and indeed mahogany for that matter, signal in their heads a sense of intelligence. However, it is a measure of the seismic changes that have occurred since then that Enda is more likely to be photographed beside a pastel lampshade.

Our Aspirant Prince will note that Enda more than any other Irish leader embraced the ideology that the best politician should be a resolutely ordinary, chillaxing fellow-me-lad who wouldn't be at all keen on the idea of a mistress, let alone ownership of an island. In opposition, such was the regularity of Enda's encounters with ladies wheeling shopping trolleys that you would wonder if the FG Dear Leader ever had the time to think about the country.

Mind you, as he indulged in an orgy of meeting the ordinary citizen, we suspect Enda actually liked to stay away from the thinking. Richard 'the lesser' Bruton, until the bad thing happened, was the 'go to' man on the Big Thoughts issue whilst Enda busied himself embracing woman with shopping trolleys, the woman outside a crèche, families in their kitchens, women stranded on motorways and women inside crèches. At times, such was the regularity of Enda's symposia with women wheeling shopping trolleys, it looked as though there would be a case for prosecution under the anti-stalking legislation.

As Mr Kenny skipped along the road less taken, developing the perception that a FG Taoiseach could be pleasant with the people, his revolution in empathy was undoubtedly facilitated by Mr Cowen. Biffo the Unready really did have the most extraordinary relationships with his citizenry of any modern democratic leader in the Western world. Were he a member of the former Russian Politburo, or the Dear Leader of North Korea, poor Biffo's utter horror at the prospect of meeting any citizens who don't come from Offaly would have been manageable. However, Paddy Mac should note that it is important in a democracy that Dear Leaders meet the citizens voluntarily on a regular basis and be seen to enjoy it.

One of the many examples provided by Biffo of his inability to manage this was when Mr Cowen was dragged by the ear to see the devastation inflicted by a sudden flood. The morale of the locals might not have been lifted by the shambling figure, tucked up protectively in the sort of greatcoat that would have been more appropriate for Stalingrad in 1942. It, alas, got even worse, for given the media opportunity that was lying prostrated like a thousand virgins in front of him, the Taoiseach, on being asked to meet further victims, instead couldn't get out of the place fast enough. As a puzzled set of mildly hurt citizens looked at the departing form, Mr Cowen's 'Hello, I must be going' stance was justified by the excuse of an incipient cabinet meeting. As if it could start without him. In contrast, the archetypal photograph of Bertie in the floods in Drumcondra provides us with a classic example of how the clever Aspirant Prince can in the most adverse of circumstances secure the pity of the electorate. The image of Bertie, gazing sadly upon the world as the waters threatened to rise above our hero's boots, meant that the citizens spent more time consoling Bertie than consoling the actual victims.

Now that he is a minister, one of the greatest talents our Aspirant Prince must cultivate is the ability to learn from error. Nothing signifies the inability of our political class in this regard more than the ongoing failure of Enda's government of the Grumpy Old Men to learn from their Rainbow past. From the start, the pervasive tone of this administration has been one of complaint about the failure of the voters to love them in the manner they believe to be deserved. Sadly, far from being the citizens' fault, it was the government who was to blame for this breakdown, for, once in power, FG and Labour promptly succumbed to their ageless fatal flaw of being unable to empathise with the real lives of the citizens they govern. In theory, the Grumpy Old Men do sympathise with the 'plight' of the citizens, but the formulaic nature of the language they use only serves to reveal the absence of a genuine sense of fret. Some will claim that their attitude is a mere consequence of the understandable inability of a cabinet of mostly privately educated millionaires to empathise with the forelock-tipping classes of middle Ireland. But, could it be the case that the real truth behind the similarity of this government to the sort of nurse who takes far too much pleasure in dosing the children with castor oil is that it has never fully forgiven the electorate for the great defenestration of 1997, when the Rainbow of FG, Labour and Democratic Left was cast out by an ungrateful electorate? They do not come out openly and say it, but the hurt emerges in subtle asides, such as the observation that in 1997 the government was creating a thousand jobs a week.

The great obsession is understandable, for 1997 was their perfect moment, when the Rainbow would reshape the future of the nation for a decade. And then, suddenly, this Eden was lost when Bertie the snake corrupted the all too susceptible Eves of the Irish electorate. Of course, the surviving Wild Geese secured some belated form of justice in 2011, when they finally managed to put their collective heels on the neck of FF. But that, alas, is not recompense enough for the hurt feelings. Instead, increasingly it appears to be the case that, in their secret souls, they believe Paddy the voter should pay a price for his 'sin'. However, whilst our Grumpy Old Men have certainly taken to the role of the scolding parents with zeal, they should not take too much pleasure out of the travails being experienced by the 'fallen' Irish electorate. Paddy the voter, being an intuitive, mercurial creature, already suspects 'the story' when it comes to this government. And if Paddy's suspicions are correct, then the Grumpy Old Men are indulging in that common sin of cutting off the nose to spite the face, for Paddy the voter is more than capable of throwing out the best government we ever had a second time. And he might even enjoy doing it.

When it comes to learning from error, Paddy Mac would also, now that he is at the cabinet table, do well to devote some time to cultivating the important art of the apology. Surprisingly, given the usefulness of apologies in creating the appearance of empathy, the Irish politician has generally had an uneasy relationship with the apology. One would have thought, given the amount of practice they have had, that they would have it mastered by now. But, the Irish TD is the equivalent of what cricketers call a flat-track bully. When it comes to the British for sins of omission during the Famine, or to the European Union for forcing us to voluntarily borrow billions of euro from *dummkopf* German bankers, we are the maestros of the art. But when it is their turn they rarely do it well, and mostly they do it gracelessly. This is strange, for a well-timed 'sincere' apologia often causes the spirit of the citizens to lift. Bertie Ahern managed it over the children, and it insulated him from any fall-out over the role of FF and the Church in facilitating the serial rape of working-class children. Not even Michael Woods's subsequent bitterly contested and costly Church–State institutions deal could fully take the sheen off that or a brief glowing moment when a normally confrontational confessional state had, in doing the right thing, enhanced our democracy.

It is annoying to be humiliating yourself in public, but our Aspirant Prince must face the reality, given the way we are governed, that he will at some stage be apologising. The injustice where you are generally apologising for someone else's blunder may explain the unwillingness, but these are the rules. If Paddy Mac is looking for the perfect case study into the difficulties and the dangers that the 'apology' poses, this is epitomised by Michael Noonan and the Brigid McCole affair. The great irony of Noonan's position was that he was dealing with the consequences of decades of, at best, benign neglect and occasional all-out assaults on the health service by FF. This minor matter did not stop that party from laying it on with a sanctimonious trowel over 'poor' Mrs McCole. But, the scampering of FF up to the high moral ground was also wondrously facilitated by the blunder where Noonan — or more accurately his scriptwriter — asked could the lawyers not have found someone in a better condition for the rigours of a legal challenge. One supposes that on one level Mr Noonan was right, for the dying Mrs McCole, who screamed at night from the clots in her legs, was in no condition to take on the apparatus of well-fed, purring State lawyers who were set on her. The problem was that from that terrible moment onwards, the minister's own goose was cooked, as everyone forgot about the misdeeds of the past and focused their ire on the more immediate target. Noonan's subsequent hepatitis C compensation scheme and the Hepatitis C Tribunal were amongst the most progressive responses to this tragedy in Europe. But the damage had been done, for politics is as much about emotion as it is about logic.

It would perhaps be of somewhat greater use to Paddy Mac if he were to consider the factors that informed Mr Noonan's blunder. Like the child who runs to Mother, the standard tactic of the politician in difficult times is to call in the lawyers, so that he can minimise the damage. But whilst our lawyer friends may achieve such an objective in a technocratic sense, the trimming, stonewalling and other legal tactics inspire such distaste in the public that any benefits derived are utterly squandered. In the case of hepatitis C, Noonan spoke the deadly words, but he was only a puppet dancing to strings being pulled by others. It did not matter, though, for when the tomatoes started to be thrown, Noonan was the guy on the stage, and that was enough for us. The most important lesson

Paddy Mac should learn from this tale is that when lawyers whisper in his deferential ear, he must always remember that politics and the law are two separate trades. And whilst politics has its flaws, the law really is an amoral soulless thing that serves the highest bidder and has no concept of morality or decency beyond that sketched out by a chequebook. Unfortunately, that is not to say that you can throw all our lawyers into the fire. The clever Aspirant Prince should, though, swiftly recognise that whilst barristers make for excellent lickspittles and reasonable attack dogs, their advice should be treated with caution.

Paddy Mac might also learn that a failure to apologise can haunt you for a decade. In Noonan's case, the ghost of hepatitis C returned to haunt him when, in an act of desperation, FG axed John Bruton. This being the age of emotion, the first demand the minister who had fixed the hepatitis C debacle faced was the call for more apologies. The jury backed Noonan, a warm, considerate politician who actually mixes easily with women, into a dark space where the FG leader, consumed by the injustice of it all, resisted. He grizzled, he growled, like a badger stuck in a burrow who hears the pad of the approaching terrier's feet, and he groused, before the apology finally dribbled out in a lukewarm sort of fashion at a Fine Gael ard-fheis. But, for Noonan, who had already been necklaced with an RTÉ 'No Tears' drama, it was too little, too tight-lipped and too late.

Paddy Mac, therefore, if he is looking for the best exponents of the art of the apology, would do better to look abroad. He would do particularly well to examine how Bill Clinton extricated himself from the consequences of getting himself entangled with the ample charms of Monica Lewinsky. It should be noted that, for all the ribald jokes, the wound caused to the Presidency was deep, because much of the power of democratic politicians is an invisible quasi-spiritual concept. Bill Clinton's exploits profoundly undermined this element of his power for no one can worship a naked king. And, in this case, the element of majesty that the office and its incumbent should retain had been stripped away by the brutal realism of the DNA of a semen stain on a navy-blue summer dress.

However, like a latter-day Houdini, Clinton used the apology to create an entirely different narrative constituting a morality tale of flaws, sin and redemption where, in a series of deft leaps, he transcended the consequences of his act by reinventing himself as a penitent American Everyman. By apparently embracing the truth of his sin, Clinton reached out to all those who had been unfaithful in America, which meant that the only ones who could condemn him were those who had not strayed themselves, and that was not a lot. Ensuring that the wife, who had Presidential aspirations of her own, stayed with him nicely facilitated the narrative of trespass and redemption, for in Oprahland everyone loves the latter concept. Mind you, though, while Mr Clinton escaped rather nicely, his is not a precedent that Paddy Machiavelli would be wise to follow. Irish wives are far less forgiving.

In fairness, there is one domestic example of the capacity of the apology to rescue the most desperate of situations. Micheál Martin's political imitation of Ronan Keating's 'sorry is all that I can say to you' appear, against all the odds, to have worked in restoring FF to some degree of semi-respectability. Like the fallen Victorian governess, the past is still always lurking for Fianna Fáil, but for now, though, they are back teaching the children. In fairness, that the FF leader's long-term aura of the good child accidentally caught up with a shower of gurriers means that Micheál was the perfect man for the job of apologising. But Micheál also took to the terrible task with a will that was almost ruthless. Of course, the good political apology should always be circumspect and, in Micheál's case, FF was the victim of a consensus where 'the biggest mistake we made … was that we didn't stand back from the general consensus in terms of raising expenditure and reducing taxes.'

The FF leader also swiftly learned that the art of the apology must also be informed by the sort of attitude where you must learn to love the apology so much that you cannot stop. Like therapy for an addiction — where addiction to the therapy replaces the addiction you are suffering from — you must continue to apologise until everyone is sick of listening to the apology. Then you can stop and return to your normal mode of operation.

It is important, even amidst this feast of saccharine, that Paddy Machiavelli should retain the critical quality of being able to retain the capacity to hate his political opponents. This should not be emotional or thoughtless. It is necessary, though, for as our Aspirant Prince will have already learned, we are all sole traders in Leinster House, and your dearest friend will crush your skull with his heel in order to get ahead. Of course, in our new world of centrist politics, hatred is technically disapproved of, for we are all working together to ensure that the billionaire and the worker will be friends … on the billionaire's terms. But, hatred is not always an ignoble political state. It is an emotion that can give you the sort of focus, intensity, drive and purpose that all natural-born political killers need. Nothing epitomises this more than the curious evolution that has taken place in the nature of Micheál Martin. During his first two decades at the top of the political tree it would not be excessive to say that bad lads like Biffo, Bertie or Charlie McCreevy treated nice Micheál like a political submissive. But if Paddy Mac is to become a Dear Leader, he is also going to have to be able to do some murdering in private and in public. Indeed our own current pleasantry of a Taoiseach provides Paddy Mac with an object lesson in this. Enda, for all the smiling, nodding, winking, fist-pumping, daydreaming and JFK-imitating is rather like JFK himself — a bit of a political gurrier — and who could blame him after three decades of being smacked on the nose by Pee Flynn? Enda knows how to hate, all right, and more important still, how to use the cold steel without taking an unseemly pleasure in it.

Ironically, it is the self-same Mr Kenny who has been the catalyst for nice Micheál's belated acquisition of the virtue of hatred. As is the case with all politicians, Micheál is not entirely good. There has always been a bit of the political rat hiding beneath the altar boy, convent-visiting, two-pints-of-Beamish-sipping, salad-and-a-side-dish-of-crab-claws dining persona. In general, were Micheál left alone, submissiveness would continue to be the order of the day, for Micheál's core philosophy is that it really is 'nice to be nice'. But Enda, mainly because he can't help it, keeps on tweaking Micheál's secret scaly tail.

In this case, the normally cunning Mr Kenny is providing Paddy Mac with an object lesson in the dangers that come if you hate not wisely but too well. Had Enda treated the FF leader with a modicum of respect, the Taoiseach would have declawed Micheál. Enda's self-indulgence in letting the old tribal instinct kick in has in this case taken a dangerous turn. Initially, Micheál appeared to be slightly puzzled by the Taoiseach's singsong-style recitation of the sins of Fianna Fáil. But, as every attempt, however false, at being co-operative was met by a litany of FF sins, the FF leader began to visibly tire of it.

Micheál may be an altar boy, but Mr Martin's ego is still sufficiently well nourished to resent being patronised by Enda Kenny of all people. It has taken some time, but the worm did turn. Micheál did not shout any more loudly, but adversity brought a new edge to his persona. Suddenly, and increasingly, he developed a visceral dislike of his Fine Gael counterpart. Micheál did not willingly embrace this new emotion. Instead, like so many other changes in his political career, it was essentially forced upon him. Though a metamorphosis of sorts has occurred it should be noted Micheál has not yet reached the zenith of tribalism displayed by the rabid Fianna Fáil man who, on his deathbed, asked for an application form for Fine Gael. When his sorrowful family asked what on earth had prompted such a decision, our man said: 'I'd prefer that the Lord took one of theirs, rather than one of ours.' However, another six months of passive-aggressive Enda continuing to rub his nose in it should complete the transformation nicely.

Chapter 8 ～

CULTIVATING THE CLOAK OF BEING AN ORDINARY DECENT SKIN

Therefore it is necessary to … be a great pretender and dissembler; and men are so simple, and so subject to present necessities, that he who seeks to deceive will always find someone who will allow himself to be deceived.

Including class and Michael McDowell's attic • an egalitarian Tiger • Jake's Peg Leg • come on and join the decent skins • better ordinary than great • reason and unreason • the Aspirant Prince and the celebrity • so who are to be our heroes? • John Bruton and the artlessness of not being ordinary • the little things that count • on picking the winner and knights versus turnips

As he matures in politics, Paddy Machiavelli will have to define his position on a series of ever more risky issues. One of the most dangerous is the concept that never dares to name its name within polite Irish society. The old Civil War parties (and Labour on a few occasions too!) have always united to deny the existence of class, but it is as pervasive and as enervating in Ireland as the caste system is in India. Of course, the political possums of FF were the most indignant serial deniers. Paddy Mac will know that few have been more anxious than Mr Cowen to claim that he was the republican child of a peasant-style Arcadia in

Clara, Co. Offaly, where all the noble savages lived in a state of pure equality. In fact, like the rest of our dynasts, the privately educated Cowen was as much a creature of privilege as any of those Tory habitués of the Bullingdon Club, such as David Cameron and Boris Johnson. In fairness, our Aspirant Prince should observe that poor Biffo is not unique, for FF's enthusiasm to be the good servant of our vested elites is one of the secret tales of the evolution of the Irish State. In many respects, the deal has been a simple one where, in return for a monopoly of power, FF has sheltered vintners, big builders and, in more recent times, barristers and consultants, whilst of course at all times speaking the language of republican egalitarianism.

In taking a position on the class issue the first thing Paddy Mac must do is avoid following the errors of Michael McDowell who, in an all-too-regular moment of honesty, once indulged in an enthusiastic paean to the virtues of inequality. Mr McDowell did not mention that if you started at the plus side of the equation, then inequality was a delightful thing, but, possibly he didn't want to complicate the argument. Paddy Mac will note that, inevitably, the hapless PD leader was savaged for his honesty. The fury, happily, did not last for too long, since it was made during the heyday, soon-to-be-goodbye day, of the Celtic Tiger, and when everyone is dipping their beaks, the impulse towards revolution is less demotic.

Ironically, the outwardly egalitarian Tiger in fact represented the high-water mark of Ireland's class system. Outside of the quasi-fascistic nature of social partnership, which ensured that the privileges of our vested interests — be they vintners, barristers, public servants, lecturers or judges — were preserved in aspic, the Tiger class system of 'chaps' looking after 'chaps' allowed a little nexus of insiders within the banking and legal system to turn a country into a casino. As per the much-misunderstood economic policies of Lemass, the subsequent rising tide did lift all boats. But, it did so in the uncontrolled manner of a tsunami, and when the bubble burst, Breakfast Roll Man and the rest of the outsiders who aspired to build something better resembled the third-class ticket holders on the *Titanic*. Paddy Mac will recall how they were locked in steerage as the ship sank, lest they inconvenience the first-class passengers being gently ushered into the half-empty lifeboats.

As for Paddy Mac, the most valuable thing he can learn from the travails of McDowell is to not speak truthfully about our class system. You would certainly secure much attention were you to try. But Paddy Mac must ask himself is he really, amidst the dynastic ones — the vintners, barristers and social partners of Leinster House — in the right place to be making such speeches? Paddy Mac, merely by being where he is, has already exchanged contracts with the Devil and, as Faustus found out the hard way, there is no point in bellyaching once the ink is dry. Our Aspirant Prince should, if tempted by the glories of class warfare, simply steel himself and realise that his job is to make his way in the world and cut out the 'champagne football' of idealism, for should he start shouting about that class stuff to his colleagues, then he will experience a similar fate to the entertainer who sang the ditty 'Jake the Peg' to an audience of amputee Vietnam War veterans. He may get a brief round of applause, but the whispering afterwards will not be warm.

Whilst the appropriate response by Paddy Machiavelli is to tiptoe away from the large sleeping pedigree dog of the class system, our Aspirant Prince should ensure that he joins one special Irish class. Among the iconic comedic events of Irish life are Eamon Dunphy's occasional explosions about the decent skins of Irish life. It is now an Irish tradition that no one takes these passionate dissertations about the blazers, con men, spivs, spoofers, five-bob-note men and shams seriously. Our Aspirant Prince, though, should carefully consider Dunphy's critique for one good reason. This is not because Paddy Mac should aspire to join in this crusade. Instead, it is because he is now one of the decent skins, stupid. This may not, alas, be pleasant, or how, in the idealistic daze of youth, he thought it might be. But Paddy Mac must understand that, in politics, to succeed you must swim amidst the mandarins, builders, businessmen, residents' association men, professionals and the others who dip their beaks so proficiently. We are sorry if that is not romantic, but that is where the critical mass lies. If, in contrast, Paddy Mac wants to keep that fine invisible thing called a soul, then we suggest he join People Before Profit.

The great triumph of the decent skins should act as a warning to Paddy Mac about the biggest weakness that politicians suffer from at the beginning of their careers. In that age of innocence, too often Aspirant Princes strive for greatness because they think that is what they are supposed to do. However, Paddy Machiavelli will not be happy if he keeps up this game. It is better instead that from the very start he tilts his lance somewhat lower, for revolutions and drama are, as we have discovered over the last half decade, seriously overrated. Bertie Ahern, as in so many other matters, provides the Aspirant Prince with a crash course in the beauty of ordinariness. The former Taoiseach's love affair with the 'hanging baskets' may have sparked more mirth than belief. But, in attempting to convince us that he wanted to do nothing more dramatic in his spare time than to hunt down the weeds in his patio, Mr Ahern was at least making an attempt to empathise with the prosaic lives of the punters.

It should be noted that even before the Bert ended up making advertisements for British tabloids in a kitchen cupboard, the 'plain-spoken man of the people' illusion was studded with contradictions. Mr Ahern may have loved nothing more than humble Sundays at 'Croker', but he was far more likely to be found in the VIP stand than on Hill 16. And whilst much was made of the quiet little holidays in Kerry, Mr Ahern was actually billeted in a not-quite-so-humble five-star hotel, as distinct from a little thatched cottage by the mountains. Still, until Bertie started the muttering about not having a palace, the voters were at a minimum charmed by the implied humility.

In contrast, if the Aspirant Prince is looking for the classic example of the dangerousness of not being ordinary, he need look no further than John Bruton. In many respects, Mr Bruton should have been the perfect ordinary Irish male, given that he is overweight, cantankerous, opinionated, and sure he always knows best — with scant reason to back it up. But, despite this running start, the electorate instinctively knew that he was not one of them.

Bruton might have been the democratic leader of a political party, but, this was a man who Paddy the voter sensed only felt he was amongst equals when he was mixing with the privately educated Sutherlands of the world as well as royalty, world leaders, judges and senior counsel. Whether they felt the same when the former Taoiseach came honking into the room is, alas, another matter.

The degree of separation these notions of superiority created between him and the electorate meant that there was a complete absence of sympathy when Bruton blundered in such matters as insulting the Peace Process. Others might have been forgiven, but in his case we smirked about the man born with a silver foot in his mouth. Ultimately, the biggest problem with John was that he reeked of privilege, and warmth is always thin amongst the plain people for those who have known nothing of the hardships of life. This meant that whilst Paddy the voter sympathised with Bertie in his anorak phase, they mocked the duck-like walk and the permanently chaotic flux of loose papers, ill-fitting suits and food particles of an uncertain date that surrounded Mr Bruton. In a better world we might say there was nothing personal in such mockery. But it was, in fact, a deeply intimate way of evening up the score by a people who suspected that their allegedly slothful ways were a constant source of annoyance to a man intent on leading a public who genuinely did not want him to get the job.

Paddy Mac should note that this distaste had nothing to do with Bruton's alleged intelligence, for the voters have a *laissez-faire* attitude to intelligent politicians and will sometimes tolerate one. The problem with Bruton, though, was that the voters knew that a man who always acquired a distressed look on his face on seeing happy working-class people was their enemy. Ultimately, their suspicions were justified by Bruton's enthusiastic embrace of the spectacle of 'Dame Austerity' being brought in to put manners on the unruly Irish. Some might be surprised that a man struggling along under the burden of having a pension for being an accidental Taoiseach, *plus* a pension for being a minister, *plus* a pension for being a TD, *plus* that directorship in the American industrial conglomerate Ingersoll Rand, *plus* the board job in the Bermuda insurance firm Montpelier Re, *plus*, that Presidency of the IFSC, *plus* we do apologise if we have left anything out, could dismiss the destruction of the lives of our aspiring class of Breakfast Roll Men and commuting country girls with such lordly ease. It was, however, merely another example of that lack of empathy where our rulers are incapable of understanding that people want more from life than mere survival as sharecroppers who serve the banks and the perks and pensions of retired politicians.

Paddy Mac should carefully observe that this fatal lacuna meant that, even when he was holding four aces, Bruton kept on losing elections. Outside of his failure to oust Albert in 1992, this was typified by his ill-fated 1997 election tour, when the FG leader was, after a week, finally hunted out the door and persuaded to meet the people. Unfortunately, his debut walkabout was collapsed by a raucous shout of 'here comes Homer Bruton' from a card-carrying, baseball cap-wearing member of the working class. Mr Bruton, in the wake of the call-out, spent the rest of the campaign safely separated from the public on a train, and FG lost the election that couldn't be lost.

The travails of Mr Bruton should also teach our Aspirant Prince that if he wishes to be seen as a man who walks with the citizen, he must cultivate a far broader swathe of company than mere barristers, mandarins and politicians. In times past, the template for this was set by Mr Haughey who, in addition to builders and millionaire grocers, also regularly sought out the company of poets, artists and painters. Happily, there is no need for today's Aspirant Prince to endure the company of poets and philosophers, since the former have been replaced by celebrity chick-lit writers. The latter, meanwhile, have been replaced by sociology, politics and media lecturers, so there is nothing of value to be distilled from their company.

In seeking direction on such matters, Paddy Machiavelli must once again look to the example set by the ward boss. It was somewhat typical that the highlight of Bertie Ahern's first general election campaign would be the opening of a Planet Hollywood restaurant. Such a decision was indicative of the carefully cultivated imagery of being an ordinary decent soul, for there is no greater signifier of ordinariness than craving the company of celebrities and fast food in the one location. This particular event was accompanied by much puzzled mockery from the Noel Whelan, Sam the American bald eagle-style school of punditry. In fact, Mr Ahern's decision to babble away excitedly to an understandably puzzled Mr Stallone put the Taoiseach that critical six inches ahead of his political rivals in a country that was about to embrace celebrity.

When it comes to his relationship with the celebrity, the one warning we will issue to Paddy Machiavelli is that, as the politician and the celebrity are often afflicted with an excess of egotism, they can be an uneasy match. But, should he manage to achieve this rare synergy between politician and celebrity, then Paddy Mac is right in there with the woman in the hairdressers that Bertie used to fret so solicitously over. For this to happen, though, the politician must be careful when deciding what school of celebrity he should cultivate, since, like the sermon about the grains of sand on the beach in Joyce's *A Portrait of the Artist as a Young Man*, there are far more than fifty shades of celebrity. If he is wise, or if he asks his wife, Paddy Mac for example will swiftly learn that cultivating the Kerry Katonas of this world will not do him any good. Far better instead that the Aspirant Prince be seen with sporting heroes such as Henry Shefflin or Ronan O'Gara, for some of the shine of their achievements will rub off upon him. Afternoon TV show hosts such as Norah Casey and Maura Derrane or even showmen like Eddie Hobbs are good.

Hanging around with chefs is also to be encouraged, for apart from the issue of the great national fascination with food, chefs are passionate, crusading, entrepreneurial types. The women like the chefs too, so that also is helpful. Given their scarcity, and the desire for them, the wise Aspirant Prince should take care to cultivate the company of as many grey businessmen as possible. They may not be celebrities, but the recession means that we are all far more interested in 'Dragons' Den'-style businessmen than in celebrities these days.

The one brand of celebrity that our Aspirant Prince must avoid at all costs is that of comedians. The problem with the comedian, you see, is that most are intelligent, logical and moral. This means that Paddy Machiavelli is generally devoured by the clowns when he appears alongside them. The only sphere of safety in this regard is if you are parodied by one of RTÉ's resident satirists ... well, with the exception of David McSavage. The rest, happily, are practitioners of the satire of the 'only slagging' variety and there is nothing to fear from that. Indeed, if you are satirised by RTÉ, you have the added benefit of having reached the sanctified heights of being a *faux* celebrity yourself.

Our earlier 'Homer Bruton' vignette is another example of how Paddy Machiavelli should, even as he reaches the foothills of high places, remember that the higher up you go, the more important it is to remember that it is always the little things that count. One classic example of the dangers of failing to recognise this is provided by the great debacle of the Labour Carton House 'think-in' of 2012. The decision by Labour to book a middle-ranking golf hotel should not, in theory, have posed Labour with any particular problems. And had it been FG or FF, say, instead of Labour, there would have been no outcry, for we associate those parties with yellow Pringle jumper-wearing, middle-aged golfers. But, the political world is not the normal world, and it is generally an even less normal place for Labour. So it was that as Mr Gilmore sported amongst the woodland nymphs (steady now, we are talking about statues), and Pat Rabbitte glided through the Rococo-ceilinged period house, it was agonisingly clear that no one had stopped to consider how the spectacle of Labour, the party of the working man, gallivanting on the golfing fairways of the spiritual home of the old Irish Ascendancy would play. This lacuna was all the more critical in the context of the small detail that Labour was living in a political world full of far colder eyes than that halcyon era of 'Gilmore for Taoiseach'.

Though Labour looked a bit woebegone afterwards, no one was suggesting that they should hunt assiduously for the foulest tenement they could find. But, the location chosen offered too good an opportunity for a barrage of *Animal Farm* metaphors. Ironically, even as the media amicably decried the party's embrace of the world of the plutocrat, one agonised spin doctor noted that part of the attraction of Carton House was that Labour's sober-side Dublin TDs, who wanted to avoid the horrors of a late-night drinking session, could drive home to their spouses. None of this mattered for it was far more interesting (and fun) to watch an event designed as a show of unity and strength turn into another lance piercing the side of poor Mr Gilmore. As for the argument that the furore was a facile one, well, of course it was. But if it is offered up to you on a plate, what are you going to do?

Disordered logic is, as Paddy Mac will discover the hard way, applicable to more elements of Irish political life than just the Labour Party. And it is particularly applicable to that most terrifying thing known as the leadership contest. This is the closest that Irish politics comes to pure socialism, in that it is equally terrifying for those who are in and out of favour in the Dear Leader's court. Whether he is in or out, when the elephants are fighting, it behoves Paddy Mac to ignore the chuckling of the media hyenas as they encourage him to leap into the fray immediately, and to think carefully about what it is he should do. This may seem to be an obvious point. However, the fret and drama of a leadership crisis addles the most cautious of minds. Paddy Mac should in particular consider the performance of the normally cautious FG TD Kieran O'Donnell during the FG leadership putsch against Enda. Having succeeded Richard Bruton as Opposition Finance spokesperson, O'Donnell resigned 24 hours later. The consequences of such a decision were evident twelve months on, when the erudite O'Donnell struggled out of Leinster House carrying six different bags as he raced for the train home to Limerick. Simultaneously, an exquisitely garmented John Perry glided by wearing a gold tie, as he strolled in to deal with ministerial questions. Mr Perry may well not be half as talented as O'Donnell, but he had chosen the right side.

The closed nature of the leadership election means that Paddy Mac must in particular ignore media prophecies on such matters. The lack of appreciation that journalists have of the importance of such events is epitomised by Enda Kenny's victory where our friend Mr Conventional Wisdom declared that once the FG cats in the sack sorted out the pecking order, everyone would kiss, make up and be friends again. It was a nice concept, which was certainly encouraged by Enda, but it did not even come close to dealing with the reality of things. The *coup d'état* of the innocents was not some form of political 'X Factor'. It was a knife fight for power, for money and for position, where the winner really did take everything and the losers went home on public transport.

Though our Aspirant Prince must move carefully when it comes to the leadership challenge, he will still have to take a public stand, for those who wring their hands and bleat, 'Boys, please stop the fighting', are despised by everyone. He should, of course, engage in some handwringing, so as to keep in with both sides, but disappearing into the murk is not an option. Happily, in deciding who will win, Paddy Machiavelli can at least be guided by history. Irish party leaders have been toppled, but generally they only go when the leader is genuinely sick at heart and desires only to leave with some dignity. The ideal precedent for Dear Leaders was set by de Valera, who resigned barely before his 80th birthday in a half-blind, enfeebled condition.

In terms of triumphant conspiracies, much was made in the past of Haughey's plot to topple Jack Lynch. But, it was Lynch himself who left, and his departure was facilitated by the expectation that hitting the road would secure the triumph of the enemies, rather than the friends of Mr Haughey. The wise Aspirant Prince will learn from Biffo just how difficult it is to take out a failing leader. When it came to the motion of confidence that the Taoiseach called in January 2011, Mr Cowen's record was without parallel. In fairness, the cast of alternatives was hardly compelling, consisting as it did of a gurning Éamon Ó Cuív, the seriously ill Brian Lenihan, the matronly Mary Hanafin and Micheál Martin. But these debilitating factors were a mere feather on the scales when compared with Biffo's role in bursting up a party and a state. Astonishingly, Mr Cowen survived, told a delighted media he was still the chosen one, and promised to lead FF into the next election, before being unhorsed a month later after another series of cataclysmic events involving the loss of half the cabinet and his coalition partners. You cannot imagine the level of disappointment felt by certain elements of the media who were planning to ensure that the first question poor Biffo would be asked when the election was called would be: 'So, Mr Cowen, do you think you can win?'

Mr Haughey, it should be noted, survived three heaves after a series of events involving the near bankruptcy of the state (before Biffo did the job properly), and the telephone tapping of senior journalists, whilst poor Mr Bruton was only defenestrated after the debacle of the Celtic Snail campaign, which attempted to claim, in the middle of the Tiger bubble, that FF was depressing the economy. Sadly, the escalating belief by the electorate that FG was a shower of molluscs meant that the prologue to the departure of Bruton was actually the Celtic Snail campaign rather than Bruton's nemesis, Bertie. The eventual denouement of the reign of Bruton's successor, Michael Noonan — which resembled Biffo's ill-starred performance in all regards except that Mr Noonan only levelled FG (not very important), as distinct from Mr Cowen, who levelled the country (rather more important) — meant that FG was so deterred from axing any more leaders that they kept Enda, who was at that point in time performing so well that the voters thought Eamon Gilmore would be a better Taoiseach.

Should Paddy Mac be agonising about his future career — sorry, we mean about who might be the most appropriate leader for the country — during the leadership challenge, he would do well to remember how the FG aristocrats fared in 2010. The media might have waved their pennants at the cream of FG's intellectual knighthood, and glared at the unreformed FG backbench turnips. The problem, though, was that, like the Battle of Agincourt, it was the churls who unhorsed the intellectuals and clubbed them into the ground. It was hardly the first time either, for the precedent had been set by Haughey's very similar destruction of the FF grandees in 1979.

Paddy Mac should learn from these events that there are always far more turnips than knights in parliamentary parties. And, following from that, he should also recognise that the churl-turnip is not a fool. Instead, within FG under Enda (and in 1979 with

Haughey too) the turnips recognised that since the aristocrats had resigned from the frontbench, it hardly served their interests to vote the same aristocrats back in to the frontbench positions they had just vacated. So, when it comes to the leadership challenge, Paddy Mac should always ignore the pundits and the intelligentsia within his own party and shout, 'Wait for me', as he speeds off in the same direction as the charging churls.

Should he escape unscathed, our Aspirant Prince, if he has been clever enough to back the *ancien régime*, should draw one other critical lesson from it all. Though all politicians are tricksters in one way or another, the most critical quality one can have in Irish politics is a reputation for loyalty. There are, of course, some forms of this particular virtue that are better avoided. Just as no one likes a man who wrestles excessively publicly with his conscience and always loses, for that sort of activity is better done in the privacy of your own bedroom, the unthinking loyalist is seen as a character-free fool who is attempting to turn stupidity into a virtue. However, the code of loyalty must never be underestimated in a Dáil where the political ideology of most members is about as complex as the rural tradition of following the local GAA village team to the end. Similarly all the Dear Leader requires of you and his other TDs and senators is that you wear his colours until the bitter end. At worst, such loyalty will secure Paddy Mac the reputation amongst the 'turnips' of being sound, and you'd never know when you might need those chaps some day to unhorse the same Dear Leader.

PART THREE: HIGH POLITICS

Chapter 9 ～

PADDY MAC LEARNS TO LOVE OPPOSITION AND TO CHOOSE HIS SCAPEGOATS CAREFULLY

Therefore if he who rules a principality cannot recognise evils until they are upon him, he is not truly wise; and this insight is given to few.

On learning to love opposition • no dirt, please • the Willie O'Dea paradox • Groucho Marx will never be Taoiseach • Pat Rabbitte's Uriah Heep problem • the virtues of the bitter jibe • madness in Davos and the great cunning of Cloyne

Just as you often find friendship in strange places, Paddy Machiavelli will, even if he joins Fianna Fáil, experience defeat. When that does occur, he must swiftly realise that defeat in politics, so long as you do not lose your seat, is not always the worst place in the world. Our Aspirant Prince's response to opposition will inevitably depend upon what part of the political landscape he occupies. In theory, he will always want to be in government, in order to transform the country. But, if he is a backbench TD in a party that has been in power for a long time, and whose ministers intended to be in office for quite a while longer, then, so long as it is confined to a brief period, opposition is the land of opportunity.

It is unfortunate to see great old servants of the party, such as the newly resigned Taoiseach who didn't make you a minister, going. Still, this does create the possibility where the voice of a young generation can be listened to and, more important still, be promoted. New ideas are required, and whether Paddy Mac has any or not, he will be the man calling for them to be listened to. Opposition is somewhat more of a horror story if our Aspirant Prince is a minister. However, if he is not a member of the top troika who are responsible for this less than pretty pass, opportunity exists there too … so long as Paddy has regularly spoken to the backbenchers once a month when he was in power.

But, no matter what side of the fence Paddy Mac is on when the great defenestration occurs, the breviary of modest phraseology about a time for humility and reflection must be brought out. Our Aspirant Prince will therefore be delighted by the 'opportunities' offered by opposition. This will offer Paddy Machiavelli an opportunity for 'thoughtful reflection' which will 'prioritise policies over spin' and 'people over policies.' There will be a 'new politics' where the 'people' will be met, listened to, apologised to and flattered shamelessly as part of the 'new straight-talking leadership strategy'. Whilst it is also critical that the electorate be listened to and 'respected' via the creation of 'a new broom' — so long, obviously, as Paddy Mac constitutes one of the bristles — the most important virtue of opposition is that it is the land where memory no longer exists. Rather like the Catholic ceremony of confession, it is the place where sins are all washed away by time and by the mistakes of your successors. The opportunities posed by this were perhaps best summarised by one of Bertie Ahern's more abstruse advisors, Gerard Howlin, who, in the wake of the debacle of 2011, said that FF would begin to recover after two years because, from that point, the voters would forget history and make their decisions on the basis of the bouquet of options available. Oddly enough, Howlin might even have been excessively pessimistic, for it is often the case that on losing power, the mourning period for 'mistakes done, errors made and the virtue of hindsight' is as long as it took Gertrude to forget Hamlet's father and marry Claudius.

During his time in opposition, the Aspirant Prince might be tempted to engage in new techniques, such as the vilification of political opponents. Before doing so, Paddy Mac should be warned that, despite our taste for it in just about every other arena of life, the Irish do not like dirty tricks in politics. By dirty tricks we mean negative campaigning as distinct from the myriad of other entirely normal dirty tricks. Mind you, Paddy Mac should also note that the electorate's 'distaste' for such nefarious acts is somewhat like their condemnation of brawling at GAA matches, where the upset of the pundits and the citizens does not stop everyone from lovingly examining a dozen slow-motion replays of the aforementioned brawl.

In truth, one of the main problems with 'dirty tricks' in Irish politics is that many of the campaigns simply weren't very good. Outside of the stellar example set by Mr Bruton's Celtic Snail, even Haughey on occasions fell prey to errors, such as the famous claim that Garret FitzGerald had been lunching with a British spy. The problem, alas, with this tactic was that such was the saintly reputation of Garret, had Haughey emerged into a press conference with a set of photographs of Garret in bed with Christine Keeler, the FF leader would have immediately been accused of photoshopping. Albert too discovered, when, with the help of some deeply puzzled British spin doctors, he tried to portray FG and Labour in 1992 as a 'lethal cocktail' that would turn Ireland into a communist commune, that even Irish voters were not daft enough to believe that John Bruton would turn the cattle fatteners of Meath into kulaks. Ironically, under the same Mr Bruton, five years later one of the better Irish examples of negative advertising portrayed FF as being the equivalent of a set of dodgy builders going uninvited into a well-ordered house, where they turned the place into rubble. It was somewhat too prescient for an electorate whose response to the arrival of FF candidates at the front door was to start making them cups of tea and ham sandwiches.

Should he have a taste for the bit of dirt therefore, Paddy Mac is simply going to have to suppress it, or he may end up suffering a similar cruel fate to that of Willie O'Dea. The former Minister for Defence may have been the most entertaining figure to dance across the stage of the Irish political pantomime in two decades, but, when it came to success at the high end of the game, there was something about O'Dea's cutting wit that made our Dear Leaders uneasy. Bertie Ahern, despite being the most loved and powerful politician since Daniel O'Connell, treated Willie with all the unease of a large land mine. Such nervousness might appear strange, but it was an inevitable side effect of O'Dea's waspish style that often left Dear Leaders such as Bertie privately fretting that Willie was thinking the same thoughts about them in private as he was saying about FF's political enemies in public. And they may not have been so terribly wrong.

It is perhaps even more important for Paddy Mac to realise, should the Dáil *dolce vita* be causing him to thicken around the waist, that another critical factor in the somewhat unfulfilled career of O'Dea was simple imagery. Willie's resemblance to Groucho Marx, crossed with a bit of an air of Rashers Tierney in 'Strumpet City', meant that he would always struggle to be seen as a heavyweight. And Bertie, being Bertie, was not at all kind to Willie in that regard by making him Minister for Defence. The broader political dilemma that this posed was epitomised by the iconic photograph of Willie pointing a *Magnum Force*-style revolver at a camera. Were it someone such as 'the Bull' O'Donoghue, it might have just managed to be realistic. Bertie might have looked even more convincing, but Mr Ahern had neither the sense of humour nor the streak of wilful madness that would have allowed the photograph to be taken in the first place, which perhaps goes a long way towards explaining why, knowing Willie as Bertie undoubtedly did, that the then Taoiseach was so loath to promote him. The dissonance between someone who looked like one of the Marx Brothers engaging in a Dirty Harry-style pose, meant that O'Dea became the victim of the sort of ridicule which meant that any progress beyond being in charge of the nation's tank collection would be difficult. But, probably even Willie knew at this stage that a man who looks like Groucho Marx will never be Taoiseach. The lesson for Paddy Mac in all of this is that if ministerial office sees him putting on a bit of weight, it is time to embrace the gym. Appearance really is everything at the high end of the political game.

At least Willie is not alone, for politicians with a tart tongue have always struggled to be loved. The sarcastic politician may wonder why they are spurned whilst terriers such as Vincent Browne are loved. But Vincent is for sport, since he doesn't actually run anything. In the real political game, though, the punters prefer the politician who wants everyone to be friends together on the same pitch. Apart from anything else, the concern is that, like Willie and Bertie, the politician who is too snarky with his opponents is thinking similar thoughts about you. Such is the strength of this particular belief, when Pat Rabbitte tore into the then FF minister Pat Carey in a famous TV debate over the collapse of the state in 2010, the sympathy of the public flowed towards Carey rather than towards Rabbitte. In fairness, despite, or perhaps because of, being in the cabinet, Carey knew very little about the great debacle unfolding before us. He was also certainly not in a position or, for that matter, capable of doing much about it. But, one could understand if Rabbitte was puzzled at the great outpouring of national sympathy for the chewed-up minister. This, however, was what happened when Rabbitte, on 'Prime Time', tore into Carey's 'auld palaver'. Rabbitte may have believed that Carey 'ought to be ashamed to show your face in this studio after you have brought our country to penury tonight and the damage that you have done to people's livelihoods and start the young people emigrating again'. Most sane people would also have understood Rabbitte's furious response when Carey said he wasn't ashamed. But, when Rabbitte snarled, 'Well, you ought to be, that's the problem with you … you're not ashamed…you don't have any shame' — as with the infamous row between Leo Varadkar and Mary Harney over Ms Harney's hairdo — we swiftly entered the territory of 'there goes Rabbitte again, playing the man, not the ball'. The whole affair left many wondering had Ireland moved on at all from the famous tale of the two peasants waiting to shoot Lord Leitrim who, when the notorious rack-renter was late turning up, became concerned as to whether 'there might be something wrong with the poor man'. Afterwards, those who were of a mind to defend Rabbitte asked, Is it the case that Paddy really wishes to be ruled by amiable dullards? It is perhaps a question better not answered.

Of course, Paddy Machiavelli should not abandon the virtues of the bitter jibe entirely, for occasional use of it within the Dáil chamber develops his status as a strong man who can rouse the troops. If Paddy Mac is looking for a role model, surprisingly, one of the finest exponents of the parliamentary jibe is the ascetic socialist Joe Higgins. In terms of oratory, few modern or even 19th-century politicians could match his magisterial critique of the infamous 'Ansbacher Man', who spent his private time 'in a secret world of offshore islands, coded bank deposits, fiddled taxes and secret loans', flitting from 'the lobbies of top hotels, restaurants, clubs and pubs' and securing 'bulky packages of tax-evading cash or more discreet cheques or bank drafts in his role as a walking conspiracy to defraud the taxation system'. The real glow of Higgins's anger was centred on the other half of Ansbacher Man — 'The Public Persona' who spent his time 'basking in the warm glow of an approving establishment' comprising 'business colleagues, priests and political party leaders'. Higgins noted sardonically that all 'deferred to him and his picture was in the business pages of *The Irish Times* every second day', generally near an article 'calling on the unemployed and the crucified, compliant PAYE taxpayer alike to tighten their belts in the national interest'.

Outside of Ansbacher Man, Mr Higgins focused his main attention on Bertie Ahern. The special nature of their relationship was perhaps facilitated by the status of Higgins as the only politician who could lay a glove on the ward boss, who was then at his peak. Outside of the comparison between questioning Bertie and playing handball against a haystack — you hear a dull thud but the ball does not come back to you — the finest exchange occurred after Bertie mischievously came out as a socialist. An astonished Higgins, who had been out of the country when the great declaration was made, said, 'You can imagine how perplexed I was when I returned to find my wardrobe almost empty. The Taoiseach had been busy robbing my clothes. Up to recently, the Progressive Democrats did not have a stitch left due to the same Taoiseach, but we never expected him to take a walk on the left side of the road.' It was indeed fun at the time. Paddy Mac, though, should note that in a classic case of

John Kelly syndrome, the ultimate denouement of all that verbal dexterity was the loss by Higgins of his seat and Joe's current status as a party of two.

Before opposition seduces Paddy Mac into getting carried away with too many Vincent Browne-style millennial fantasies about honesty, our Aspirant Prince must also swiftly learn that, in Irish politics, the theory of the voters wanting their leaders to be truthful, and the practice, are somewhat different. Like all manic depressives, the Irish are great enthusiasts for extremes of self-flagellation or manic displays of self-confidence. Simple, level-headed analysis of our flaws is something that our national psyche struggles to deal with. The Irish voter is like the patient who asks the doctor to 'give it to me straight up', until the diagnosis arrives, whereupon the screaming and the lawsuits begin. The fate of Enda Kenny in Davos provides Paddy Machiavelli with a classic case study of how in politics truth is not a defence against trouble. This experience was all the more ironic since the election that had brought the long-term Playboy of the Western World over the line had been fought on the basis that Irish citizens wanted a more honest school of politics than that practised by Bertie.

Our Aspirant Prince must qualify the lesson of Davos by remembering that at the best of times it has always been risky to let Enda out on his own talking about that economic thing. Some might be concerned by the scenario where it is dangerous to let the leader of a country speak his mind without having a stair gate of advisors to cushion any falls. But, we all know that when Enda is left to his own rhetorical devices, odd things happen. It is something we are used to and comfortable with and, rather like sexual practices, once it is consensual and safe no one has a problem. In fairness, no one could say either that Enda unleashed his Chauncey Gardiner gene in Davos. The worst that he could be accused of was admitting that the problem with Ireland's economy was that 'Irish people simply went mad to borrow... which spawned greed to a point where this went out of control and led to the spectacular crash.' It did not help perhaps that Mr Kenny had, little more than a month earlier in his national address to the nation, told the public that 'it's not your fault', but Enda was hardly the first Irish politician to embrace the view about the hobgoblin of consistency.

The air can be thin in Davos, and perhaps Enda was light-headed on hubris when he dared to flirt with speaking truthfully to the public. It didn't last. The applause of the mandarins and millionaires had barely faded away before an immediate fatwa of advocacy groups came howling down the road. The most delightful *amuse-bouche* of 'outrage' came from the Sinn Féin TD Pádraig Mac Lochlainn, who said: 'This analysis that people in Ireland went drunk with credit, were reckless and they have to now be cleansed by a decade of austerity to clean them of their sins is very worrying.' That it was also very accurate was apparently immaterial. Mr Kenny engaged in a swift tactical retreat as he explained: 'Our people have been the victims of this situation. We are left with the circumstance of cleaning this up and explaining the truth of that scale to our people.' Happily, Mr Kenny had learned a valuable lesson and we've heard no more straight talking about Paddy's vices since. Whether it was a good parable to learn was a moot point, for our inability to respond well to being told the truth about ourselves played a key role in getting us to the land of 'we are where we are.'

Intriguingly, our Aspirant Prince should note that the wisest comment of all during the furore came from the Minister for Finance, Michael Noonan, who when asked about the world-wide coverage said: 'I didn't hear his comment. I'm not going to comment on something I didn't hear.' Of course, once the recording was kindly played for him, Mr Noonan took the even wiser position of not commenting on something he had heard by declaring: 'I'm not going to comment. Ministers don't go around the place commenting on the Taoiseach's remarks.'

Mr Kenny secured a very different response after his Cloyne speech. The latter provides Paddy Machiavelli with a critical lesson in another of the virtues that our Aspirant Prince must develop. This consists of a cunning ruthlessness in the selection of national scapegoats that he can beat up in order to prove his virility. When it came to Kenny's Cloyne address, like other aspects of Mr Kenny's reign, there was rather less to the speech than first appeared to be the case. It was a pity too, for listened to in the first flushed afterglow of a still-believed-in new government, we appeared to be in the territories of Grattan. The effect was enhanced by the comparison with some two years earlier, where after the first Murphy Report into child abuse, an addled and eternally deferential Biffo, still apparently residing in 1950s Ireland, had appeared to almost apologise to the Vatican for the annoyance he had put them through.

Kenny, in contrast, managed to achieve an impressive fusion of righteous anger and impressive empathy as the new Taoiseach was reinvented as a latter-day St Patrick, chasing ecclesiastical snakes out of their boltholes. Building on his successes in America, it appeared that, despite all our doubts, Mr Kenny possessed the potential template for, if not greatness, then some mild level of dignity. The language was certainly a tart experience for a church which, up to five years earlier, still basked in the delights of cosy phone chats between the Taoiseach's office and All Hallows. Our bishops were certainly not used to governments slamming the 'inadequate and inappropriate response' which contributed to the undermining of 'child protection frameworks'.

The contents of Mr Kenny's speech were revolutionary, when compared with the era of John A Costello and his cabinet hiding so as to avoid the funeral ceremony of the Protestant Douglas Hyde, as Kenny warned the 'revelations in the Cloyne report have brought the Government, Irish Catholics and the Vatican to an unprecedented juncture'. As the Taoiseach claimed that the report 'excavates the dysfunction, disconnection and elitism that dominate the culture of the Vatican to this day' an astonishing thing appeared to have happened. In one sentence Mr Kenny seemed to have removed himself from any connection to the clericalist world of the old Irish state, or the happy days of Enda playing golf with the local Monsignor on Sundays. Enda did not stop there, as the Taoiseach slammed the scenario where 'the rape and torture of children were downplayed or managed to uphold the primacy of the institution, its power, standing and reputation'. Kenny might have been lightly rated prior to taking office, but at this point it seemed possible to believe that a new republic might genuinely be at hand. Such was the elevated level of the Taoiseach's moral indignation there were even trace elements of the cut-throat severity of a Michael McDowell surrounding the acerbic warning that Ireland 'is not Rome'.

Significantly, however, the Taoiseach was talking about history when he criticised the world of the 'industrial school or Magdalene Ireland, where the swish of a soutane, smothered conscience and humanity and the swing of a thurible ruled the Irish Catholic world'. Still, one could hardly blame a people thirsting for leadership after the vacuum of a Biffo if we allowed ourselves to be seduced by the grandiloquent declaration that this was now 'the Republic of Ireland in 2011. It is a republic of laws, rights and responsibilities and proper civic order where the delinquency and arrogance of a particular version of a particular kind of morality will no longer be tolerated or ignored.' The echoes of McDowell continued, as Kenny warned that, 'growing up, many of us in here learned that we were part of a pilgrim Church. Today, that Church needs to be a penitent Church, a Church truly and deeply penitent for the horrors it perpetrated, hid and denied — in the name of God, but for the good of the institution'. With a rare frankness, he told the various prelates that, when it came to the citizens, 'their law, as citizens of this country — will always supersede canon law that has neither legitimacy nor place in the affairs of this country'. Compared with the eclectic emotion displayed by the Taoiseach, the speeches of others appeared to be somewhat dry. The Tánaiste was caught so flatfooted by the affair that the Labour leader nearly had to declare war on the Vatican in order to regain the initiative.

Sadly, later events indicated that there was less to the speech than met the inquiring eye. Mr Kenny's subsequent purse-lipped response to the Magdalene scandal — where the Taoiseach metaphorically patted his pockets to make sure his wallet was still there when the elderly ladies came looking for justice — revealed that the denunciation of gimlet-eyed canon lawyers was informed by rhetoric, rather than a desire for revolution. Indeed, even prior to that, a truer measure of the Dear Leader's radical instincts was uncovered after Mr Gilmore pledged that gay marriage was the civil-rights issue of this generation. As we were subsequently treated to the spectacle of the Taoiseach of the land falling over a flowerpot outside the National Library as he tried to evade the media pack's queries on the gay marriage thing, the key lesson for Paddy Mac is that if a clever Prince wants to look courageous, he should always declare war on Great Powers who are now weak. Mr Kenny, in going to war with the Church, was taking on an institution hollowed out from within by depravity and weak leadership. Indeed, it is a measure of the fallen state of the institution he assailed that Mr Kenny was far more unnerved by the prospect of the pink wedding reception than by the imperial purple of an angry prelate.

Paddy Mac should also note that scapegoats can come in the most intriguing of forms. Economists and intellectuals have recently declared that 'when future historians look back at the big-picture history of Ireland, they are likely to conclude that Ireland in 2010 to 2014 enjoyed a golden age of enlightened governance'. Before you start to blush modestly, Enda, they are not referring to you, but to the Troika. Yet, intriguingly, the poor Troika has become the flayed donkey of Irish political discourse. This might appear to be all the more surprising for Paddy Mac, given the failure of the Coalition to live up to promises of reform made prior to the 2011 election vote. But, once they experienced the shocking discovery that reform tends to irritate the citizenry, the Coalition, having sniffed the political air and found it foul, turned on the Troika and made it their priority to get them and their reform tomfoolery out of the country as swiftly as possible. Mind you, smarter elements, such as Michael Noonan, were more reluctant to see the Troika go, for before the Troika left when there was bad news to be delivered, the Coalition could, like the old trade union leader, go to the electorate and claim, 'It's not us, lads, it's the gaffers.' Some will say that it is surely illustrative of the incorrigible nature of the Irish that the greatest complaint is that the Troika is making us live like Germans. Paddy Machiavelli should leave aside such critiques and, like de Valera accepting the oath, simply recognise that he lives in a country where reform is always seen as a school for oppression. Alternatively, our Aspirant Prince can take the responsible position, argue how water charges, property tax and third-level fees are good, and that this is how a mature state that isn't fiscally incontinent governs itself. However, if Paddy Mac has retained any of the cunning that got him to where he is, he will go to the electorate wringing his cap as he bleats about how the Troika made us do it, your honour, and if we get e'er a chance at all we'll get back to ruling ourselves in the fine old style that originally landed us into the land of 'we are where we are'. That, after all, may actually be what the voters want. We will find out soon enough, for the Three Horsemen of the Troika, having cast a cold eye upon our variant of crony capitalism, and attempting to force us to behave like normal states, have gone. And intriguingly, they were as anxious to go as our elite were to see them leave. Mind you, whilst the latter's view on the Troika was clear, we never really found out what the Troika made of exotic creatures like us. Perhaps it's best not to ask.

Chapter 10 ⌒

SINBAD'S MONKEY AND WHY ASPIRANT PRINCES SHOULD STEER CLEAR OF BEING TOO CLOSE TO DEAR LEADERS

From this a general rule is drawn which never or rarely fails: that he who is the cause of another becoming powerful is ruined; because that predominance has been brought about either by astuteness or else by force, and both are distrusted by him who has been raised to power.

On the politics of Sinbad's monkey • now you are a strong man • the Biffo-Bertie paradox • special friends • the dangers of seeing a Dear Leader when they are weak • a Noonan necessity • be semi-competent • spotting disfavour • outside friends and how Máire Geoghegan-Quinn is the best friend a future Dear Leader can have

One of the tales Paddy Machiavelli should always carry around to inform his dealings is the story of Sinbad's monkey, where the legendary mariner helped carry a demon, masquerading as a frail old man, across a river. Sadly, far from securing any gratitude, Sinbad discovered that once the monkey leaped onto his back, he could not shake the creature off until, like the death of many another Irish leader, he got it drunk and murdered it with a rock. In time, Paddy Mac will find that the thing he has yearned for most, the friendship of the Dear Leader, can, when it arrives, be somewhat like that of the monkey. It may well begin with smiles, affability and guarantees of a better future, but be assured, for all the protestations of gratitude, any Dear Leader will see you as nothing more than a permanent taxi to a better place … for him. The even worse news on this front is that the frailer he gets, the more tightly he will cling on to you. The problem, alas, for poor Paddy Mac is that if a Dear Leader takes this decision, Paddy Mac will not have any choice in the matter.

Still, should Paddy Machiavelli become the Prince's designated 'strong man', it will provide the outside world with the first indication that he might be one of the 'special ones'. The even better news is that it is not so difficult a task to become a strong man since Leinster House is so full of invisible men. Paddy Mac should not, of course, appear too eager to secure this honour. Instead, being the party leader's strong man must fall upon our Aspirant Prince's shoulders like the white man's burden. Paddy Machiavelli must also be cautious about the motives of those who would suggest that he be a 'strong man'. This is particularly the case early in his career, for if our aspirant strong man moves against someone and is taken out, the ramifications can continue for a decade. The classic example of this is somewhat surprising, for we suspect Micheál Martin has never defined himself as being the Taoiseach's bailiff. However, back in the pink of his political youth, the then popular young Minister for Health set himself up for a tilt at Charlie McCreevy. It was an unusually brave decision, given that Bertie's Cardinal Wolsey was still at the height of his powers. Micheál, though, was emboldened by the apparent tacit support of Mr Ahern, who was not at all displeased by the prospect of a wounding conflict between Bertie's most likely successor and an increasingly bumptious Minister for Finance. Like the infamous battle of the Widow McCormack's cabbage patch, the resulting denouement was a short and bruising affair in which, once Bertie had helpfully opened the window, Micheál and his big new budget were sent flying towards the nearest dungheap. Micheál continued to be a minister for a decade afterwards, but, in a strange way, he never fully recovered his authority. Ironically, in the long run, peripherality was to become Micheál's friend, but it is doubtful he felt that way at the time.

Paddy Mac might note that being the Dear Leader's special political friend does not mean that you are genuine friends. There is no better example of this than the famous Biffo-Bertie paradox. The then Taoiseach, Mr Ahern, had little respect for poor Biffo, and Mr Cowen, in a rare display of prescience, found Bertie to be an incomprehensible, slippery, insubstantial force. Mr Ahern, however, on the rare occasion that the FF sheep showed their teeth, tended, particularly in his declining years, to use Cowen as his enforcer. In a strange way, given his other failings, the template for the leader's enforcer at a senior level is provided by the same Mr Cowen who made it clear that he was simply acting as his master's barking dog. It is important for Paddy Mac to adopt a similar 'it's not me, lads, it's the gaffer'-style when he is dragging some partying TD out of the bar. Indeed, it may, courtesy of some sympathetic nods and winks, even allow Paddy Mac to seduce future supporters.

It might appear to be the case, now that Paddy Machiavelli is seen to be the leader's special friend, that he is on a certain road to the top, but is this really the case? Dear Leaders, you see, are mercurial, dangerous sorts of animals. That, after all, is how they got there. They are, therefore, quick to be suspicious, egotistical and terribly needy. Paddy Mac has all those qualities too, but he must sublimate them, or the ice of the Dear Leader's disfavour will freeze the wax on his political wings. There is no finer example of these dangers than the travails experienced by Phil Hogan. After all the years of plotting, mooching, grinning, conniving and strong-arming in the service of Enda, it was thought that Phil would be Enda's Richelieu once FG secured the less-than-holy grail of power. Or, to put it more accurately, Phil certainly thought it was the case. There was always the possibility of trouble, for rather like Bill Clinton, not-so-cute old Phil always had a reputation, in political terms, as being a hard old hound to keep on the porch. But, after his role in securing the Taoiseach's job for Enda, it might have been thought that the celebratory evening where Enda trotted in to Phil's 50th birthday party, saw their mutual pal Michael Lowry in the audience, and asked, 'Is that an application form for FG I see in your pocket?' was a prologue to greatness.

And yet, it has utterly not turned out that way. Instead, as the Dear Leader smiled upon Noonan, Joan, Mr Gilmore, the rest of the obedient Labour ministers, not-so-cute old Phil found himself resembling that Dickensian urchin who, with his nose pressed against the sweetshop window, can only gaze wistfully at the delights within. It is difficult to say what precisely the problem is with Phil. Some say it is a woman thing, and Phil undoubtedly has had his share of scrapes there. Nothing epitomised this more than the scenario where the environment minister might have thought he was engaging in harmless banter at an Oireachtas golf outing with the former administrator to John Bruton, Anne O'Connell. At the outing Ms O'Connell had noted she hoped Phil wouldn't screw property owners in the planned new tax. Referring to her partner, Máirtín Mac Cormaic, the minister had jibed, 'I have no problem screwing you. Hasn't Máirtín been screwing you for years?'

No harm had been meant, but, it was inevitable that from this moment on that the matter would end up in the media, that Phil would apologise for what Ms O'Connell found to be a degrading, insulting and abusive remark by saying that he meant it as a joke, and that despite all the apologies no one would be happy. The subsequent furore which occurred when, after being texted about the evils of the new property tax by a woman — again! — Mr Hogan issued the tart reply, 'Would U ever relax and feed the children', was silly-season material. But, as Paddy Mac will recall, we have previously warned that being seen to be positive on the women front is one of the most critical actions our Aspirant Prince must take.

Mr Hogan's rap sheet in that regard is unfair, for it's not that Phil hasn't tried with the women. In fact, some would say he's always trying, with all that legislation about gender quotas. The problem, though, is that like that poor dog on the porch that is kicked every time he wags his tail, on the premise that bad plans are afoot, Phil has acquired a reputation for not being 'progressive', and once that happens, you are slipping down the greased pole. The other great problem that has afflicted Phil is that it is important for the Taoiseach's special one to have the appearance of being at least a semi-competent confidant. Dear Leaders like their chosen ones to bring a hint of sunshine with them. Sadly, Phil is surrounded by a somewhat murkier atmosphere. There is nothing bad there but, like the classic, old-style FF minister, Phil is messy. It is not that FG is a flag of convenience for Phil, for there is no more ardent Blueshirt; the problem is that he is too old-fashioned, too tribal a true blue for the new breed of ethical FG aristocrats.

For Hogan, alas, the messiness even extended to his rows with those Irish farmers who believe it is their inalienable constitutional right to use the nation's rivers as a personal latrine. Septic tanks were only the start of it, as other furores over the household charge and property tax swiftly followed. The problem for Phil in all of this was that whilst incompetence or simple bad luck can be survived, an unloved minister is, in the eyes of Dear Leaders, like a cat bringing home a live mouse. Indeed, some will say that in Phil's case, his woes started when Enda's special one ruined the Dear Leader's homecoming ard-fheis. Enda had been basking in the tolerance, if not love, of the citizens. He was a friend of the Chinese top man, Xi Jinping, of Obama and even of the Queen of England. And then, like a thunder cloud suddenly appearing in the middle of blue skies on the first day of cutting the hay, cute old Phil came in the door and the landscape turned dark with distant boos.

Ultimately, the main lesson provided by Phil is about the dangers faced by 'special ones' who see the Dear Leader at his weakest and most open moments. In the case of Enda and Phil, they had, as the poet Patrick Kavanagh said in 'Advent', 'tasted and shared too much'. That is all well and good whilst one is in opposition, for a parity of sorts exists between all opposition TDs who are, ultimately, even when on the frontbench, still merely TDs. But, on assuming power, Dear Leaders swiftly become uneasy with any ongoing notions of egalitarianism. Even in a republic, becoming Taoiseach is like some secular ordination where all flaws associated with the normal race of mortals are erased. However, in the case of Dear Leader Enda, not-so-cute old Phil is like the courtier who has seen the king naked. Both may laugh initially, but, over time, trouble begins to fester, as the Dear Leader considers the importance of his dignity. And, in this regard, suddenly and quite often swiftly, the once closest one becomes a difficulty and a source of displeasure.

The other problem Paddy Mac must be aware of is that if you have been seen as the Taoiseach's confidant, you will have few friends to protect you or put in a quiet word once you are in trouble. Instead, your 'colleagues' will step on your head to secure that precious spot beside the Taoiseach's well-nuzzled earlobes. In a variant of the power of groupthink, the consequences when that occurs resemble the pig pen, where all the little hogs queue up to secure their status by nipping the tail of the weakest one. And, inevitably, it is your own litter that are the worst. So it was that when the first problems began, sources delightedly murmured about how Phil was 'in real trouble in the constituency'. Meanwhile, within the party, our man found himself accused of being a 'messer rather than an enforcer'. Suddenly, the new wisdom was that 'Hogan and Enda are not as close as you would think. Don't forget that Enda sacked Phil as Director of Elections after the 2007 election right in front of the parliamentary party. Poor Phil didn't see it coming until Enda said he would have bet his house on FG winning two seats in Carlow-Kilkenny and sacked poor Phil on the spot.'

The measure of the utter cruelty of politics consists not so much of the swiftness of the decision, if that is not putting it too strongly, of Enda to elbow not-so-cute old Phil off the political magic carpet. Paddy Mac will note that what will have stung even more, however, is the replacement of Phil with Michael Noonan. A cold war might have existed between the Dear Leader and his finance minister for a decade, but, when Enda decided that Ireland needed somewhat different qualities, Phil was invisibly elbowed out of the way, as Noonan became the Dear Leader's chief consigliere. The first critical factor in Noonan's rise was that, whilst Enda is not good on the sums front, he is a dab hand at understanding the strange politics of national morale. In particular, he noted that a people somewhat short on the self-confidence front were relieved when Noonan, the national comfort blanket, returned from another bout of kissing the cheeks of Christine or nodding gravely in the company of Mr Schäuble to tell us that the foreigners think we're quite respectable again. Phil, in contrast, was getting involved in fights with farmers over sewage. The Dear Leader knew what he wanted to be associated with, so in a classic case of 'needs must when the devil drives', the former Robinson Crusoe of FG became the centre of gravity in the government and Enda's new 'special friend'. Sadly, Noonan's delight at this new status has been unrecorded.

In defining his relationship with the Dear Leader, Paddy Mac must also bear one other critical matter in mind. He should always be aware that the time will come when the Dear Leader himself may fall out of favour. It may never do Paddy Mac harm if he is seen to be favoured by power, but if he is seen to be nothing more than the Dear Leader's little doppelgänger, he will, should troubled times arrive, be seen by those who desire a change in dispensations to be the mere continuation of all that has gone before. So, when the Dear Leader's candle gutters, as it inevitably will, Paddy Mac will not want to be too near when the castle collapses, because the Dear Leader will, like Sinbad's bad monkey, try to cling on, even where the love is gone. Instead, as Paddy's colleagues watch carefully, he must tread along the acutely narrow fence of offering change combined with a peaceful transition of power, unity and no blood at all on the carpet. After years of being in the safe centre, Paddy Mac, in short, will position himself as the man to deliver change.

When it comes to seeking his own 'special friends', Paddy Mac must carefully target those whom he will embrace. In this regard, those he should be most anxious to please are junior rather than senior ministers. The problem with cabinet colleagues is that they will know our Aspirant Prince too well and will still retain notions that he is an equal. Another difficulty posed by the *ancien régime* is that, in seeking to become Taoiseach, the Aspirant Prince will never be thanked for giving people that which they already possess. Like Haughey, when he took on Lynch by stealth, and Albert when he took on Haughey openly, it is instead the new to whom our man must look, for in their avaricious eyes he must retain some small quantity of stardust. The junior minister, who is generally as talented as his designated senior, is always ripe for the plucking because, like

Aesop's fox, he is within touching distance of the grapes. But, whilst Paddy Mac is on the stepladder that will facilitate the final great leap, he should never be so uncouth as to tell the junior minister this directly. Instead, a small little display of warmth, such as a brief conversation detailing Paddy's incomprehension at the junior's absence from cabinet, will earn their loyalty for a decade.

Of course, as our tale of not-so-cute old Phil demonstrated earlier, the Dear Leader is far likelier to fall out of love with Paddy Mac first. In this regard, one of the earliest signs of disfavour occurs when our man is namechecked with a challenging ministry like Health. Paddy Mac should note that many suspect to this day that 'honest' Jack Lynch's decision to restore Charles Haughey to the cabinet was primarily motivated by the desire to see how Mr Haughey would fare with such delights as the legalisation of contraception. Outside of Micheál Martin, Bertie Ahern also used Health as a panopticon for Brian Cowen. And on those rare occasions when our current Dear Leader fears that the Mr Sheen is beginning to wear off his bodywork, curious leaks appear from 'senior sources not at all close to the Taoiseach' over how, were James Reilly to suffer a similar fate to that which befell poor Humpty Dumpty, then young fellow-me-lads like Leo Varadkar and Simon Coveney could surely rise to the challenge.

Should the Dear Leader indicate that Health is the direction in which he is sending Paddy Machiavelli, the response must be one of unalloyed delight at this 'challenge'. And Paddy should be delighted, for within the wink and nod land of Leinster House, putting him into Health means that he is now the designated unofficial official opposition to the ailing regime. There is, however, one challenge that he must resist totally. Some virtue can come of requests to reform a dysfunctional Department. But if Paddy Mac is mentioned as being the contender for a top European job, though he may continue to appear to reside in the bright land of the living, he has, in reality, joined the undead. Europe is the pleasantly apportioned elephants' graveyard where the wise prince buries his little difficulties and prays that such difficulties don't return to haunt him. And if he finds his name being attached to Europe, then the Aspirant Prince, if he still intends to be leader, must either kill the notion or kill the king who has designated him for such an appalling fate.

As he reaches the anteroom of real power, one other key complaint that Paddy Mac must ignore is the bleat that some of our gamier politicians indulge in about how your private life, or your friends, is your own business. In the modern age, everything is of public interest, particularly if it has an association with business. And sometimes, such is the power of that which Bertie called 'ettics', mere association, as distinct from friendship, can damage you. When it came to that controversial New York stock-exchange balcony scene involving Enda and Denis O'Brien, the furore, astonishingly, allowed Fianna Fáil to briefly take the high moral ground on ethics. Friends, or rather bad ones, have also done the career of not-so-cute old Phil (again!) little good, for unlike Macavity the cat, he is constantly, as with the Lowry birthday farce, being found grinning beside the scene of the political crime.

We understand it is a trial for our Aspirant Prince, as he accustoms himself to the centre of power, to be wary about his friends, for what is the point of being politically successful if you must continue to mix with the peasantry? But Paddy Machiavelli will at some point have to make a value judgment. If he wants two terms as an EU Commissioner, he should follow the path set by Pee Flynn. But if he is betting on the jackpot, then the priestly caution of Enda is the better route to take.

Curiously, one of the better examples of the importance of being cautious about friends is provided by the normally incautious Charlie McCreevy. The Galway Races was that Gatsby-style theatre of illusion and dreams where Fianna Fáil unveiled itself to the world. This folly was the great canvas on which FF painted its deepest desires for money, power, excess and, occasionally, sex in a public space. The problem, of course, was that the braying about their wealth and status actually turned into the most visible symbol of FF's separation from the people. Throughout all of it, though, one cute operator was noticeable by his absence. Charlie McCreevy may have been FF's king of the racing fraternity, but, even in an age that was chilly about ethics, McCreevy was wily enough to realise that this could only end in tears. He indulged in a fair few follies himself, but, enough of McCreevy's old cunning remained for him to realise the people are ill at ease with politicians who are too close to affluence. And, generally, given the consequences of our love affair with crony capitalism, who could disagree with them?

Others, alas, were not so wily, for there is no clearer example of the dangers inherent in becoming too friendly with the wealthy and the subsequent trappings of wealth than the fabulous tale of John 'the Bull' O'Donoghue. It would have been harder, at the start of his career, to find a more plain Jane-style republican than the same 'Bull'. In a regime which contained no shortage of Wolseys, O'Donoghue was the living child of de Valera. But, slowly, a great change gathered itself over O'Donoghue, who mirrored the calcification of a party that became all too aware of its power and position. The denouement was bitter, as the tales of ministerial expenses of €126,000 — including limousine rides between airport terminals, using the government jet on one six-day festival of flights where our hero jetted from Cannes to the Heineken Cup final and then travelled back to Cannes before going to London for a Ryder Cup event — were regaled to the rapt habitués of Cahirciveen who, on the first chance they got, kicked 'the Bull' out of the Dáil. Ironically, the terrible defenestration occurred in the very sports hall which had been built courtesy of the politics of the pork barrel that the Bull had licked so assiduously. A stony-faced electorate were, and continue to be, utterly indifferent to O'Donoghue's observations about the irony of the location. Sadly, they remain equally unconvinced by the protestations of O'Donoghue that he lived a frugal lifestyle. In their eyes those rides in a Venetian gondola told a different tale.

In contrast to the poor Bull's difficulties, one set of friends that Paddy Machiavelli should cultivate as assiduously as possible is able women. This is not just because he will receive great credit in being supportive of an increased profile in politics for the ladies. What is more important is that he can do all this without running any risk that his own ambitions will be thwarted, for a woman will never, under the current political dispensation, be Taoiseach. It should be noted that our prophecy in this regard is informed by reality, rather than sexism. Or to put it another way, the reality we are describing is informed by the endemic sexism of Leinster House. Some women have had a tilt at the top job, but Mary O'Rourke, despite her current status as the national Queen Mum, was always too tart for the delicate tastes of that school of FF deputy whose dream woman consisted of an expert maker of sponge cakes. In fairness, unease with powerful women is not just a Fianna Fáil fetish. Within Labour, Róisín Shortall also tried her luck, but there was too much lemon attached to Róisín for the National Women's Council, let alone the Labour Party. It would be unfair to merely single out Labour, for FG, the designated progressive party of Irish politics, has never managed to have a female contender, even at the low point of 2002 when anyone could, and did, become leader.

One compensation for 'the ladies' is that there are always openings aplenty to become the Tánaiste or the Deputy Leader. Be it Nora Owen, who was John Bruton's deputy, or that political canary in the coal mine, Mary Coughlan, Dear Leaders like to have a few women around the top table, for they take the bare, or rather, the masculine look off the place. And it is, or rather was, nice to be able to say that a woman is the head of state, even if she has fewer powers than the last Emperor of China. However, should our Aspirant Prince be fretting about the threat posed by any female challenger, the fate of Máire Geoghegan-Quinn provides us with the truest template of his safety. Geoghegan-Quinn, who had, unwisely, from an early age put everyone on notice that she intended to be Ireland's first female Dear Leader, had all the qualifications for the post. Such was her political subtlety, she was clever enough to back Haughey when he was on the rise and, two decades later, to also mark out the contours of his political *in memoriam* at a warm-up speech at Haughey's last FF ard-fheis, where she spoke in front of the stony-faced Haughey in the past tense, about how 'there will never be a time like it again: never such excitement, never such achievement, never such heartache, never such happiness, as the time they will talk of as the Haughey era.' Afterwards, one admiring figure noted that it was the first time he had ever seen the leader's adoring followers applauding the public execution of their man.

It is a measure of how swiftly her career imploded that, just over half a decade later, Geoghegan-Quinn was gone from politics, unless being an EU Commissioner counts, and it doesn't. She might have been a politician who could fillet a bruiser like Michael Noonan to the point of almost finishing his career, but the distaste of 'the lads' for uppity women meant that she ended up writing books and a column for *The Irish Times* before finally being appointed as the Commissioner for Something or Other because Biffo could not find anyone less embarrassing. It is often said that the measure of the sexism that is endemic in Irish politics was provided by the sight of Bertie succeeding Albert, when it should have been Máire Geoghegan-Quinn. In truth, the real measure of the strength of the 'men need only apply' ethos is that Biffo, rather than Máire Geoghegan-Quinn, succeeded Bertie.

Chapter 11 ～

LEARNING TO BE A STRAIGHT TALKER WHILST EMBRACING THE JOY OF VAGUENESS

… that hatred is acquired as much by good works as by bad ones, therefore, as I said before, a prince wishing to keep his state is very often forced to do evil.

So *do* speak, but only if you have something important to say • and only if you choose the correct issue • a Green tail • Labour's gay times • on the dangers of excessive optimism • death by waffling • a straight-talking iconoclast • Quinn the alter ego • you're right, so what? • do manufacture your own controversies • Noel's third-level lesson • never ask till you know, and on being unloved

At some point around now, Paddy Mac will be raised to the heights of a middling ministry, such as the Environment or Transport. No, he is still not important but, like the teaser who sets the mood for the stallion, he is beginning to get a sniff of the action. Now that he is a Middling Minister, Paddy Machiavelli may start to fret again about whether he should take a more dominant position in the Dáil chamber. If he is uneasy about such a prospect, our Aspirant Prince should be consoled by the overwhelming view that being a star in the chamber is the political equivalent of what natural puritan John Giles called 'champagne football'. Like the frothy stuff, it may look good and impress those pundits who know little about the great game, but that which bubbles on the floor of the Dáil often turns sour once it hits the cold air of the voter's judgment. Two decades of champagne from a variety of Labour leaders, such as Ruairí Quinn, Pat Rabbitte and Eamon Gilmore, produced a Labour Party that resides at the edge of extinction whilst the roar of other big beasts, such as the Brut, the Biffo and the McDowell, often only appeared to have the effect of scaring off the electorate.

Despite these precedents, Paddy Mac should be wary of the bona fides of the 'speak softly but carry a big stick' argument, if only because too many Irish politicians speak softly and carry a small stick. Instead, our Aspirant Prince should observe that a critical flaw in the champagne football analysis is that it confuses the making of much noise with dominating the Dáil. Mr Bruton, when he was haranguing the then permanent FF government, may have generated a level of decibels that would silence a donkey braying for a mate, on the not entirely incorrect basis that a much larger donkey is hanging around. But, you only dominate the Dáil chamber if you instil fear and Mr Bruton did not possess that trait. Paddy Machiavelli will therefore not be as clever as he might think if he actively avoids the Dáil chamber. He should note, though, that those who really did dominate the chamber, such as Dick Spring, Charlie Haughey and Garret, did so because they captured in some transcendental manner the spirit and conflicts of the age. Their unique personalities helped, but the themes and issues they fought over were what drove their dominance. Haughey's snarling persona was driven by the desire for secrecy and self-preservation, whilst Garret and Dick Spring were the white knights of the other side of Ireland's ghostly civil war.

Paddy Mac need not fret too much if he cannot find a similar zeitgeist, for a host of Taoisigh ranging from Jack Lynch to Enda have always been ghostly presences in the Dáil. Indeed, some, such as Bertie, made a positive virtue of it. But Paddy Mac should still attempt to occasionally shine in the chamber, since no one is impressed by a zombie. However, if he is to do so, the Aspirant Prince must discover an issue he is comfortable with. The best news we can give our friend Paddy Mac is that this issue does not have to be the dreaded beast of economics. This is epitomised by Enda Kenny's speech on IRA decommissioning in 2005, for getting Enda to make a coherent argument about economics, or anything to do with sums, was always a frightening experience. But, when it came to morality or law and order, Mr Kenny, or to be more accurate his excellent speechwriter, was on home ground. The issue of the McCabe killing fitted that particular bill. An unrepentant, politically irresponsible Sinn Féin had evolved into the political equivalent of some holding company for an IRA that was robbing banks to fund its members' pensions. We know now that banks were operating in a remarkably similar manner to the IRA but, at the time, Kenny's anger chimed with a public who wanted peace but not with dishonour, and so he laid into the reprehensible capitulation of the sovereign government in the face of IRA intimidation. Paddy Machiavelli should note that the speech was valuable on two fronts. Firstly, given the semolina-style standard of bland political discourse that was the defining feature of the Ahern era, Enda's passion stood out. And it served to indicate that there was more to Mr Kenny than nodding, winking, smiling and bucklepping.

In contrast, the unfortunate Greens provide Paddy Mac with a critical case study in what happens if a party or an individual becomes obsessed by that which is not of interest to the voters. It is easily forgotten now, but in the Cowen administration, the Greens' status as the voice of reason, God help us, meant that the now-disappeared party had been holding their own up to 2010. And then, suddenly, in a country where the middle classes possessed genuine fears that they would be soon dining on the contents of the nation's dustbins, the Greens started to obsess about the docking of dogs' tails and banning property developers from hunting deer. The Greens might have wanted to end the practice of docking little dogs' tails, but, instead, a bemused electorate took the view that it was the Greens themselves who should be docked, and what sane person could blame them?

Paddy Mac might be inclined to believe that such errors were a mere once-off that can safely be explained by the simplistic wisdom that the Greens are mad. He should, however, note that all political parties are susceptible to this strain of political myxomatosis. Garret had his constitutional crusades, Albert had Harry Whelehan, and even Bertie, the most cunning one of all, had his Bertie Bowl. Ironically, it took a former Green Party apparatchik to define the similar factors that led to Labour's debacle in Meath East in 2013. Labour might have started with modest ambitions of beating Sinn Féin into third place. But, by the close, the poor candidate, Eoin Holmes, an impressively pink-shirted, 'Cool Hibernia'-style, very talkative, film-producing, coffee shop-owning advocate of same-sex marriage, was in fifth place behind the political eccentrics of Direct Democracy Ireland, and damn glad to get in ahead of the old Workers' Party.

In the wake of the disastrous campaign, Steve Rawson, a colourful former Green Party strategist, noted that the 'Cool Hibernia' thing was possibly not the best strategy to be adopting at a time when 'property tax notices come dropping through Meath letterboxes'. Rawson's diagnosis was chilling for Labour, as he dolefully recalled that 'the Greens, as junior coalition partners to Fianna Fáil, eagerly promoted civil partnership and a Lord Mayor for Dublin, during the worst economic meltdown since the foundation of the State, to a bewildered and angry electorate'. The similar spectacle of some Dublin 4 chap trotting into the despairing Meath homes of those jobless, despairing collateral victims of the Tiger and wittering on about gay marriage meant that Rawson was, to put it mildly, not being cruel when he warned that 'Labour's messaging and optics depicted a leadership and campaign team out of touch with the general mood'. Rawson would have found many an echo in the Labour benches when he warned that, in attempting to evade their economic failures by moving to the famous 'gay civil marriage is the civil rights issue of our generation' line, Labour was in real danger of becoming totally alienated from an electorate who were already existing pretty close to the edge of reason.

The voters might prefer to hear good news about the economy rather than a lecture about the joys of gay marriage, but Paddy Machiavelli should, in seeking the love of the citizen, be careful to not be too seduced by the cherub of optimism. Paddy the voter will always prefer fairy tales to Gothic horror stories, but our Aspirant Prince should always apply some minuscule degree of quality control to his narrative, or he will end up casting his sweetness upon the desert air. In the case of Charles Haughey, for example, during his first incarnation as Taoiseach, after the famous 'living beyond our means address', Mr Haughey experienced a bounce in popularity. The citizen felt that after the drift surrounding the gentle death of 'honest' Jack, Ireland had finally secured the sort of plain-speaking autocrat who would do our thinking for us. But, as an election neared and Charlie's political legs turned to jelly, he decided that speaking pretty to the voters about all the nice things he was going to do for them might work a little better. Oddly, though, the more he spoke of boom and bloom, the more Stygian the state of national depression became, as the voters fretted about the likelihood that Haughey's boom and bloom would catapult them into the poorhouse.

The classic modern example of the dangers of excessive optimism is provided by Brian Lenihan. Our deceased former Minister for Finance may now reside in the same iconographical closet as Robert Emmet, but it was all rather more equivocal in 2009 when, six months after Mr Lenihan's Emergency budget signalled the end of the boom, on presenting our second austerity budget in a year, Mr Lenihan claimed that 'notwithstanding the difficulties in the last eight months, we are now on the road to economic recovery'. The script veered further towards the fantastical as Lenihan bragged about how 'though our self-confidence as a nation has been shaken, the Government's strategy over the last eighteen months is working'. Sadly, the real state of confidence amongst the citizens was epitomised by the urban non-myths about how Paddy the voter was busy hiding his euro coins in the attic even as Lenihan somewhat despairingly repeated, 'We have a plan ... to take us forward on the path of sustainable economic growth'. Lenihan, by simple acts of courage and a sense of sustained personal sacrifice, would transcend the bitter mockery he faced on a day when even the likes of James Reilly left him looking like a fool. However, the lesson Paddy Machiavelli should learn is that attempting to beguile the voters with the false rhetoric of optimism, based on nothing more concrete than the hope that the world might accidentally transform itself into that which he desires, is more likely to have an unhappy ending.

Apart from Brian Lenihan, the career that epitomises the importance of securing the reputation of being a straight talker, as distinct from a weaver of pleasant fairy tales, is that of Eamon Gilmore. We may be a nation of Berlusconis, but the voter likes the theory (as distinct from the practice) of being led by a man who tells it as it is. In the year prior to Election 2011, Eamon Gilmore had reached that elevated state to such an extent that he was the man the people wanted as their Taoiseach. Significantly, and perhaps even mischievously, Brian Cowen, in the early months of Gilmore's leadership, also made it quite clear that he saw Gilmore as being much more of an equal than Enda. At the time, it even seemed as though the compliment mattered. In those initial blissful days, there certainly was something about Eamon that was perfectly 'connected' to the concerns of the citizen. After the great age of the elegant 19th-century-style sound bites of Rabbitte, the bracing but clever simplicity of Gilmore's critique of the government was like a breath of fresh air. Then, sadly, after the initial 'pink but perfect' phase, something strange happened, as fresh air was replaced by hot air. In retrospect, the change may be traced back to the moment Gilmore accused Cowen of being guilty of 'economic treason'. The problem for Mr Gilmore, alas, was it became increasingly difficult to top such a claim, except perhaps by the implicit promise that by declaring war on Berlin, Eamon would lead Angela by the nose towards Labour's way. But, as the language became ever more heightened, unfortunately, our wary voters began to suspect that they were hearing rhetoric, as distinct from ideas that could actually change the place we were in. Though, like the villainous Hedley Lamarr in *Blazing Saddles*, Mr Gilmore continued to use his tongue 'purtier than a ten-dollar whore', the voters, divining a terrible absence of solutions, began to melt away. And the more that evolved, the more Gilmore fell into the dangerous place of being open to the most wounding accusation that can be made in Irish politics. Surprisingly, this was coined by the non-confrontational Bertie Ahern who, on being goaded shortly after the fall of Albert Reynolds's government, lost his temper in public — the only occasion this occurred in Bertie's political career. Turning on Gay Mitchell, he snarled, 'You're only a waffler, you've been around here waffling for years'. Though no one ever said it directly to Gilmore, as the Labour Sir Lancelot turned into a Sir Talks-a-lot, more and more of the plain people began to believe that, when it came to the vice of death by waffling, Mitchell had finally found a successor in Mr Gilmore.

If he wants to acquire the reputation of being a straight-talking iconoclast rather than a waffler, Paddy Mac should cast a beady eye upon the career of yet another ghost — Charlie McCreevy. The most important thing our Aspirant Prince should note about Charlie McCreevy's persona is that this was not a creation of fiction or spin. In his earlier political incarnation McCreevy did not merely rebel against Charlie Haughey, he also kicked a fair few bishops and the fearful conservatism of a society that would not let people alone to live their lives as they desired. Indeed, such was McCreevy's iconoclastic fearlessness, he was not beyond kicking the voters for their indolent acceptance of the various tyrants who bound their lives in chains. The electorate might have responded gleefully to the pointing out of their vices, but his own were somewhat less sanguine. Outside of forfeiting ministerial office, McCreevy's honesty meant he suffered quite a few real kicks and thumps. Such a process might not have been too enjoyable for him at the time, but it built up an enormous treasure trove of credibility with the electorate.

If Paddy Machiavelli feels McCreevy is a little too iconoclastic, he should note that speaking freely is a form of liberation. McCreevy might not have secured office during the Haughey era, but the Cheshire Cat grin of cheeky satisfaction, and the mischief that winked out from sparkling eyes, suggested that despite the absence of a Mercedes, he had chosen a happier route than those who served out of fear and desire. In a curious way, this ebullience added to the impact of his rebellion, for often Dáil outsiders are afflicted by that Eeyore gene, which means that they are half in love with disgrace and exile. In the case of McCreevy, though, the sparkling nature of his public discourse added credibility to his opposition to Haughey. It was suggestive of a man at ease with his position, who was acting out of honest motives.

The virtues of McCreevy's sunny-side-up personality are best understood by the decline in public support that hit Enda's government of Grumpy Old Men. They should of course know that already, for nothing epitomised the importance of that quality more than the war between Charlie McCreevy and Ruairí Quinn. This was a brief conflict that lasted just two years, but it was a rare elemental division between the straight-talking Mr Angry from Sandymount and the FF Joker, who knew better than anyone else how to stroke the Irish id. The final battle which settled the fate of the State for two decades occurred in 1996. Things back then were so good the Rainbow did not even need to talk up the budget in order to bury Bertie and FF. Instead, Quinn's incapacity to move beyond an utterly professorial persona meant that a budget, driving a revolution in Irish governance and the economy, utterly failed to enchant the citizenry. Ethical Labour finance ministers may always be reluctant to use vulgar phrases such as tax cuts, but if you are giving things to people, there is nothing wrong with letting them know about it. Instead of musing about investing in our society, Quinn should have been talking about your money going into your wallet. But, when you are a political altar boy, it is terribly difficult to be using vulgar phraseology such as this. So, instead, the most successful finance minister in the history of the State drifted off into a soliloquy about confounding 'those commentators who said that you cannot achieve social progress and fiscal responsibility at the same time'. On one level, Mr Quinn should not be criticised, for he is instinctively of the altar-boy class. Paddy Mac should observe, however, that there are consequences when there is neither theatre nor magic in a style of public discourse that seeks only the approbation of the mandarin class and contains nothing of interest for the people. Paddy the voter will sometimes listen respectfully to the ego, but when the pied piper of the id trots along wearing the finest of motley, he will follow the merry tune without a critical thought.

Of course, you can overdo the straight talking too. One of the few politicians who was completely correct about the Irish fiscal crisis was Richard 'the lesser' Bruton. Paddy Machiavelli should remember that it was Richard, five years before the great implosion began, who prophesied that our new prosperity was being driven by the 'here for a good time, not a long time' fiscal principles 'of the hog cycle, fuel the boom, suck poorly informed people into taking a chance, and when it gets difficult, renege on the promises, pull all the credit lines and let the innocent be crushed'. In his time in opposition, Richard was also one of the few to attack the Ceauşescu-style misgovernance of social partnership. Sadly, the fate of Richard indicates that being right in politics is only an opening negotiation strategy. Despite all the 'book-learning', when Richard 'the lesser' Bruton had to leave pleasures such as the making of jam in order to issue his milk-and-water-style challenge to the Playboy of the Western World, the turnips of his own party slashed the stirrups of the politician who was right, stuck their pikes into the royal one, and laid him before the current Dear Leader. Enda did allow Richard to live, but a high price had to be paid, where the lesser one had to swear allegiance to such an extent that Richard's main task as Minister for Jobs is to get out of the way when Enda is making all those good news announcements.

Now that he is of middling rank, Paddy Mac must learn to master the art of creating his own controversies, for the cabinet minister who simply runs his own Department quietly and efficiently will never be noticed. The Aspirant Prince must therefore ensure he is embroiled in occasional conflicts and dramas. Paddy Machiavelli should, however, make sure that he is not constantly in trouble, or he will get a reputation for being truculent. Our Aspirant Prince should instead recall the art of Bertie in those infamous social partnership talks, where our hero would arrive late at night rubbing his eyes, engaging in much downcast, doleful muttering about the difficulties that he, a man alone, faced in coming up with a resolution to a problem that had in reality already been solved, for, if it hadn't, then Bertie wouldn't be there in the first place.

Paddy Mac would be wise, though, to note that self-generated controversy can be a dangerous affair. Noel Dempsey discovered this to his cost when, in the middle of the Celtic Tiger, he decided to reform a system of free third-level fees where the wealthy used the funds saved from third-level fees for private second-level education. There's social reform for you, Paddy Machiavelli-style! The fate of Dempsey's solo run was decided by the minister's utter failure to follow another key political principle of never asking a question without knowing the answer. Had Dempsey looked before he leaped, he would have seen both Mary Harney and Liz O'Donnell waiting with the purring chainsaw they kept especially for socially progressive acts. And no matter where he looked, he would have seen no sign of Bertie at all. It all ended in an inevitable sort of way when Dempsey 'put his cabinet career on the line', unleashed a blistering attack on his critics inside and outside the government, and put it up to his Fianna Fáil ministerial colleagues to support him. Bertie supported Noel in the way that only Bertie could, with some fretful mutters about how he wanted the issue out of the way before the poor Leaving Certificate students sat their exams. His little dance having been done, Noel then did a humiliating U-turn, consoled a little by a few bob from the bulging Exchequer. Whatever about Noel, it all ended well for everyone else. In the case of Bertie, Dear Leaders are never too unhappy to see ministers with notions being turned over — particularly if the knife is wielded by a coalition partner. The Regressive Plutocrats were allowed to continue to pose as the egalitarian defenders of the Yummy Mummy private-school-fee-paying habitués of south Dublin. The last we saw of Noel, meanwhile, was the spectacle of the then Minister for Transport refusing to return from a foreign holiday when Ireland froze over during the harshest winter since the 1940s. As the photographs of the minister's gritted drive and road were lovingly spread across the newspapers, it was clear that iron had entered Noel's soul a long time before our hero walked away from the battle for FF's survival in 2011.

Surprisingly, perhaps the finest example of a politician

seizing the zeitgeist, and making it his own, is provided by Garret FitzGerald. Up to that moment when Haughey seized the Taoiseach's office, FitzGerald had been seen as a pleasant, woolly sort of a fellow. But then, in a stark attack whose lines resonate even today, the opposition leader set the political battleground for a decade. The wily FitzGerald did not, of course, dive straight in. Instead, he began with some *faux* reluctance about the 'difficulty of responding adequately or sensitively to this unique situation'. This was followed by the assumption of the status of the Father of the Nation, as Garret claimed he had to speak 'not only for the Opposition but for many in FF who may not be free to say what they believe or to express their deep fears for the future of the country'. The sense of macabre drama can only have been intensified by FitzGerald's expression of the hope that he 'may be equal to it, that I may say what needs to be said and can be said, recognising how much I cannot say, for reasons that all the House understands'. The fact that most of the House didn't, and those who understood would have preferred not to, made it all the more menacing. White Knight Garret, though, was bravely prepared to take a Black Knight possessed by 'an overweening ambition … a wish to dominate, even to own, the state'. Paddy Machiavelli will note that Garret also deployed the great virtue of empathy as he professed his sympathy for 'the feet that will go through that lobby', which will 'drag', and the hearts that will 'be heavy' as they give 'their formal consent' but 'withhold their full consent'. Garret often had a good old run at the innocent-abroad game, what with the odd socks and so forth, but despite his outward guilelessness, FitzGerald knew well that the politician who can define or discover an enemy has an identity and a purpose.

In the age of consensus it is sometimes claimed that it is harder these days to find a common enemy. But, as the case of Michael D and the war on the limits of austerity proves, if you look hard enough, there is always some dragon hanging around a corner waiting patiently to be slain. Sadly, it is the measure of where we are that sometimes it takes a septuagenarian President to decipher and find our moral crusades. But they still exist. And some would say that, in the age of consensus, we need to find them more urgently than ever.

Though he will have his great days as he tiptoes towards the top, it is important that Paddy Mac realises that no matter how carefully he treads through the political land mines of the world, at some point in his career he will be unloved. This might not even be his fault. It may be that the government itself is hated, and he has just been caught up in the debris. When that unfortunate moment occurs, there will be no point in our Aspirant Prince flapping around the problem like his colleagues. Instead, if Paddy Mac is to stand out, he must confront the problem by evading it. The best methodology in this regard is for our Aspirant Prince to come out and openly tell the people they are correct in their desire to disembowel poor Paddy Mac, watch him die slowly, and then stick his head on a spike. He should adopt a generalised air of fretful concern, to indicate that the citizens' unhappiness has impacted upon his very soul. And Paddy Machiavelli, to ease that pain, must then promise that the government will try to listen to the people. The latter is a particularly good promise, since listening is not a commitment to actually do anything. If the mood is particularly bad, he should even take the brave step of going before the cameras to accept full responsibility for whatever disaster in troubling the people. In doing so, however, Paddy Mac must restrict himself to accepting responsibility. Never, if he wants to keep his job, should he go so far as to accept the consequences of accepting responsibility.

In these unfortunate times, there are two critical things that our man absolutely must not do. The first is that he must evade all attempts to confront this mood or engage in any sort of mature rational discourse with the angry citizen. The second error that he must not make is to display fear, run, hide, or attempt to secure any form of personal escape. It is not just that the party hierarchy, as was the case with all those disappeared ministers during Albert Reynolds's campaign of 1992, will note Paddy Mac's disappearance. The unhappiness of a cabinet about to lose office is the least of his problems. Instead, the problems will come from those TDs who, having noted the similarity of his spinelessness to their spinelessness, are unlikely to be too roused should he ever go mooching around the leadership.

The Aspirant Prince should also note that if the voters perceive Paddy Mac to be a fearful creature, they will impose their wrath on him for fun. In that regard, Michael Noonan is the best case study for Paddy Mac. It is easy, or perhaps it is more convenient, to forget that in 2002 today's National Grandfather was a lonely, reviled figure. The response to the existential crisis faced by the leader and his party by Noonan was one of open terror until the desolate acme was reached, when our current, great panjandrum of a finance minister had a pie squashed into his face. Happily, two decades on, Mr Noonan learned a very different fundamental truth, that no matter how unloved you are at a particular point in time, this may actually not be a permanent state. It is a lesson that Paddy Mac would do well to remember, for whilst the winds of adversity may sometimes blow hard, they always eventually blow themselves out.

Chapter 12

FOR GOD'S SAKE, MAN, NEVER LEAVE YOURSELF OPEN TO THE ACCUSATION OF ACTING POLITICALLY

Nevertheless, our experience has been that those princes who have done great things have held good faith of little account ...

On taking the moral stand • the virtue of depoliticising politics • art and deceit • why the Aspirant Prince should have a maverick as a pet • eats, shoots and leaves • Sir Talks-a-lot • Biffolinguistics • the virtue of being a doer • legacy builder or optimistic spoofer, and why the Aspirant Prince really should avoid a life of vice

One danger that comes with growing power is that carelessness may infect our Middling Minister. The first symptom of this is that our Aspirant Prince, now that he is a public figure, may be tempted to take a moral stand on some issue. In this regard, Paddy Mac must be utterly careful in his courage, for nothing destroys the reputation of a politician more swiftly than securing the reputation of being some sort of Joan of Arc who hangs around disparate piles of faggots, waiting to be burned.

Happily, the real danger period for our Middling Minister occurs earlier in his backbench career, for by the time he reaches the top table, Paddy Mac will be well housetrained. His time of political youth is somewhat different, however, for there are always rebellions, no matter how prosperous the times are. And it is tempting to join the fun when a normally well-behaved group of government TDs start to resemble the ballad about the mice in the pub who, after sipping on spilt porter, start bellowing, 'Bring out the f**king cat'. Paddy Mac, though, should be aware that, generally, by the time the pad of the cat's paws is heard, the poor hungover mice, having by now sobered up, bolt for the hole behind the skirting board. So, by all means, Paddy Mac may flirt with rebellion, but he should be careful, because if he doesn't race inside the wainscoting fast enough, the paw may clamp down on his tail, and poor Paddy Mac will find himself engaged in a face-to-face conversation with the cat.

In fairness, sometimes, no matter how hard he tries or how carefully he treads, the utterly unexpected occurs, and the Aspirant Prince is confronted with that appalling vista known as 'the moral issue'. This, of course, has nothing to do with finance or banks or white-collar crime. Morality and finance are not close bedfellows in Irish politics, due to the wise decision by Irish politicians to outsource that sort of stuff to clever people like central bankers or powerless marks, such as crusading journalists. So, Paddy Mac should never fret about having to take a more complex moral stance on the finance thing, beyond noting that the banks, like the weather, are very bad. Instead, our moral furies are generally confined to the arena of 'abortion' where, if Paddy Mac is not terribly careful, he will have to confront political spectres like 'freedom of thought' and 'matters of conscience'.

So, how should our Aspirant Prince respond to this less than pleasant new world? His first instinct will rightly be to run away fast as he can. Though this would be both logical and nice, if our man is to be a Dear Leader he must take the harder road of running away in the intellectual sense, whilst appearing to engage with the terrible thing in public. Although his responses will vary, depending on whether our Aspirant Prince is in government or in opposition, two key constants transcend these vastly different scenarios. The first is that Paddy Machiavelli will, above all else, be 'concerned'. And far more important still, our Aspirant Prince will also be anxious to ensure that no one attempts to 'play politics', for God forbid that politics might ever be deployed to resolve a serious 'moral issue'. Having erected that bit of decent drapery, if he is in opposition, the priority of Paddy Mac must be to mine much political capital by noting in 'concerned' tones that the government has a responsibility to deal decisively with a problem which he has absolutely no intention of going near.

For the government, this, alas, is not as easy as logic might suggest. Ireland's centrist, not-so-cute old Phil Hogan-style school of politics, where everyone within Labour, FG and FF is essentially on the same side, is not designed for difference. So, when the 'moral issue' arrives, the fellowship of Leinster House 'lads' are, like the crew of the *Starship Enterprise*, flying blind into a galaxy they know nothing of. The 'moral issue', particularly if it is the abortion thing, is not a problem that can be solved by a deal, or a few quid, or the nuzzling of a few TDs' ears in the Dáil bar. Instead, it will expose our poor TDs to 'angels on a pin'-style debates over whether we should have flying columns of doctors to ascertain if heavily pregnant women are suicidal or not.

When it comes to morality, therefore, Paddy Mac must at all times be aware that he lives in a political system where the real 'moral issue', let alone an independent conscience, attracts the same fearful wonder as the Aztecs felt when they saw Cortés on a horse. Amidst all this chaos, be he a minister or a TD, the one thing that Paddy Machiavelli must not do is to take a personal stand or be in any way outspoken. Morality in this regard is a matter for 'the boss' and Paddy Mac's role once 'the boss' has spoken is to remember that, in matters like this, the ethos of all the lads together means that the 'turnip' who puts his mind away in a dusty corner — and votes, speaks and thinks in the same way as his betters — is far more valued than the Peter Mathews variant of the species.

The dangers posed by the 'moral issue' should confirm for Paddy Machiavelli how important it is to fully absorb the ethos of affable pragmatism. Indeed, if it does not sound contradictory, its central theory — that in times of crisis the worst sin is to act politically —

should be Paddy Machiavelli's core value. A simple person might think it is odd that politicians, when they condemn each other for 'acting politically', are in such a rush to denigrate that which they are theoretically supposed to do. But, outside of noting that they are just getting in ahead of the queue, the greatest virtue of never being 'political' is that it exorcises ideology and all the trouble that *that* brings from the political system.

Ideology in politics will still have its advocates, but, as he sits decorously on the fence, Paddy Mac should note that the problem is that ideology is far too restrictive, for if you stand for something, then you cannot stand for everything. Paddy Mac, in contrast, must swiftly learn that if he stands for everything then there is at least a chance that he will not be hated by everybody. In practical terms, the joys of being apolitical also mean that if Paddy Machiavelli is faced with some slavering beast, such as a banking crisis, corruption in politics or that feared 'moral issue', he can, with the straightest of faces, geld the awful problem by condemning any attempt to 'play politics' with an issue which should instead be referred to a committee, a review group, an outside inquiry of 'experts', or if he wants to bury a particularly rank bone for 15 years, a barrister-filled tribunal of inquiry.

As he moves towards the centre of high politics, Paddy Machiavelli must grow up in other respects too. In particular, he must, if he is to be respected a little, learn the art of deceit, because he and his colleagues will need him to practise it. Deceit may have a bad reputation, but should Paddy Mac be a capable practitioner, he will swiftly secure the invaluable reputation of having a facility to glide both himself and the party out of trouble. Though this is a fine trait to have in Leinster House, we will issue one caveat. If he is to be a maestro of deceit, our Aspirant Prince must retain the public profile of being an honest dealer, for the attitude of the electorate to honesty is a curious one. They can accept roguishness, and indeed they often demand it, but, rather like the nice girl in the 1950s who was unfortunate enough to become pregnant, if our Aspirant Prince is publicly branded with the *fleur-de-lis* of dishonesty, his career is over.

The most critical aspect of deceit in politics is that good politicians never lie. They may misconstrue a question or, worse still, be asked the wrong question when they are anxiously waiting to give the right answer. Or, if asked the right question, they may 'misunderestimate' the question they are asked and reply to the far more pleasant question they thought they were asked. In time, they can get so good at the art it could even take a tribunal of inquiry, staffed by the most expensive barristers money can buy, several months to secure an accurate answer to a single question. But, no politician ever lies deliberately. Indeed, the Aspirant Prince will note that such is the anxiety with which politicians approach the concept — akin to the way superstitious actors always call *Macbeth* the Scottish play — the word 'lie' is actually banned in exchanges in the Dáil chamber.

However, rather like the difference between venial and mortal sins, the good politician knows that deceit is occasionally a necessary kindness when it comes to the promissory notes, the Peace Process, or the ongoing state of hopelessness the country finds itself in. Within the current administration, after a somewhat shaky start where they were far too open about their enthusiasm for reform, the lads swiftly acquired a fine facility for the art of necessary deceits. Nothing epitomised this more than the promissory notes saga. The choreography was perfect, as just prior to the 'triumph', insidious little whispers emerged about how two years 'have passed since the fine morning of the democratic revolution' and when it comes to our cherished banking deal 'the Messiah' Noonan has turned into Old Methuselah 'still wandering around the desert'. Suddenly, if the government's subterranean narrative was to be believed, the great deal was in danger of slipping away. A nervous electorate was told that strenuous efforts in the great art of diplomacy by Mr Noonan, and in particular Enda, would be required to save the 'prom notes'. Solemn warnings were issued about the damage that any failure in this regard would do to our relationship with Europe and, more important still, to our compliance with the less than belle Dame of Austerity.

Mind you, as we neared the close, the real situation was somewhat given away when the European Parliament President, Germany's

Martin Schulz, told the Dear Leader, Enda Kenny, that the time had come for 'Paddy' to make an assertive case for Irish debt relief. The inability of our German friends to understand the real subtleties required in the wink-and-elbow language of Irish politics meant that, from that moment, everyone knew the deal was done. But, there was reasoning behind the delicate foreplay that led to this consummation, for what triumph or medals would have been secured from an easy victory?

This meant we had to have theatrical public displays of wrangling and private spin-doctor-driven whispers about hard 'tangling' by Enda and long dark nights of the soul before Enda and Michael finally brought the golden child of the 'prom note' before the adoring Fine Gael backbenchers. And, in terms of the art of politics, one had to think of our German bankrollers too. Life for Angela is always going to be immeasurably easier if Paddy is seen to have to 'dance for the money'. Not, mind you, that you'd need too many six-shooters to get Enda's feet a-tapping.

Far from believing that deceits such as flattery and dissimulation are vices, Paddy Mac should take the view that they are pragmatic virtues. It is hardly so terrible a thing, for example, to tell our electorate that they are the smartest fellows in the world. How could they not be? They have elected our man Paddy Mac to run the shop. The electorate are, alas, somewhat more suspicious these days, for the times when you could still secure a cheer by listing their sacrifices and praising them for the measured nature of their response to the economics of austerity — otherwise known as being clubbed into fiscal insensibility — are now gone. But, that is not to say the alternative position of giving out to them for their failings would work any better. It might make for an interesting spectacle, but how well would it go if Paddy Mac were to ask the voters just how stupid they were in thinking that the banks would not want to be paid back for the decking, the new car, the apartment in Lagos, the island kitchen, the Italian tiling and the four holidays a year? Enda tried a bit of that in Davos, but not any more since then.

That said, whilst Paddy Machiavelli must develop an aptitude for gentle deceits, he must take care not to be too open. Nothing does more damage to the politician than being seen to be openly cynical (or honest!) about the political games they must play. In this regard, Paddy Machiavelli should look closely at Labour's Derek McDowell, the favoured child of that wing of Labour who believe that Ireland shall never be free until every man in the gay and bisexual-friendly, non-competitive-sports-supporting, females-served-first, Susan McKay Women's Council Memorial Lounge of the Working Man's Arms raises a cheery white wine, diluted with sparkling water, to the passing of some future Gay Civil Rights and Abolition of Blood Sports Bills.

Mr McDowell, after a long disappearance, returned to our attention in the wake of the Meath East by-election when he wrote in *The Irish Times* (where else?) about how Labour needs to 'refute the nonsense, which has become a mantra in some quarters, that it has broken its promises'. As Mr McDowell tartly added, 'It hasn't, or at least none that matter', in a single sentence he summarised the reason why Labour is in the land of where it is. It might have appeared to be a fine barrister's trick to dismiss child benefit or a euro on a bottle of wine as being small issues that only affect small citizens, but a million ordinary — well, in Derek's eyes — mums make for a great deal of voters. And their small annoyances may yet result in an awful lot of awfully small Labour backbenchers losing their seats.

Ultimately, Paddy Mac should always remember that when it comes to deceit, the truth of things is that people soon tire of the truthful life. If we were like the logical horses in *Gulliver's Travels* we might get used to it, but human nature is not easily transformed. This endemic dislike of too much truth goes a long way towards explaining why FF was in power for 62 of 78 years, for no other Irish party has come close to mastering FF's facility for hiding in full view. This means that Paddy Mac should treat deceit as a form of insurance. After all, if a man's house goes on fire, there is much sympathy. But if it is not insured, pity is swiftly withdrawn from the fool who has not prepared for such a possibility. So, it is at the higher echelons of politics also that no one will trust a Dear Leader who has no facility for deceit, on the wise grounds that such fine

Michael Foot-style role models cannot be relied upon to preserve their interests.

One of the gentler deceits that Paddy Mac should engage in is the keeping of company with mavericks. Though he should never be one of them himself, the wise Aspirant Prince should always try to keep a couple of them as pets, for whilst they can bite, exotic pets secure attention and denote status. It is like the keeping of tigers by boxers such as Mike Tyson. However, there are real benefits too, for, by cultivating the company of the maverick, Paddy Mac is like the old aristocratic lord who acted as the patron for an impoverished poet. As with the best of aristocrats, Paddy Mac can create the impression of being a freethinker who is iconoclastic and receptive to new ideas without uttering any himself. But, though it gives him a vicarious reputation for radicalism, he must be prepared to drop his maverick pets at a moment's notice should they threaten to cause him any form of political embarrassment. After all, pets, though pleasant, are always disposable.

Paddy Mac, however, should also realise that some mavericks, when kept as pets, may be more dangerous than others. The classic example of this is Lucinda Creighton who, in a FG party dominated by the turnip class, is seen as a maverick because she both possesses and speaks her mind. Paddy Machiavelli should recognise that hanging around with Lucinda will be of great value if he wants to differentiate himself from the herd. But, though life will never be dull, our Aspirant Prince must approach someone like Lucinda with great caution, for the problem with Lucinda is that she might expect him to act as he speaks. And, worse still, she might be quite vocal if he doesn't.

As he climbs ever so carefully towards the top of the political tree, it is all the more critical that Paddy Mac keep a careful eye on both the small and the big things. Were Lynne Truss, the author of *Eats, Shoots and Leaves*, ever looking for a sequel to her tale about the great destruction wrought upon the English language, she would do far worse than to examine the Irish political system. In particular, she might inquire into the strange pride the Irish politician displays in acquiring an incomprehensible language known as mandarin-speak, which reduces the listener to insensibility. It is almost as if, like the wearing of a verbal tuxedo, our politician believes that being impossible to comprehend is a signifier of importance. Sometimes, mandarin-speak is of use if you desire to be incomprehensible. But, as Paddy Mac reaches the shores of middling importance, one of the threats he must be cognisant of is the motivation behind the attempts by the civil service mandarins to force poor Paddy Mac to learn a language not known to mortal man. He would do well to remember that he secured public office courtesy of his reputation for being a hard-hitting, plain-speaking man of the people, who would change things. So, why is it that, so often, Paddy the minister finds himself talking about 'paradigms of expectations'?

The reasoning behind sending Paddy Mac out to babble about 'cross-structural, interdepartmental synergies' is simple. When the smiling mandarin sends out our man the minister with this tofu in his mouth, he is acting with malice aforethought, because one of the critical tasks of the good mandarin is to separate politicians from the citizen. And, if the politician who dutifully accepts his script constantly uses language that the electorate cannot understand, the latter simply become cross with Paddy Mac. Sadly, too often our politicians conspire in their own downfall, for, like all magpies, the Irish politician is a great imitator. That, allied to his essentially submissive nature, means that should he spend a sufficiency of time with his civil service betters, eventually, like the docker wot lairnt to speak proper, he will begin to sound like them. That is the greatest triumph for the hairy spiders of the mandarin class, for, from that moment, our Aspirant Prince is one of theirs.

Retaining the capacity to use the sort of language that other human beings deploy is one of the disciplines that the Aspirant Prince must rigorously impose upon himself. The unfortunate fate of Mr Gilmore provides us with an intriguing example of how a politician who secured his success on the basis of plain speaking somehow managed to lose the props that had secured his happy position in the first place.

In his prime, Mr Gilmore, like a slightly more rotund Jimmy Stewart in *Mr Smith Goes to Washington*, was the people's man in a Dáil full of overly plump unfeathered hens. For example, on the banking bailout the metaphor might have been homespun, but the Labour leader's observation that this resembled the scenario where 'many people at some stage in their lives have been approached by a family member ... who has asked them to be a guarantor', and that one was often reluctant to do this, hit a nerve. It seems odd now, but back then there was a real resonance behind Gilmore's simple analysis of the banking guarantee that, 'Frankly, the Labour Party is not prepared to do with the taxpayers' money what it would not be prepared to do with personal money', and behind his warning that 'the Taoiseach is proposing to hand over the deeds of the country to bail out the banks'. One of the mysteries of Irish politics is what happened to that man. Whatever the cause, Paddy Machiavelli should be warned that if you flutter into the Venus flytraps set by our mandarins, once you cut the golden thread of plain speaking, you are going to slowly drift away from the citizens.

The most curious phenomenon, when it comes to the inability of our political class to understand the virtue of straightforward sentences, is the fate of Brian Cowen. The myth surrounding Mr Cowen before he took office was that we were getting a man who used the language of the people. That was certainly not to be the experience. We will not repeat the vast reams of statistic-riddled terminology that Biffo read out to us in such stentorian tones. All we will say instead is that one could only marvel at the colossal failure of imagination and collapse in desire that fed such inarticulacy. In a real sense, that might have been the problem. The politician who falls out of love with his trade is inarticulate, because he has nothing to say and nobody to say it to. Mr Cowen's woes were, in a strange way, a confession of incipient failure and a plea that his vocation had been lost, had we the wit or the kindliness to see it.

The great suspicion of fancy-talking politicians that exists amongst the voters means that Paddy Mac must strive to cultivate the reputation of being a 'doer' rather than a talker. Of course all politicians set out to acquire the status of a 'doer' on the lines of an Albert or a Haughey although obviously minus the corrupt stuff in the case of Haughey. But, if the wise Aspirant Prince watches carefully, he will see that most leave with their tail between their legs as accusations of 'time-server' are thrown at them like glass confetti. The key to acquiring the reputation of being a 'doer' is actually remarkably simple. Our Aspirant Prince will note that many new ministers enter their Departments thrusting grandiose objectives into the grateful arms of wily civil servants. Dr James Reilly, for example, wished to become the new Noël Browne, and for some this would have been seen to be admirable. It does, however, seem like a bit of an ask to impose the health service of a civilised country like Holland on the HSE without at least getting the HSE to reform itself first. And, sadly, in the case of Dr Reilly his 'my way or the highway' attempt to bustle through the razor wire of HSE ineptitude without a wirecutter saw him acquire the reputation amongst the voters at least of being the cabinet dunce.

The Reilly dilemma epitomises the uncertain stance of the Irish politician who actually tries to do something. Leinster House, you see, is strewn with the corpses of legacy builders, most of whom actually were — if we are to be honest — optimistic spoofers. One of the finest examples of this is Martin Cullen, who built a career on the promise of bringing PD-style private sector efficiency to FF and to the public sector. As we alas know, it didn't end too well for Martin, FF, the PDs, or for a vast number of 'efficient' electronic voting machines. The problem was not so much Martin's own attributes, although those didn't help, but the vastness of the declared objective, because efficiency in the public sector was always going to be a counsel of perfection too far. Indeed, given that imposing efficiency on Irish governance has been beyond the capacity of the Taoiseach (should he want to), or Germany, the Troika, the IMF and the European Commission, the declaration by a mere Middling Minister, such as Martin, that he would secure this boon left Cullen terribly open to the charge of being nothing more than an optimistic spoofer.

If Paddy Mac is intent on acquiring the reputation of a 'doer', he must first of all ensure that his objectives are few, and more important still, that they are achievable. Albert Reynolds originally managed this trick with the phones, and then came the Structural

Funds, and after that the Peace Process, and then after that anything was possible. However, sometimes the small things can count for a great deal more than you might think, for Mr Haughey managed to secure a similar legacy via free travel and free electricity for the 'old folks'.

Given the circles in which he is moving — and what he has had to do in order to get there — it might seem strange to warn Paddy Mac about the dangers of being excessively amoral. But, as he approaches the summit, if it is not to his political loss, the Aspirant Prince would be wise to take the moral road, for vice in politics generally brings nothing but sad denouements. This is typified by the ongoing fascinating tales of the life and times of Michael Lowry. The then Wild Colonial Boy from Tipp may have started life as a humble refrigeration engineer, but by the time the sainted Rainbow was ushered into power without having to annoy themselves by asking the electorate, the man known as Lowry was surrounded by a diffident but intriguingly menacing sense of destiny. Few ministers were ever as loved or as trusted by their Taoiseach, though, mind you, few Taoisigh were ever as guileless as the poor old 'Brut'. The fall was as fabulous as the rise as Lowry's fate became intertwined with that of Ireland's biggest tycoon, Denis O'Brien. The subsequent 14-year tribunal wrought a series of changes that were as much physical as psychological, and Lowry became the latter-day equivalent of the portrait of Dorian Gray. Today, however, the world is a changed place for Lowry. The man who rocked the cradle of the future FG does occasionally surface as a school for scandal, such as that delightful vignette where, at Phil Hogan's 50th birthday party, an ebullient Enda entered the room, saw Lowry and asked if he had an application form for Fine Gael. Sadly, in a real respect, the centrepiece of the joke was the implicit acceptance by Kenny and Lowry that the latter was a political scarecrow. And, had Lowry agreed, the room would have turned silent with horror.

Like Haughey, the question that will always be asked is, What could Lowry have achieved without all the messing? Instead, the real standing of Michael Lowry is epitomised by the moment, in the wake of the swear-filled Lowry tapes, when Lowry was being pursued by Ronald Quinlan, an old south Co. Dublin matriarch looked over at the hunted form and declared with all of the sweetness of her tribe: 'Ah, Michael, it's yourself, the man with all the fucks.' Corruption, and sometimes merely messing, exacts a cruel price. The dream of that old FF renegade Ray 'Rambo' Burke was to retire to the respectability of the south of England and spend lengthy summers watching white-flannelled cricketers. Instead, the last image the public saw of Rambo was of him being launched into a prison van. Of course, the most dramatic lesson in the foolishness of vice is provided by Mr Haughey. The old Kinsealy fox was well into his last and final run before the hounds dug him out of the covert and chopped him up. But, whilst the collapse of Haughey's fabulous hall of mirrors and the unveiling of the naked, shrivelled form occurred late in the day, a political connoisseur such as Haughey knew well what a historic legacy he would leave.

Paddy Mac must therefore realise that whilst corruption may provide present pleasure, outside of damaging your judgment and corroding your reputation, it offers almost certain future misery. And if that does not convince, then he should always carry the image of Lowry, the man many thought would be Taoiseach some day, being stared down upon by a south Dublin matriarch and dismissed as 'Michael, the man with all the fucks'.

PART FOUR:
THERE AT LAST, THE FINAL STEPS

| THE MEDIA MEDUSAS

Choice of servants is of no little importance to a prince, and they are good or not according to the discrimination of the prince. And the first opinion which one forms of a prince, and of his understanding, is by observing the men he has around him.

On media • the real issue • the terror of the doorstep • being anti-social • publish and be damned • avoiding the impulse to self-pity • choosing the correct spin doctor • avoiding doppelgängers, the wise prince should really cultivate the media • how they actually treat the media • on being injured • the divine rule of editors • death of a political lamb • flowerpot diplomacy and head-buttery • feasting with panthers and free at last

It is a measure of the nature of modern politics that we are going to devote a chapter to our Aspirant Prince and the media. In a better world or, more accurately, one designed by Fintan O'Toole, we would be discussing the politician's relationship with history, poetry and philosophy. We are, though, where we are, and that is a different place from the one where Mr Haughey would talk to terrified FF backbenchers about the Medicis, and Garret would talk to an even more terrified set of FG backbenchers about liberation theology. When it comes to the Media Medusas, Paddy Machiavelli can get all high-minded about the virtue of 'deeds' over 'words' and how the good politician should never be concerned about these creatures. But, should he do so, Paddy Mac is like a man fishing in a river without a hook.

In learning how to make love to the media, the first principle Paddy Mac must accept is that the plain people are not intrigued by politics. It may come as a shock to some of the more elderly TDs, namely the cabinet, but life in Ireland, as Paddy Machiavelli knows all too well, has moved on since the days when all the peasantry had for diversion was Michael O'Hehir on Sunday, Din Joe's 'Take the Floor' music show, religion, the *Irish Press* and politics. Now, to secure the attention of the public, Paddy Mac must, on a quiet day, compete with Sky Sports, Gordon Ramsay, Gordon Ramsay's mistress, the views of Gordon Ramsay's wife on Gordon Ramsay's mistress and the views of Gordon Ramsay's mistress on Gordon Ramsay's wife.

In fairness, it must also be realised that since, in the deodorised age of centrism, all politicians essentially say the same thing, one should hardly blame the people for their lack of interest. Our politicians meanwhile must also deal with the difficulties where, in tandem with the death of ideology, the tactical nature of political warfare in the media has changed. In the past, these resembled old-style battles where two armies dressed in different colours would square off against each other and fire at will until one lot ran away. In contrast, the modern theatre of conflict is diffuse, involving air, sea and ground battles, and, on occasions, elusive guerrilla operations where the politician must seamlessly deal with the divergent interests of air, print and internet media.

The changed nature of the modern media is epitomised most appropriately by the terror of the doorstep. Our Aspirant Prince will not know a lot about this until he becomes a minister, whereupon he will learn that this occurs when a dozen competing media outlets shout incoherent questions for two minutes. The problem with the doorstep is that politicians, in dealing with the media, generally like distance, preferably incorporating a raised dais and a desk behind which they can shelter. This means that our ministers often play hard to get and make quite the fuss about these events. But, were Paddy Machiavelli to think more deeply, he would realise that the doorstep is rather less terrifying than politicians imagine it to be. This is not a place where the media are on a search for knowledge or exclusives. Instead, all they are looking for is two facts, or variants thereof, and then the politician and the hack are friends for ever, or at least until the next news bulletin.

The strange fear that our political classes suffered over these harmless doorsteps was inevitably epitomised by the response of Biffo to this torture. It was, even for the hardest heart, a study in bathos, as beads of sweat curled into little rivulets above the nervously squinting eyes of Mr Cowen. Second by second the eyes turned into the sort of narrow defensive slits one would associate with the small windows in a medieval castle through which archers would fire at the approaching enemy. Poor Biffo, of course, had no arrows, so it was just a case of him melting away gently, rather like an abominable snowman who has found himself trapped on a South Sea island. Consequently, when Paddy Mac finally faces his first flying column, he must, unlike poor Biffo, display genuine delight, and avoid any displays of fear or trepidation. The one thing he must not do is to attempt to run away from a doorstepping because, like all retreats in war, this is the position where the most damage — such as falling over a flowerpot whilst trying to avoid questions on the delights of gay civil marriage — is done.

At the beginning, our Aspirant Prince is a long way away from such territories, for Paddy Machiavelli, unless he is a lunatic or a 'character', arrives at the Dáil with absolutely no media profile. Given that he is starting at the bottom, the first thing he must do is to embrace social media. Necessity can be a virtue here, for using social media means that our politician is an automatic member of the 'smart' society. In spite of such prospective riches, nothing epitomises the caution with which politicians approach the web — which they urge everyone else to embrace — more than the strange fate of the Pat Rabbitte Twitter account. The intriguing feature of this account is that whilst it was set up in Mr Rabbitte's name some years ago, the Labour Lothario of the one-sentence quip did not post a single tweet for a number of years. It is somewhat poignant to think that, rather like those who in a previous age waited for the statue of the Virgin Mary in Ballinspittle to speak, in some place in the cybersphere thousands of devotees, like Narcissus by the pond, gathered to wait patiently for the first words of wisdom to emerge from the cybershrine of Rabbitte. What may be even more intriguing is that despite the absence of a single quote, Mr Rabbitte's stable of followers consistently increased. Some would say there is a message there.

In fairness, the caution is somewhat understandable because it is certainly a triumph of hope over experience to call the web a 'social medium'. Should Paddy Machiavelli ever have the misfortune to read the Muppet Show known as Politics.ie he will swiftly realise that it is as social as a punishment beating. Despite what he must endure, our Aspirant Prince should not be seduced into the good old boys' belief that what Vincent Browne quaintly calls 'the Twitter machine' is a waste of time. The great drama of Biffo's Galway lock-in would never have been articulated were it not for a tweet by Simon Coveney, of all people. Paddy Machiavelli must, however, use Twitter with a purpose, as ever-so-nice Simon did on that occasion, for if he is not careful and engages too enthusiastically, he runs the risk of being sucked into any variety of internet rows. This is a form of Joe Duffyism where those you are having the row with never have, and never will, vote for you. Instead, the best thing Paddy Mac can do is advertise himself as a man of action who is engaged in critical events. Circumspect entries such as 'in the Dáil chamber this morning, hot and heavy exchanges' or 'PAC meeting on now, serious matters are being raised' establish your status as a participant in the great events of the day who has been kindly enough to provide the little watcher with a bird's eye view. And happily, once you have twittered a little and facilitated this illusion, you can put the computer down and return to your more usual Dáil chamber task of reading the *Racing Post*.

At some point, Paddy Machiavelli will have to abandon the internet and meet real journalists. Our man will be naturally suspicious and fearful, if only because the rest of the herd are. However, Paddy Mac's attitude should be informed by the fate of that child who suddenly wonders if there is a monster in the bedroom. Inevitably, whilst the initial level of terror is low, the more the child fears the imaginary monster, the more real the gremlin hiding in the closet stroking a chainsaw becomes. In contrast, if Paddy Mac bravely dips a toe into the icy waters of treating journalists like human beings, he 'normalises' the media and learns what journalists' needs are.

In trying to calibrate his overall strategy, Paddy Mac can, if he wishes, choose from thousands of books. Yet, one simple phrase from the 19th century best defines what his appropriate baseline should be. Granted, few modern politicians have had a career that encompassed defeating the greatest military strategist in history or a ten-year peninsular war. But it is a measure of the degree of simple manliness that has been lost from political life that no Irish TD would dare to indulge in a reprise of Wellington's warning to a notorious courtesan, who intended to refer to him in her memoirs, that she should 'publish and be damned'. If our Aspirant Prince thinks that there is something unnerving about the softness of our political elite who, like the current Taoiseach, take to a metaphorical sickbed if they are even looked at in a cross manner, he would be correct. The media is a rough old beast to tame, but bleating like a lamb when some internet road warrior compares you to Herod merely results in raising questions as to whether such an alabaster thin skin is capable of dealing with all that rough trading from Angela.

It might appear obvious that if Paddy Mac is to curb the tendency of all politicians to bruise too easily, one of the most critical decisions our man must make is to pick the sort of spin doctor who can rein in the politician's instinct for self-pity. It is no easy task, for in the end the political class tends to unanimously find that the injustice, the cruelties, the maltreatment and the poor terms and conditions become too much to endure. And no, before you ask, our politicians are thinking about their terms and conditions, not about the state of the country. The plaintive bleats of the unhappy politicians — with their salaries, pensions, expenses, free dinners, foreign junkets, constituency-office expenses and allowances for everything from sighing to breathing in air — are never liked by a public who are far too engrossed with their woes to have time to dress another man's wound. But, self-pity about their status in the world is the honey that politicians cannot avoid. Instead, even those who are as wily as Bertie fall prey to musings about the unfairness of the failure of the Irish taxpayer to provide him with yachts, islands, palaces (as distinct from St Luke's) and the rest of the booty that Mr Haughey appeared to believe to be an entirely normal part of the democratic process. Paddy Machiavelli would do well, therefore, to keep a wintry eye out for any rise in the self-pity gene, for it is the first symptom of a politician being no longer at the top of his game.

If he can find the sort of spin doctor who will ensure that Paddy Mac avoids the self-pity error, our Aspirant Prince will have chosen well. He will also be unique, for few of his colleagues will choose correctly. The weakness displayed by our politicians in the choosing of spin doctors is strange, given the role that illusion must play in all political life. Inevitably, the primary cause of this phenomenon is the simple one of ego. Because the politician believes they are a perfect sphere, the last thing they see themselves as needing is some latter-day equivalent of the Roman slave in the chariot whispering about their blemishes. This gap in comprehension means that one of the more intriguing features of our various princes is that, when it comes to cultivating a relationship with a media whom they genuinely fear and dislike, they tend to have a preference for hiring as media advisors those who detest the media with an equal passion. A clever Aspirant Prince will therefore follow Machiavelli's rule on advisors, think carefully, overcome any feelings of nausea, and appoint someone with the capacity to actually tolerate those whom they must make love to.

Rarely, however, does that leap of the imagination occur. Instead, and particularly when it comes to FG and Labour, the spin doctor acts as a little doppelgänger to the distaste that the politician feels for his unwanted Boswells. This sin is particularly prevalent amongst inexperienced spin doctors. Such uncertain souls feel that if they are to be viewed with warm eyes by their masters, they should attempt to become mirror images of the greater deities they serve. This, allied to the natural desire of most to appear better than their opposites, means that they soon acquire a supercilious style where the talk is of 'feeding the animals' and the 'media zoo'. Oddly enough, such an attitude is not at all conducive to generating any great warmth from the poor chimpanzees on the other side of the cage, particularly given that most of the media monkeys feel they should be running the country themselves, rather than fighting over the bananas being thrown into the tea party.

Of course, it would be better if politicians did not need spin doctors at all. But, few indeed are the politicians who, like Bertie at his peak, are so tuned in to a country's psyche that they have no necessity for one. When it comes to Paddy Mac, the three templates for serving his needs in the spin doctor class are provided by PJ Mara, Fergus Finlay and Seán Duignan. Critically, all three possessed minds of their own and, better still, were clever enough to disguise this unfortunate trait. In choosing a spin doctor — outside of looking for that rare creature with an independent mind — Paddy Mac should try to secure an advisor whose essential traits are different from his own. So, if he is a technocratic, policy-driven figure, such as a Brendan Howlin, the ideal spin doctor would be a cross between PJ Mara and Seán Duignan. Paddy the technocrat will need the guileful cunning of a PJ to sow confusion and uncertainty, whilst the scrapes that Paddy will get into if he tries to reform things means almost inevitably that he will need Duignan's Charlie Chaplin tramp-style mix of pathos crossed with dignity, in order to secure the pity of his media enemies. But if, in contrast, he is an affable pragmatist, Paddy Mac will need the brimstone and fury of a young Finlay to at least create the impression that he is intent on changing things.

In choosing a spin doctor, our Aspirant Prince should also be guided by one critical final talent. He must try to choose someone who knows a little of the world that exists far beyond the confined cloisters of Leinster House. Intriguingly, before he became Haughey's boon companion and town crier, PJ Mara, in his initial career, was a salesman. Some would say that this perfectly qualified poor PJ for the illusions he would have to create, but it is unlikely that such a past would impress today's saccharine politicos. Instead, the modern spin doctor is too often little more than a lay equivalent of that cardinal's secretary who has never seen a world beyond the corridors of the Vatican. And politicians then wonder why they are accused so often of being out of touch.

Having a spine does not mean that the Aspirant Prince cannot be friends with the media. But what is he to do in order to reach this Parnassus? In this regard, it would, of course, be a wonderful start if Paddy Machiavelli were to ask what the poor dispirited journalist requires, for, like the peasant who just wants milk and potatoes for supper every night, the necessities of the journalist are simple. What they desire is to hear interesting things, whilst an arm around the shoulders, rather than a suspicious squint, is also always pleasant. And the hack also likes tales of infighting and derring-do where the minister is the hero. Sadly, the template for media management is set by Phil Hogan who, in the middle of one of the many uneasy periods in Environment, informed one particular journalist that he was part of a set of media 'knackers' whom Phil was intent on putting 'manners' on. The 'onslaught' worked so well that Phil's promise made the front page of that 'knacker's' newspaper. In passing, Paddy Mac might also note that this policy of reminding the media of their 'place' is particularly popular with FG and Labour governments, none of whom has ever been re-elected.

Paddy Mac must learn that whilst demanding that 'manners' be put on the Irish media will always raise a cheer from his colleagues, this is emphatically not the public position he should take. He must instead make it clear that he is the friend of the free press. Of course, this is not true, for if you have the characteristics required to reach the top echelon of Irish politics, the media is absolutely not your friend. But, it is wise in public at least to swiftly adopt the position that the innocent man has nothing to fear from his 'brothers' amongst the 'independent' media. Happily, our Aspirant Prince would, for the most part, be right because, thanks to the Irish libel system and the lawyers who suckle on that capacious tit, a guilty man, let alone the innocent, has little to fear from the Irish media.

Though necessity means that Paddy Mac must always treat the media with a false bonhomie, there will always be tears at some point. And, when a journalist has written something injurious about him, there are any number of responses that the wise Aspirant Prince can adopt. If he is a plutocrat, he can use the courts as a willing cat's paw to drown his enemy in litigation. However, seeing as most politicians are not billionaires, few will be able to follow that enchanted road. The Aspirant Prince can follow the road of open confrontation, but, this is not a wise road to take. You see, a war with the media can take a number of equally impotent forms. Paddy Mac can write a letter of complaint, but that will simply be put in the bin. If he complains to the editor, they will be happy that the journalist is doing their job. And if he rings the journalist's office directly, he will be put on speakerphone, so that everyone can listen to Paddy Mac making a fool of himself. He can decide to follow the FG route of chilly silence, or casually libel journalists by claiming that what they have written is a lie. But, by following that path, Paddy Mac will inevitably experience the fate of the child who, on seeing an incurious wasp, runs around waving a jam sandwich, attracts the wasp's attention and ends up being stung.

The Aspirant Prince would, when injured, be far better to follow the Bertie route of padding up to the journalist who has just written 2,000 words of his finest vitriol about Mr Ahern. The then Taoiseach would place his arms, or one arm, around the shoulders of the errant hack and murmur, 'Fair play to you'. This would be followed by a sibilant chuckle of 'that's great stuff you're writing, keep it up' before the then Taoiseach would glide away, buoyed by opinion-poll popularity ratings of 90 per cent. Like many of Bertie's other actions, this had a multiplicity of objectives. It not only confused the enemy but also damaged the spirit of the journalist who, confronted with such bonhomie, suffered from feelings of inadequacy that his best efforts had so little effect upon their target. Pleasantry will also confuse the media in one other manner. Journalists always ascribe malevolent purposes to a politician, but when a politician displays warmth and humanity, journalists are confused by that which is unexpected.

One problem Paddy Machiavelli is incapable of dealing with is that the fearful level of ego of politicians is actually only surpassed by the higher echelons of the media themselves. The ego of the latter is accentuated by the fact that whilst politicians possess some power, unless they are Germans they are inured to the reality of regular defeats and the occasional hasty retreat. In contrast, newspaper editors live in a world that is not dissimilar to what governance was like under the divine right of kings. This means that when they propose that social partnership should end, or that Ireland might declare war on Europe, or that all taxation be abolished, newspaper editors are left in a state of somewhat anguished bafflement when such fiats are disobeyed by mere ministers and Taoisigh. This generally provokes a brief eruption of fury, before a butterfly or something equally minor captures the attention of our editor, and the politician is summarily dismissed as a lightweight and a dead loss.

The reality of this particular complex was explained to one distraught politician, when she unwisely asked why she had been cast into outer darkness by a previously supportive newspaper. The politician was told that she was the equivalent of an orphaned lamb who is adopted as a family pet by the farmer. For six months, the lamb is fed warmed milk from a bottle, bathed with the children, who pet its downy wool, allowed to sleep in front of the Aga, and generally cooed at as it follows the farmer and his family around the place. But the day inevitably comes — even in the kindest of farming households — when, without warning, the farmer or his wife grabs the lamb by the scruff of the neck and, minutes later, she is inside the Aga that she previously used to doze beside in her special basket. This cruel truth should not stop the ambitious prince from trying to build some relationships with the media. We are, after all, the drab Michelangelos who will design the frescoes of our politicians, which the outside world will, hopefully, watch with awe.

The building of such relationships is not easy, however, for when it comes to this dialogue of the mutually deaf, if the relationship goes wrong it goes terribly wrong. Nothing epitomises this particular danger more than the infamous 'Flowerpot Fracas'. This occurred when, having been spooked by an unruly question about the delights of gay marriage at a doorstep outside the National Library, the Dear Leader Enda Kenny appeared to stumble backwards over a tripod near a large flowerpot. That was unfortunate enough, but then Mr Kenny's press machine decided to escalate the incident out of all proportion by complaining to TV3 chiefs about the highly respected political editor Ursula Halligan, who, they said, had engaged in actions 'tantamount to assault' on the Dear Leader by asking him a question. One supposes they were at least sincere in the allegation, for this administration does appear to be of the view that the difference between being asked a question and a physical assault is essentially a technical one.

Unsurprisingly, the Taoiseach and his advisors, who believed themselves to be victims in all of this, were confronted by a media backlash from political correspondents, who believed that if anyone had been subjected to a couple of off-the-ball shoulders it was Ms Halligan. The unwonted display of trade union-style rancour was undoubtedly assisted by a letter sent by the then 'newbie' Government Press Secretary, Feargal Purcell, to the remote souls of the Press Gallery regarding the 'collectively disgraceful' behaviour of journalists at the event. Of course, it all ended with collective wails from the media about sinister allegations and a swift U-turn by the defeated forces of the government camp.

Sadly, politicians rarely learn. The classic modern case of the dangers of appointing your own doppelgänger as Government Press Secretary is the decision of Mr Cowen, who had the same relationship with the media as Socrates had with hemlock, to appoint the ex-army man Eoghan Ó Neachtain as his main press advisor. It obviously was never going to be the happiest of times, but the decision of Mr Ó Neachtain to set upon the gilded high priests of the press with the sort of vigour normally seen in front-row exchanges in Munster rugby derbies did not improve relations. In fairness Mr Ó Neachtain may not have had too many options in the matter, for Mr Cowen would have been placid, or certainly not displeased, had his spin doctor taken a meat cleaver to the political correspondents. But in terms of the then urgent need to win the hearts and minds of the media, the abrasiveness was not the road to take.

Even when intentions are good, however, Paddy Machiavelli will discover that dealing with the media can be as unrewarding as feasting with panthers. Enda Kenny, on becoming Fine Gael leader, attempted to cultivate the media by calling 20 selected hacks in for some fine dining accompanied by very stilted conversation. In fairness, our sense of distance was understandable, for the hacks knew that the 'social event' was false, and that after the excruciating pleasantries and the foie gras that was already turning to ash in our mouths, we would return to calling Enda the most stupid leader of FG ever and everyone would end up feeling betrayed. Of course, after the food was consumed, the media inevitably returned to their traditional tasks and, oddly enough, the experiment of our future Dear Leader was not repeated.

Happily, there is another route whereby good politicians can free themselves from the all-too-gentle 'tyranny' of the media. For that happy state of affairs to be secured, all that needs to happen is for the prince to act in a courageous, independent fashion. This, however, happens so rarely in Irish politics that one hesitates to mention it for fear of being accused of naivety.

Chapter 14 ~

CONTRASTING TALES OF A COWARDLY BIFFO AND AN ENDA NOT FIT FOR PURPOSE

A wise man ought always to follow the paths beaten by great men and to imitate those who have been supreme, so that if his ability does not equal theirs at least it will savour of it.

On taking leadership positions • must you really be Minister for Finance? • how you must deal with MIADS • the terror of the truthful official • not part of the team • the U-turn • Biffo Agonistes • avoiding the Peter Pan principle and the virtue of pomposity

At some point the great change occurs and Paddy Mac becomes a Minister for Serious Things. Generally, the signal for this is that he either has become Minister for Finance, or some journalist, casting around desperately for names to pad out a piece about a possible leadership challenge to Paddy's own Dear Leader, decides to include our Aspirant Prince's name because there is no one else left. When it comes to the latter, which might be termed the Jim Hacker route, the most important thing is that when Paddy Mac's name is mentioned, nobody laughs. Should that boon occur, then he really is on the road.

One positive development Paddy Mac should take advantage of is that whilst it was once de rigueur for Dear Leaders to serve in Finance, the happy ascension of Enda Kenny means that this no longer is the case. In truth, we and Enda are probably both better off that the Dear Leader was never put in charge of the nation's sums, for had Enda been Minister for Finance, he would most assuredly have not been Taoiseach. The achievement of Mr Kenny was undoubtedly facilitated by the none too unimportant reality that FG had been out of government for so long, there was no former Minister for Finance available for the boss's job, unless they sent for Alan Dukes, and not even 113 seats would be a sustainable majority in circumstances such as that.

Intriguingly, this lacuna is one that Charles Haughey would agree with. He may now be one of our designated national scarecrows, but, Mr Haughey, who knew more than any other politician about the art of governance, held the view that accountants who became Ministers for Finance made for poor Taoisigh. It was an interesting view, given that Haughey himself was an accountant and a former Minister for Finance. Mr Haughey, though, realised that being a Dear Leader requires different qualities from merely balancing books. As poor Paddy the voter continues to dine on the ashes of austerity, who could blame him for feeling nostalgic for an old gallant like Haughey, who dared to mention issues such as art, culture and the importance of leisure in a budget speech, and who also possessed the imagination to realise that government should at least aspire to enhance the happiness and moral sensibilities of the citizen. In that regard, despite all his other flaws, Mr Haughey is a role model that Paddy Mac should not ignore.

Of course, once anointed to his new status as the Minister for Serious Things, Paddy Machiavelli must immediately embark on a swift process of reinvention. A critical first step here is the curious art of taking up 'leadership positions'. This delicate process should only occur if the party is in trouble, since, if you are popular with the people, there is no need for leadership. In fact, quite often the reason you are popular with the people is because of the absence of leadership. Should the opposite be the case, our Aspirant Prince must make it utterly clear that any taking of positions should be informed by the innocent desire to give the Dear Leader a hand. Others may speculate all they want (and hopefully they will), but Paddy Mac is helping the struggling Dear Leader by articulating the plaintive cries of the citizenry that the Dear Leader is too busy to hear.

In taking some of the burden off the leader's shoulders, it is generally better that Paddy Mac should follow the cunning Noonan precedent. This occurred during one of the many difficult periods of Mr Bruton's leadership, when his aspiring replacement said he would be taking 'leadership positions'. A great, or rather a modest, level of excitement followed the Noonan declaration for a number of months, until the absence of any 'leadership positions' — or more importantly a leadership heave itself — saw the drama die away.

Some TDs were critical about the absence of bright new ideas but Mr Noonan was actually to be commended. It is, as the spectral history of Enda Kenny's 'democratic revolution' indicates, rare for grandiose policy declarations to be followed up with practical actions. And, as the even spookier travails which afflicted Garret's constitutional crusade indicate, actually trying to implement grand designs can be the source of even greater troubles. This reality means that Paddy Mac is far better off declaring he is taking 'leadership positions', for he at least has shown willing. But, he must then surround the actual ideas, should he actually have any, with a sensuous shroud of mystery lest they be found wanting in the balance.

Intriguingly, Joan Burton may provide Paddy Mac with an even better template for the taking of a leadership position. When Ms Burton, in the wake of Michael D's critique of austerity, engaged in her own 'we have reached the limits of austerity' speech, she did not talk about taking leadership positions. She merely did it and then let everyone else talk about how she had just taken that position. The even better feature of this decision is that, given that Burton was echoing the views of a Labour President, she could not be accused of disloyalty to the Labour Dear Leader, unless the sainted President was part of the non-existent plot too.

A far more pragmatic skill that Paddy Mac must learn when he has reached the top branches of the tree is how to deal with 'failed mandarins', for he may have to do it quite a lot. Paddy Machiavelli will not, if he knows what's good for him, use such a vulgar phrase. Instead, he will prefer the somewhat more circumspect phrase of 'mandarins in a difficulty' (MIAD). When it comes to the issue of a MIAD, three time-honoured techniques generally suffice. If possible, Paddy Mac should move heaven and earth to shift them to Europe, for in addition to getting them out of the way, the EU will foot the bill. In the case of Kevin Cardiff this, of course, is informed by anxiety to indicate just how highly you rate the Dear Mandarin … and of course Europe too. Sadly, this has all become somewhat more difficult, owing to Europe being somewhat wiser about the malice that lies behind those beguiling Irish eyes.

Failing that, Paddy Mac should take two other routes. One is to invent a fine new quango, where the unwanted one can be shifted out of public view. There is also the Rody Molloy option, where the no longer desired heroic mandarin departs with the praise of a Taoiseach and a Tánaiste ringing in his ears. The problem with the spectacle of a mandarin disappearing with saddlebags stuffed in a manner that resembles Mr Creosote in 'Monty Python' is that the collateral damage for Paddy Machiavelli over the going often outweighs the benefits of the departure. If there is one consolation for our Aspirant Prince, it is that the furore over the €630,000 golden handshake and €143,000 pension paid to a failed Financial Regulator will fade. Critically, even as Paddy Mac defends this and other payoffs with all the conviction of the Greek finance minister presenting the budget, there is one other consolation to be secured. If you protect our MIAD comprehensively enough, once the mandarins realise that under Paddy Machiavelli there is no chance that the flames of reform might lick their feet, they will turn him into their little protectorate.

The importance of such an outwardly lowly status is epitomised by the far more serious terrors posed to our Aspirant Prince by the mandarin who is not a team player. Generally, such mandarins are easily recognised because of their iconoclastic truthfulness. The dangers posed by such a figure are encapsulated in the case history of the former senior Department of Finance official Robert Pye, who repeatedly warned his superiors about a possible property crash and its effects on our banks. In seven separate briefing papers written from 2004 onwards Pye warned that there was a 'real risk' that a collapse in the property market could cause one of the banks 'to go under'. Mr Pye, who was senior enough on the mandarin front, also warned the Department of Finance that the reliance on 'windfall' taxes like stamp duty had left the country on a financial knife edge.

Sadly, the misbehaviour intensified as Pye then suggested that the National Pension Reserve Fund should move away from shares to precious metals, in order to avoid the pending stock market crash. In the same document, he suggested that the benchmarking process would have to be halted before the country reached a point of 'inability to pay'. The even worse news was that a lower-ranking Department of Finance official, Marie Mackle, also warned her superiors that Ireland was heading for an economic crash. In her briefings, the Assistant Principal Officer repeatedly stated that she had only a BA in economics and 'is not an expert', but evidence from various bodies such as the IMF, the OECD and the Central Bank warning of great risks 'deserved attention'. Paddy Machiavelli will understand that had such information reached Mr Cowen and his cabinet squadron of poltroons, this would have been deeply embarrassing, given that they claimed the civil servants had never warned them of the imminent crash. And in truth, such information would not have been terribly welcome before the crash either. Happily, none of this unfortunate speculation reached the higher echelons. Instead, Mr Pye was marginalised, transferred internally and given no further work, whilst gratitude was only distinguished by its absence when it came to the prescient Ms Mackle.

There are important lessons to be learned here for Paddy Mac. For all politicians, one of the greatest terrors that causes them to waken at night is the possibility that some whistleblower will tell them an inconvenient truth. The only thing they fear more than that is that they will be shown to have failed to deal with or understand such an inconvenient truth. Luckily, should Paddy Mac reside in a place of friendship with his mandarins, the courtly eunuchs will, if someone has to be silenced, do the job themselves.

They will, in fact, do the silencing so effectively that Paddy Mac will not even know it has been done. And, of course, should the views of any whistleblower emerge, the best solution to that problem is to commission an *internal* review.

Lest he be too grateful, though, Paddy Mac might stop for a second to ask just whose interests the mandarins are really serving. Mind you, on second thoughts, maybe it is better that he does not.

Now that he is at the edges of the top, Paddy Mac must also master the important art of the U-turn. His first act must be to disregard the unpopular press that the U-turn suffers from. The fundamental flaw that undercuts the sighs, mostly in media and academic circles, for decisive government is, as Paddy Mac knows all too well, that the voters have never, except for brief interludes under Lemass and Haughey, expressed much of a taste for such a bracing experience. Our media idealists may yearn for the virtue that comes from the strong leadership of a Thatcher-style figure. But whilst Mrs Thatcher may famously have said, 'U-turn if you want to; the lady is not for turning', Paddy the voter is always for the U-turning if the road looks a bit difficult. Should Paddy Mac be looking for a role model in this regard, it would be hard to surpass de Valera, who fought a civil war on the issue of whether we were a republic or not. Then, suddenly, in 1927 our man serenely turned around, said essentially that the matter was a bauble to him and could we start getting our government jobs and the rest of the good stuff now, thank you?

Whatever about the rights and wrongs, de Valera provides us with two critical lessons on how to perform the perfect U-turn. Firstly, to qualify, the U-turn must be successful. Secondly, and this is more important still, the very existence of the U-turn must be denied. It is critical that Paddy Machiavelli also understands that these two acts are intimately intertwined, for the politician who starts denying that a U-turn has been committed before the job is done resembles a man caught with his trousers down in his neighbour's wife's bedroom. In such circumstances, no amount of explanation is likely to placate the enraged husband. Similarly, in politics if the U-turn has been accomplished before the enraged husband of the

Irish electorate races in the bedroom door, then it is a fait accompli that is not worth talking about.

When it comes to the U-turn, Paddy Mac therefore should not attempt to engage in obfuscation or rhetoric, for that will only confirm the suspicion of the voters. Paddy Mac should also utterly avoid the 'we didn't know how bad things were' line of defence, for, at best, Paddy the voter will condemn the Aspirant Prince for being stupid. Instead, on such occasions, he should be guided by the resolute simplicity of Bob Hope who, when caught in bed with a starlet by his wife, uttered the immortal phrase 'Honey, don't believe your lying eyes'. Oddly enough, despite our status as the most sophisticated electorate in Europe, Paddy may find that a similar series of blank denials, if they are definitive enough, may actually work.

Two of the better examples of the U-turn are inevitably provided by the FF party. When Mr Haughey devised the infamous 'Health cuts hurt the old, the sick and the handicapped' slogan some innocents may have thought this meant Charlie would be cherishing the nurse and not closing the hospital. In fact, Mr Haughey was simply making a factual statement, and he proceeded to prove in spades that health cuts do indeed 'hurt the old, the sick and the handicapped'. Subsequently Mr Haughey deployed two methodologies to deal with the unfortunate accusation that he had been fibbing to the electorate. Firstly, in a more subtle variant of the Bob Hope defence, the promise was contemptuously denied and consigned to history. Once that had been done, the voters, and, more important still, the media, were dazzled by a great list of other triumphs the administration had secured, until time and sheer boredom meant angry articles about the old folks, the sick and the handicapped were gazumped by mock heroic profiles of Monsieur Haughey, le Petit Président de l'Europe.

Bertie Ahern provided Paddy Mac with an even finer example of the great art of the U-turn when he managed to execute a perfect volte-face right in front of his deeply suspicious Labour Coalition colleagues on the issue of a second tax amnesty. When Albert first began to talk about the desirability of this intriguing notion, such was the doleful nature of the sheepish eyes which Bertie, the defender of the working man, threw about his implacable intent not to introduce such an amnesty, that the Labour Party were entirely cozened by the promises. Then, Mr Ahern trotted into the cabinet one morning, announced the amnesty, and Labour were so stunned they were entirely incapable of opposing this fait accompli. Though Bertie subsequently fired a lot of diesel under the noses of the slowly wakening Labour hounds, with mutterings about being the unwitting victim of vast cosmic forces, what Paddy Mac should learn from this is that speed of execution is a key feature of the successful U-turn. It should be done without any foostering, for like the pulling of a tooth, the faster you slam the door shut, with a string tied to the tooth, the easier it will be for everyone.

As he starts to glide ever so gently up the final furlong, Paddy Machiavelli should also closely consider the careers of great Irish politicians, so that he might learn that which is necessary in order to advance to the highest office. This is not such an easy task in Irish politics, and in particular its modern variant, for somewhat obvious reasons. Indeed, it might be more accurate to suggest to our Aspirant Prince that he should study the careers of high-profile politicians, so that he may learn what not to do. In this regard, although Mr Cowen may be a political Banquo (and, worse still, a Biffo), our Aspirant Prince, if he is wise, should carefully study how the leader who was loved more warmly by his own than any other Taoiseach turned into poor Biffo Agonistes.

Biffo's bleak storyboard provides Paddy Mac with a particular lesson in the underrated virtue of courage. It might seem strange — given that in general our advice to Paddy Mac is to follow a policy of evasive trimming — to suggest that our Aspirant Prince should on occasion act courageously. Sometimes, though, like that first meeting between Enda, Angela Merkel and Mr Sarkozy, even the Irish political hind must turn and face the pack. From the start, though, that was absent from the irresolute Mr Cowen. In 2008, when a country that instinctively sensed harsh times were ahead sought its leader, he melted away into some caravan in Connemara. It did not help the morale of the public that, rather like King James at the Battle of the Boyne, the Taoiseach had fled the field before the battle was even over. Indeed, such was the absence of fight in Mr Cowen that he proved incapable of even dealing with Niamh Horan, the then *Sunday Independent* Entertainment Correspondent, who visited his holiday caravan. All was going well until Ms Horan divulged her identity, whereupon, in her own words, 'a deafening silence' ensued. Ms Horan's colourful description of how 'the Taoiseach sat frozen to the spot. His partially dunked biscuit remained suspended in the air, held halfway between his cup and his mouth as his ashen face tried to take in the awful realisation' did not suggest that Ireland had elected a new Putin. The scene became even more surreal as, before Cowen could 'utter another word the soggy piece of Digestive — which had been left too long … dropped to the floor.' Even when poor Biffo did recover, his instinctive response was to start to fret about the trouble he would be in with the wife. For those who remember the old saying about how 'it's not the size of the dog in the fight but the size of the fight in the dog that matters' the entire episode was not exactly a good omen for Mr Cowen's capacity to take on the dragons racing towards his teetering State.

The career of poor Cowen should also warn our Aspirant Prince about the danger of falling too much under the spell of the sanctuary provided by the Dáil's high walls. Once in Leinster House, you are to a certain extent in an enchanted place where, particularly if you are a minister, there is always someone around to do something for you. Paddy Machiavelli should therefore be constantly aware of how easy it is to end up living in a world as divorced from reality as that of Peter Pan. It might seem strange to associate Brian Cowen with the fantastical child-centred world of JM Barrie's fairy tales. But, though he looked more like Captain Hook, Mr Cowen really was the Irish Peter Pan. An ocean of newsprint and amateur psychologists' reports might have been applied to the great 'What is wrong with Brian?' question whilst he was the Taoiseach. But, put at its simplest, and tragically for us, the problem with Mr Cowen is that he really is the boy who never grew up.

Paddy Mac should note that this explains how Biffo was tailor-made for the post of being the FF leader, for it too is a party which, from its adolescent beginning as the facilitator of an utterly irresponsible civil war, has, with the exception of the occasional flirtation with maturity under Lemass and Albert, never fully grown up. Paddy Machiavelli, hopefully, will realise that these characteristics set the country and the Taoiseach on a certain road to our current Via Dolorosa. The post-colonial state of arrested development that characterised the Irish State was all well and good whilst we could live in our own Neverland. But, when we ventured out into the real world to play fiscal poker with the pirates of the ECB and the German banks, they fitted us up and are now chopping us up.

The key Peter Pan principle that must guide Paddy Mac is the need to maintain an equivocal edge in his relationship with the enclosed nunnery of Leinster House. It was said that communication was the be-all and end-all of Cowen's troubles. In fact, the seed capital for that downfall was Cowen's belief that the Dáil bar was a sanctuary that could keep the world at bay. The problem, however, was that when the world knocked down the door brandishing a banking crisis, Biffo and the rest of that ill-fated bar lobby were utterly unable to deal with it. The rest of us then became the fiscal experiment which finally proved that the fairy-tale politics of Peter Pan always end with the chaotic nightmare of a Biffo Agonistes.

One of the happier lessons that Biffo teaches Paddy Machiavelli is that intelligence is not a determining criterion of the qualities required to be Taoiseach. When it came to the cult of worshipping Biffo's brain, something of the credulousness of Oliver Goldsmith's village peasants informed the belief of the FF backbenchers who, when drinking with Biffo, 'gazed, and still the wonder grew, that one small head could carry all he knew.' In contrast, cleverness was not something that has ever been associated with Dear Leader Enda. But, whilst a spooked public continuously shied away from the notion of Taoiseach Enda, and still do, Paddy Machiavelli should note that Mr Kenny is the Taoiseach and is likely to be in the box seats for some time.

Intriguingly, Enda is not the only example of how you don't have to be a genius to be Taoiseach. During the increasingly uneasy lead-in to the Lemass succession, when compared with the three musketeers of Haughey, Donogh O'Malley and Brian Lenihan — or Neil Blaney, for that matter — 'honest' Jack Lynch was hardly the pick of the intellectual litter. But 'honest' Jack, with his pipe, his small Paddy and lunch at home with Máirín every day, was the political equivalent of comfort eating. No one supported Jack because he was clever. If you wanted that, then you would be better off trotting over to say hello to the guy in the sharp suit making love to all the builders. In fact, many of his enthusiastic supporters predicated their support on the fact that Jack, because he wasn't bright, would be an awful lot safer.

Some might suggest the preference for Lynch, Enda or Liam Cosgrave, whose attitude to Garret's intellectuals bore a more than passing resemblance to that of a terrier padding into a fox's den, is indicative of the electorate's mistrust of radical intellectuals. But, a slightly different argument could be made that the respective strengths of that less than glamorous troika are best captured by the fable about the respective differences between the clever fox who knows many things lightly and the slow-moving hedgehog who knows one big thing. In all three cases, the political priorities of Lynch, Cosgrave and Enda were inculcating respect for public office and securing the institutions of the State. They were and are no ignoble objectives, the importance of which was far too easily forgotten by others.

Seeing as how he is now a Minister for Serious Things and a leadership contender, Paddy Machiavelli must face another transformation. If he is to be the Dear Leader, there is a point where he too must begin to cultivate a sense of distance, no matter how sociable he may normally be. The cruel truth about life as a Dear Leader is that, like judges, Paddy Mac must become a man without friends. Just ask Bertie, if you can find him these days. It is not that Paddy Mac shouldn't talk to his old pals, but, as the Falstaff dilemma kicks in, he must start to become preoccupied. His friends, or rather his colleagues, will be somewhat puzzled when, instead of the hurling or the gossip, he begins to chat to them about policy and positioning. They will, with the exception of a couple of the more knowing ones, be even more startled when he starts to muse about how politics is not so much a game as a form of vocation. Nothing definitive will be stated, but, almost imperceptibly, Paddy Mac will acquire a responsible air. He is now a man carrying new burdens and dealing with different preoccupations. What these are, nobody, least of all the man himself, knows, and though the burdens are not defined, they are real. Paddy Mac should note that such a process was even experienced by the Dear Leader Enda. There are those who still argue that poor Kenny Lite is a man of hidden shallows rather than mysterious depths. But whilst it might be excessive to suggest that Enda is the Irish equivalent of Churchill's famous description of Russia as a riddle wrapped in an enigma, from the moment he became leader he secured that critical air of separation from the herd that all leaders must acquire. And, ironically, Enda's 'man of hidden shallows' reputation may even have facilitated this process, for how can you know what the motives of a leader are if he actually doesn't have any?

Paddy Mac should also be warned that embracing the virtue of pomposity is unavoidable if he is to become a successful Dear Leader. Nothing epitomises the great caution that Paddy Machiavelli must bring to public affairs, and the utter imperative to avoid humorous intercourse with the media once he is near the top, more than the furore that followed the same Enda over his infamous 'nigger' joke. The ruckus began when Enda, who was still the bright new FG leader, told an anecdote that included the 'nigger' word during a function attended by parliamentary colleagues, party workers and political journalists. The circumstances in which the remark was made arose out of a personal memory Mr Kenny had of his friend and former Fine Gael colleague David Molony from Tipperary, who had died suddenly that week. The already struggling FG leader recalled that during a holiday of the 'liquid variety' in a cocktail bar with Molony and the human rights advocate Maurice Manning, Mr Manning had spotted that the name of one of the cocktails on the drinks menu was a 'Lumumba'. When Mr Manning asked the Moroccan barman if this was a reference to Patrice Lumumba, the assassinated Prime Minister of the Congo, the barman dismissively replied that

Lumumba was 'some nigger who was killed dans la guerre'. On one level it was an amusing meditation upon how transitory the fame of politicians can be. But, as Kenny would find out the very hard way, it was also an anecdote best told at the bar counter with friends, as distinct from being declaimed out loud in front of a hundred individuals, many of whom sported hostile feelings towards the new FG Dear Leader. Like Con Houlihan's famous housewife racing in from the garden in a futile attempt to save the burning cakes in the oven, Mr Kenny sensed too late that he could be in trouble here and swiftly noted that this was not a racist story, which it wasn't. Not that this was to matter too much.

Instead, within a day, Enda found himself fighting with the Labour Party, the league of journalistic literal simpletons, the Refugee Council and the Irish Council for Civil Liberties, who said they could think of no circumstances in which the use of the word was appropriate. They should perhaps have considered asking the American Afro-Caribbean community who, oddly enough, use it on a regular basis without fainting. Enda did try to defend himself via the bleats of a media spokesperson who noted that the media were 'misconstruing a word and taking it in isolation'. That lasted for about as long as the lifespan of the male wing of the praying mantis family before Mr Kenny bowed to mounting pressure and 'unreservedly' apologised. The apology didn't really matter, as poor Enda found himself being compared to a schoolyard bully or barstool bowsie and was also linked to the recent random murder of a long-term Chinese resident of Ireland. Still, Mr Kenny had learned a valuable lesson. Under the new Puritanism, outside of being found in bed with a live boy or a dead girl, the most dangerous thing any politician can do is to tell a joke.

Chapter 15 ～

PADDY MACHIAVELLI SECURES THE TRUST OF THE CITIZEN

… nor is genius or fortune altogether necessary to attain to it [power], but rather a happy shrewdness.

On the need to secure a sparse sense of authority • grandfather Noonan and trust • temper desire with caution • of course you don't want to be the leader • the politics of 'all I want to do is me budget' • cultivating hope • behaving with your coalition partners and the importance of being lucky

If Paddy Machiavelli is to reach the final level which proves that he really can be a Dear Leader, there are still some final frontiers he needs to conquer. Though he might not want to, he particularly needs to acquire that pale ghost known as authority. The problem our Aspirant Prince faces is that authority resembles the 'it' factor in politics. This is not necessarily good news for Paddy Mac, since 'it' is impossible to define. The other great problem the practical politician has with 'it' is that this 'it' cannot be bought or measured or imitated. Some even doubt that 'it' actually exists. And sometimes when you think you have found 'it', the glitter you see turns out to be fool's gold. But, like Clinton or Blair or Bertie, if you have 'it' then you know 'it' is real. However, either you have 'it' or you don't have 'it', and if you don't, you can never be taught to acquire 'it', for the harder you try to grasp, the swifter 'it' flits away, as though frightened by the unmannerly nature of your avaricious desire.

Like our friend 'it', the same criteria apply to authority, but with one caveat. In the case of Paddy Machiavelli, acquiring a sense of authority is complicated by the fact that, unlike Angela's Germany or Britain, Ireland is a Mediterranean-style state with an ongoing weakness for political Casanovas until the crisis strikes, and then suddenly the rush to authority begins. This means that, like the wise virgin, our Aspirant Prince would be wise to retain some vestige of steel inside the velvet glove he uses to massage Paddy the voter, lest this steel be required some day.

In examining the complex way that this authority thing works, Paddy Mac will find no better example than Ray MacSharry. Our Aspirant Prince should note that whilst MacSharry had a speckled career, this counted for little when a strong man was needed to save the state. MacSharry is also the original case study in how authority is a first cousin of our friend authenticity, for you cannot construct it on foundations of spin. Authority can also spring from the strangest of places too, for originally, when he became Minister for Finance, there was some fluttering in Dublin 4 over MacSharry's status as part of the Haughey-Doherty litter. The critics missed one fundamental point, for in that sort of company only rough but clever men who know their own minds would survive. It was a form of training that would prove invaluable when it came to dealing with the tough decisions MacSharry had to face.

MacSharry's authorative persona was also helped by the belief that he was ideologically closer to the old school of republican FF than the new 'soft FF lads' who dream only of playing golf with bishops and bank managers as a sign of social acceptability. Yet, up to 1987, despite a latent sense of potential, MacSharry appeared to be travelling to no particularly interesting destination. There is no doubt that he could have gone to his political grave having been nothing more than a junior minister and there would have been no defining sense of a lost legacy.

However, when faced by a challenge that had defeated Garret, Haughey, Dukes and Bruton, MacSharry, perhaps because he was an outsider, found himself right at home. Others would have indulged in windy appeals and calls to arms. Paddy the voter, though, has always believed that when it comes to fancy speaking, generally, if a fellow is doing a lot of speechifying, it is because he is trying to disguise the fact that he has no intention of implementing anything he is talking about. In the case of MacSharry and that famous 1987 budget, the most intriguing feature of his speech was the absence of any ornate rhetoric. Instead, rather like one of Beckett's plays, sparseness became a political style which conveyed on him, in the manner that a thousand speeches conveying a willingness to die for Ireland never could, that invisible cloak of authority. Garret FitzGerald might have been a deeper thinker, and Alan Dukes somewhat more clever, but MacSharry was that thing known as a doer. He had a plan and a strategy and that was a rare enough sight in Irish politics. What was even rarer, though, was that people realised MacSharry, courtesy of that lightly worn air of authority, was going to implement it.

A sense of authority may be the key that unlocks the chastity belt of the citizen's trust. It is not, however, the sole quality our Aspirant Prince must cultivate, for the citizens' views on what they need from our politicians is a fickle thing. Dick Spring's sherriff riding in to clean out the Haughey whorehouse act charmed the nation for a time. Once that had been secured, however, the voters could not wait to snap the sheriff's badge off Dick, and place all their trust in a different, more genteel political whore-master called Bertie. By 2010, however, a traumatised people needed to be reassured, and no Messiahs need apply. Instead, serendipitously for FG, just as Ireland decided she needed a National Grandfather, Enda chose Michael Noonan to chart his party's economic course.

For a country that was dealing with the consequences of the Butch Cassidy and the Sundance Kid-style economics of Bertie, the stolidity of the Captain Mainwaring school of Noonan economics acted like Viagra on FG's poll ratings. Suddenly, a distressed citizenry had its own ancient sage dandling the child on his knee, reassuring it, telling it fairy tales and funny stories about how when he was canvassing and mentioned Anglo Irish Bank, even the dog would start to bark. Though Noonan didn't smoke a pipe, he probably should have, for it would have suited the village schoolmaster persona of a man who was 'severe … and stern to view' when dealing with the reprobates of Fianna Fáil, whilst the electorate 'laugh'd with counterfeited glee, at all his jokes, for many a joke had he.'

Noonan, however, did not merely steady the tiller or put a smile on our faces. The new, almost septuagenarian, Finance spokesperson seized the day to such an extent that he took out Joan Burton, the real architect of Labour's rise to first place in the polls, and he almost delivered a majority to FG. Paddy Machiavelli will see many queer things in his time in Leinster House, but few will surpass the scenario where, a quarter of a century after he opposed Ray MacSharry's famous 1987 budget, Michael Noonan became the comeback grandad of Irish politics.

Outside of the importance of winning the trust of the voters, Noonan also provides us with a critical lesson in how our Aspirant Prince must learn to marry the differing impulses of desire and caution. Back in 2001, Noonan took that which he most desired from John Bruton and walked into a desert. Had he waited until 2002 and the aftermath of the inevitable defeat heading Fine Gael's way, Mr Noonan would have been the pick of a united party that would have been kicking itself for its failure to take the wise decision of making Noonan leader in 2001. However, Mr Noonan could not refrain from seizing that which he had wanted for so long but with so little reason.

Mr Haughey also provides Paddy Mac with no shortage of lessons on the importance, at the highest end of the game, of tempering desire with caution. In the 1960s, Mr Haughey wanted the leadership of FF too intensely and offered too few reasons outside of a desire for self-advancement as to why he should get it. Now, all political leaders are driven by ambition, but most cloak it with some decent drapery of deference. Sadly, Mr Haughey's inability to create the slightest pretence of chaste intentions meant that too many people speculated too correctly on his motives. It ended somewhat badly with the victory of 'honest' Jack. In the aftermath, the drama of the occasion was captured by James Dillon's *oeuvre* about the machinations of 'Deputy Haughey and his Camorra,

Deputy Lenihan, and Minister for Justice, Deputy O'Malley', who had stalked the corridors of the House telling some of the younger members of the FF party to 'vote for Charlie, because if you vote for Charlie and George Colley is elected he is not vindictive, but if you vote for George and Charlie gets elected he will follow you to the death'. Whilst Dillon had seen some 'young inexperienced members of FF quail at that', it had not worked, and he had witnessed the moment of recognition. He recalled seeing 'Haughey's face white as parchment, and I said, Haughey has gone down the sink. Remember, when he failed to land his fish last Wednesday night he will never land it. He is finished. He stinks politically.'

In fact, Mr Dillon was somewhat inaccurate, and a key factor in that regard was Mr Haughey's own capacity to learn from failure, to such an extent that one of the better examples of political humility and the capacity to restrain the political id is provided by the same Haughey. This occurred when, in the wake of the Arms Crisis and the subsequent 'vindication' of Mr Haughey, a motion of no confidence was placed in 'honest' Jack Lynch. As was intended, all eyes were upon Lynch's enemy Haughey, who had made it eloquently clear that he rated 'honest' Jack rather in the manner of how the owner of a pack of stag hounds would view a King Charles Spaniel trotting over to join the pack. But, whilst the hopeful eyes of a capricious combination of dreamers were on Haughey, the future Taoiseach had done the maths. Were he to vote against Lynch, Haughey, who was at this point the member of a gang of one, faced a future involving all the creature comforts of St John the Baptist. Though Jack Lynch made for an unlikely Salome, faced with a denouement, Haughey engaged in a de Valera-style U-turn. Out went all that spirit of the nation — or Mr Haughey as a latter-day Cú Chulainn fighting to the death, back against a rock, with a raven croaking on his shoulder — stuff. Instead, Mr Haughey went, head bowed with the rest of the flatfoots, through the Tá lobby and, like Slattery's Mounted Foot, lived to fight another day.

The imperative of caution therefore means that when his name is first listed in a leadership contest, Paddy Mac should cloak his desires with a cunning air of puzzlement over the rationale behind this great boon. It is inevitably a matter of some concern that the party is at 10 per cent and the Dear Leader has a 5 per cent popularity rating. But, until such time as he knows he has more votes in the ranks of the party than the Dear Leader, this is the fault of the people. Unsurprisingly, the template when it comes to avoiding any dangerously premature strike against an ailing leader is provided by Bertie Ahern. After the fall of Haughey, it had been thought that there would be a contest between Bertie and Albert until, suddenly, Bertie declared he would be a non-runner, just after a substantial number of FF TDs had wagered their political future on Mr Ahern. From that point on, every response by Bertie on the issue of the leadership considered the claim that Bertie had no interest in that leadership thing, despite the counting of heads that his own mafia had been so vigorously engaged in. In contrast, the only counting Bertie was interested in was doing 'me budget', which was due shortly. So it was that our hero wandered around, like a dishevelled variant of Johnny Forty Coats, and informed a totally disbelieving nation that 'all I wanted to do was me budget', were he to be left alone. Of course everyone, well, except Bertie apparently, knew that Bertie had a deep interest in the FF leadership. And everyone except Bertie also knew Bertie had stepped aside because Bertie — not that he knew it, seeing as how he had never been interested in the leadership — feared he did not have the numbers. Not, of course, that Bertie would have known this, since the only thing he had been counting was the numbers for 'me budget'.

Anyway, that aside, as is always the case in Leinster House the truth of things did not matter that much. The muttering about 'me budget' provided Bertie with some decent drapery to mask the U-turn. But, whilst Bertie had stepped aside, he had done so on a promise, for he was clearly Albert's most dangerous opponent. And the place for a Taoiseach to keep his most dangerous political opponent is safely occupied in Finance doing up 'me budget'.

Ultimately, if Paddy Mac is looking for the perfect role model for appearing reluctant to secure power, he should note that few displayed greater abilities in this regard than FG's lachrymose Taoiseach John A Costello. In Mr Costello's case it probably helped that he was genuinely reluctant to give up a lucrative career in the Law Library to be insulted at will by de Valera's semi-literate street gurriers. So, on two occasions when he secured the highest office in the land, Mr Costello submitted us to doleful orations about how this was a place he did not wish to be near at all. It was a performance that did not remotely improve the mood of the FF benches, and the tongues hanging out of them for a taste of a ministerial Mercedes. But, such is the contrarian streak in the Irish electorate, they made Mr Costello the most successful leader of FG since WT Cosgrave.

Because he is now at the edge of the boss-man's chair, Paddy Machiavelli is going to have to refine his position on the art of the false promise, for a real danger now exists that what he says may actually be remembered. It would be a better world if he did not have to make promises. But, the politician always has to do this because the *raison d'être* of his existence is the promise. In truth, for the voter, since 1977 and Jack Lynch's great giveaway manifesto, the political promise carries a similar currency to the unfortunate tale of Patrick Kavanagh and the neighbour who asked him to write a poetic curse on a neighbour. After much labour, Kavanagh produced the poem, requested some cash for his efforts and secured the somewhat chilly response of 'Ah, Jesus, I thought you'd do it for a couple of bottles of stout.' Ironically, despite such an absence of faith, an electorate who make a terrible flap when promises are broken are even unhappier if you don't make them.

The complication Paddy Mac must deal with is that false promises are sometimes necessary to deal with present exigencies. Nothing epitomises this necessity more than Ruairí Quinn's famous pre-election claim in 2011 that third-level fees would not be restored. The subsequent outworking, where third-level fees climbed up the drainpipe back into the bedroom of Middle Ireland, has evoked many loud complaints from FF, who really should know better. There has even been more clucking from those Labour backbenchers who don't know enough to realise that politicians cannot always be moral about such things. Indeed, the latter would do well to recognise that they would not have their seats were it not for Quinn, since the tide was heading inexorably towards a single-party FG government. Many subsequently believed that Labour would actually have been better off in opposition anyway. But, given that they had already been in that wilderness for 14 years, one could understand if Mr Quinn and the other Grumpy Old Men were not in the mood to be seduced by the suggestion from Labour's many 'friends' that they should wait another four.

Wouldn't that have gone well?

Of course ethicists will bleat, but Paddy Mac's position should be that so long as the promise secures victory and is made with a contrite heart, and that the intention is to fulfil it should this become possible through some miracle, then no sin has been committed. It might be claimed that in embracing the 'moral reservation' theory of promises we are being too cynical, for at least one Irish politician, Garret FitzGerald, was honest with the public. But, the voters threw him out in less than a year when he got too honest about the children's shoes. Enda Kenny may claim that 'Paddy wants to know the story', but if our treatise has taught Paddy Mac one thing, it is that, as we noted earlier, Paddy the voter only likes to hear a nice story. Paddy Machiavelli's attitude to the promise therefore should be informed by the premise that if men were good, there would be neither alehouses nor whorehouses nor political promises. But we are where we are and we must deal with the demand that exists for all three.

A wise Aspirant Prince should, however, always apply moderation when it comes to the provision of promises, if it is at all possible. The electorate will not let him get away with generalities such as 'for better days'. But, if he has a track record of modest success then cannily vague promises such as Bertie's 'A lot done. More to do' slogan may work. Even the elliptical nature of Mr Ahern's first electoral slogan of 'People before politics' carried weight, for it hinted at the weakness of a Rainbow government that secretly always preferred reading a nice ESRI report to meeting the proletarians in their public houses and bingo halls.

The one sin that is unforgiveable for our Aspirant Prince is to make excessively exuberant promises when there is no need to. The politician who is tempted in this regard should realise that for all the claims about the guileful nature of the Irish electorate, you can rarely make enough promises to satisfy your voters. But, you will ultimately earn their contempt if you plead too openly with them for their support. And, as the denouement to Election 2007 shows, if it all goes south, the voters will glare at those political floozies who made them an offer they were too selfish to refuse, even though they suspected it was not in their best interest.

Care about promises should not be confined to tax cuts either, for if Paddy Machiavelli is in opposition he will experience occasional urges of the reforming kind. However, whilst the leader-writers of *The Irish Times* may dream grimly of a Savonarola-style bonfire of the citizens' vanities, Paddy the voter is generally suspicious, and rightly so, for such experiments may force him to be purer but they rarely add to the sum of his happiness. So, unless he is a member of the Labour Party, the Greens or the PDs (and, oddly enough, two of that particular troika are defunct and the third may soon follow suit), the reform agenda should be kept at a chilly distance.

Caution about the consequences of promises should not deter Paddy Mac from attempting to create a spirit of optimism amongst the people. Rough pragmatists may laugh at such soft thoughts, but the absence of a politics of optimism can have real effects. When it comes to our present crisis, for example, how can the much-desired 'confidence fairy', which is such a necessary feature of growth, thrive when a faint mist of depression now hangs over Irish politics in a manner not seen since the 1950s? On one level the air of depression is entirely understandable given the scale of the mess our Grumpy Old Men fell into. But when we are almost casually informed that the State could face another lost decade on top of the already lost half decade, it represents an astonishing failure of politics surely that again, as in the 1950s, a country of vanishing youth is being led by a gerontocracy that is far too comfortable with the politics of elegant pessimism.

There was a time when Brian Lenihan would have been an unlikely role model for Paddy Machiavelli. Even the beginning of the dramatic denouement of his career was farcical, dominated as it was by the late-night, garlic-eating scene with David McWilliams, which resembled a cross between the witches in *Macbeth* and *Carry On Up the Department of Finance*. The journey from hubris mixed with innocence to nemesis, disaster and redemption was a rare one within an Irish political tradition that scarcely makes it as far as the territories of redemption. However, from the original, frankly less than convincing 'our plan is working' budget speeches, Lenihan's determination and sanguine courage provided the electorate with an all too rare point of light. He was, in truth, rarely correct and often too guileless when dealing with the villainous cast of Bertie, Jean-Claude Trichet, Biffo, the Anglo bankers, the failed mandarin class and the social partners. Such, however, was the transformation from the somewhat soft, self-indulgent barrister, bullied so mercilessly by Bertie, that at Mr Lenihan's funeral, even as the party's last hero was eulogised, we were simultaneously burying Fianna Fáil. Though Brian brought philosophy, learned guile, charming elusiveness and perhaps even a little bit of theology to the political table, Paddy Mac should note that what elevated Brian Lenihan above the herd was that he was a man visibly trying to do the right thing. And more important still, he was also one of the few politicians in that strange administration who was optimistic enough to believe that there was a way out of the mess he was trying to resolve.

Mr Lenihan's colleague Eamon Ryan was, in that cabinet of the damned, a second prodigy in the art of generating optimism. Ryan, however, also provides Paddy Machiavelli with a stark tale about the fickleness of the voter and the speed with which those powers can dissipate. Eamon was once the metrosexual minister who left tongues in FG hanging out with the hope that he would join and lead them. Paddy Mac should note that the fall of Eamon and the Greens occurred because, despite their youth, they became politically dated with an alarming speed. In 2006 the Greens were on the rise because they were the bespoke Italian designer-kitchen party of Irish politics. They were the political sign that Ireland was so wealthy it could now, like normal countries, move beyond the comfort blanket of Civil War politics. The civility was to reach as far as Fianna Fáil, who, having treated the Greens in the sort of manner last seen during the Red Scare in 1950s America, began to realise that they could safely intermingle with those strange creatures. But, despite their youth and obvious abilities, when the great fall came and the Greens became the political equivalent of fine dining at a time when Paddy the voter was in more of a soup-kitchen mode, nothing could save them.

The somewhat tortured relationship of the Greens with FF should inform Paddy Mac that another test of his capacity to thrive in the thin air at the top of the political mountain is the level of cunning he displays in the treatment of coalition partners. This has been an evolving art since the 1980s, when FF and FG believed that the role of the coalition partner was not to let the door hit them on the ass as they backed deferentially out of the Taoiseach's office. After many catastrophes and break-ups, it is all a little more polite these days. Paddy Machiavelli can, of course, if he wishes to secure popularity amongst his own, though certainly not the Taoiseach's office, treat his 'partners' with bellicose hostility. This incorporates the patented school of 'Bull' O'Donoghue rhetoric about Green slugs or Biffo's 'if in doubt leave out' stance. However, before Paddy Machiavelli fancies himself too much in this regard, he should remember that coalition partners can be like the stickleback. They may be small, but they are still capable of slicing up your underbelly. Paddy Mac should also recognise, though, that if you are loyal to your coalition partners, apart from enjoying the delights of the quiet life, you will acquire their respect. And more important still, when it comes to your colleague TDs, you will also arm your allies with precedents as to how you might behave as leader when it comes to your own internal coalition.

When he begins to enter the endgame, the Dear Leader's slowly disappearing acolytes will be considering one particularly serious issue. Put bluntly, they will in particular want to know if Paddy Mac is lucky when it comes to the winning of elections, for this, far more than any series of successes in Leinster House wars or budgets, will decide the views of the backbench 'turnips' on Paddy Mac's capacity to be the next Dear Leader. The political idealist might imagine that qualities other than luck should come into issues such as by-elections, and referenda, for that matter. But, in a political system without ideology, luck plays a significant role in determining the fate of individuals and parties. Of course, in this regard, the plotting of a Dear Leader may scupper Paddy Mac's hopes. This is a particular danger should a Dear Leader who is in trouble wish to shorten a couple of tall poppies. A far more desolate scenario still may be that the Dear Leader wishes to avenge some imagined, or worse still, some real slight. The finest example of a Dear Leader seeking to punish a political reprobate is the decision by Enda Kenny to put Charlie Flanagan in charge of the less than easy task of convincing the Irish people to love Gay Mitchell in that ill-fated Presidential election campaign. In scenarios such as this the inevitable defeat is greeted with much disappointed head-shaking over how our man has failed the impossible test. Sadly, such egregious failure also inevitably justifies the continuing exclusion of the Director of Elections from ministerial office. And whilst colleagues will be sympathetic, the taint of failure will still be attached to the Director of Elections' political record.

Of course, all electoral exercises are accompanied by risk. Sometimes, even the easy test, such as a referendum to give the Dáil the powers to attack — our apologies, conduct an inquiry into — the banks can prove problematic. Whatever about the referendum, if Paddy Mac is in charge of a by-election, he will often need to be lucky on several fronts, for quite apart from the malice of the Dear Leader, Paddy Mac can only pray that he does not have to contend — our apologies, work — with a strong local TD. Nothing epitomises the risks involved in this regard better than the example of the Tipperary South constituency where Bertie, at the peak of his powers, lost two by-elections in a row. And it, of course, had nothing to do with the sitting FF TD Noel Davern that the two FF candidates in these by-elections would have struggled to secure a seat on the local council, let alone the Dáil. They were, after all, democratically chosen by Noel's FF delegates and, having been selected for the by-election, oddly enough, they never ran for the party again. In situations such as this, where Paddy Machiavelli's fellow TDs head off to campaign lustily in the pub, no one will criticise him too much for losing. However, even if the candidate our man is landed with is a 70-year-old, half-blind, limping, artificial-insemination man, once again, defeat means the blossom of our tall poppy has withered somewhat.

Though the by-election may be noticed by few in the normal world, how Paddy Machiavelli performs in this play within a play will be critical in deciding his political future. If Paddy Mac is lucky, and generally this is secured by being in charge of by-elections when in opposition, the rewards are immense, for he will secure a reputation for being a great winner of elections. Of course, in the aftermath of the happy event, all eyes will be on the appalled sitting TD, the delighted new TD and the 'relieved' Dear Leader. Paddy Mac, however, would be better employed casting a couple of winks in the direction of the backbench turnips as they nod and grunt happily at each other.

Chapter 16 ~

BE PATIENT AND CUNNING AND STILL, AND ALL THINGS COME TO THOSE WHO ENDURE

And as experience shows, many have been the conspiracies, but few have been successful; because he who conspires cannot act alone ...

On how the prince creates the good republic • the true importance of authenticity • youth will not have its fling • endurance our finest trait • Enda and resilience • etiquette • trust not plotters • cold lovers are not appreciated • the *coup d'état* • endgames, scarecrows and timing • the best time to become leader • chairman or chief • the final leap and a certain future

It might seem surprising, given what has gone before, for us to suggest that, as he approaches the prize, Paddy Machiavelli should begin to consider how he might build the good republic. But outside of noting that once he becomes the Dear Leader he will be kept far too busy to have time for such abstract notions, Paddy Mac should note that whilst the protection of one's personal sanity means cynicism is necessary in politics, the politician whose mindset is informed by nothing but cynicism is a stunted tree. Our Aspirant Prince will, of course, have learned much on his journey to the top that will incline him towards the cynical road. He will have also noted the dangers of being brave (because the brave perish) and the importance of not being ideological because ideology makes the people unhappy. Paddy Machiavelli will also know that, too often in Irish politics, where courage is required the response is one of caution; that innovation often only inspires the desire to quash it; and that where there is discord the wise slip away quietly. He will know that those who believe themselves to be smart respond to thought with populism, to truth with pay-offs, to the need for action with review groups, to despair with sympathy (but no commitments) and to doubt with focus groups. Meanwhile, those who vote him into the job will, for the most part, hope that Paddy Mac, being properly housetrained, will not be a danger to anyone. Instead, they will want an affable, pragmatic, willing instrument of the voters who is never so impolite as to believe excessively in anything, but who also possesses all the tricks, all the appropriate sentiments and clever catch phrases that are necessary in order to survive.

That, at least, is what politics will attempt to do to him. But, of course, it doesn't always end up that way. Sometimes a Lemass or an Albert arrives out of nowhere and surprises us all. And even if Paddy Mac turns out to be a slightly lesser grade of prince, such as a Lynch, affable pragmatism and a keen knowledge of the people are not the worst of political philosophies. When he reaches the Taoiseach's office, should the going get tough, Paddy Mac will be tempted to plea that 'they' (whoever they might be) will not let him behave in a courageous manner. However, the tough resilience of a Cosgrave should remind Paddy Mac that the Taoiseach should always be his own man rather than a bought and purchased man. Outside of retaining that small degree of independence Paddy Mac must always remember amidst the flux of political life that his primary task is to build and defend the republic. And, to do that, he must retain some capacity for idealism.

Oddly enough, even though he is trading in a palace of deceit, for Paddy Mac to reach that final goal he must also retain a central core of authenticity. And if he is looking for examples of the importance of authenticity, nothing epitomises its virtues more than the delightful denouement of the career of Michael D Higgins.

The theatrical nature of the personality of Michael D has often led to claims that he is not authentic. But, authenticity is not merely confined to horny-handed sons of the soil, and, in his case, the flapping, the poetry and the musing represent the authentic nature of Michael D. The 2011 Presidential election confirmed that even in an age of spin this authenticity is a critical virtue, for it was his authenticity allied to suspicion over the bona fides of Seán Gallagher that carried Michael D over the line. It helped that on this occasion Michael D's school of authenticity was particularly suited for a job where the main requirement is a capacity for the occasional bit of theatrical rhetoric and the capacity to articulate fine thoughts. Ultimately, though, the critical factor was an electorate who were utterly mistrustful of politicians in general; they knew that if you pricked Michael D, the blood would match his DNA.

In contrast, the problem with Gallagher was that, under the heat of the campaign, the authenticity of his persona began to unravel. And, even in Irish politics, there is no more dangerous moment than the point where the electorate begins to suspect that you are not what you are presenting yourself to be. Gallagher understandably used his status as an entrepreneur to bathe his Fianna Fáil DNA in more pleasing colours. However, this position was always going to be utterly undermined by the inevitable discovery by the electorate that he was of the FF tribe. This fatal flaw meant that, at the slightest strain, the structure would crack and begin to unravel. And, in truth, even before the theatrical RTÉ 'Frontline' implosion, the electorate resembled the sort of salmon that deceives the hopeful angler by surging towards the bait before, spooked by some imperfection, it turns with a disdainful swish of the tail.

So, apart from authenticity, what precisely do our electorate, and far more important still, Paddy Machiavelli's colleagues, require of our man before they usher him into the Dear Leader's suite? There is, of course, much wish fulfilment by our intelligentsia in this regard. Many quills are dipped and much ink is wasted prophesying that what the people want is youthful, reforming vigour. Paddy the voter, of course, is for this in theory, but only if it does not affect his perks and privileges, for, rather like our 19th-century peasantry whose core political value was the keeping of the land, Paddy the voter today is happiest when politicians leave him alone to live in a gentle, amoral, Mediterranean sort of way.

This desire means the only honest answer to any *cri de coeur* for youthful radicalism is that in Irish politics, with rare exceptions, youth will not have its fling. The UK and America may have a tradition of youthful leaders, such as Thatcher, Blair, Obama, Clinton and Cameron. We, however, prefer our leaders to resemble the elderly habitués of a bishops' conference. That FG soberside, Liam Cosgrave, even when he was young, was not youthful; Garret was a national grand-uncle; Jack Lynch came draped in the sepia of de Valera's Ireland; whilst Albert, though lively, was a child of the showband era ruling a country nudging the envelope of the Celtic Tiger. Lemass might have been in a hurry, but he was an old man. Haughey too was past his best by the time he secured power, though that might have been a good thing. Mr Bruton, though youngish in years, was a figure who gave the impression of a man who would have been more at home within the Irish Parliamentary Party. Bertie Ahern was seen to be a man who belonged to a youthful age, but he too was a creature who resided intellectually in the age of putting posters of de Valera up by gaslight. As for Enda, he is a child of flaming turf sods and Liam Cosgrave.

So, should a young Paddy Mac come trotting in the door planning to shake the thing up, well, you can forget about that, for young men in a hurry come to a bad end in the land of 'whoa, what's your hurry, son?' Instead, Paddy Mac must learn from, and accept, the Bertie Ahern School of Political Apprenticeship, where the excited, newly elected TDs cool their heels for a decade on the backbenches, serve a five-year apprenticeship as a committee chairperson, a further five to ten years as a junior minister and then, 25 years after entering the House, emerge as bright, reforming new ministers. Paddy Machiavelli should note in this regard that whilst Michael Noonan may never be Taoiseach, he is an apt role model for another critical trait that is required for an Irish Dear Leader. If you want to be Taoiseach in Ireland, you must have a capacity for endurance beyond a level that is healthy. The importance of this trait was epitomised by the sight, in the wake of what was supposed to be one of the most revolutionary elections in the history of the State, of Noonan, two decades after he accused Ray MacSharry of engaging in 'grand larceny' of FG policies in the 1987 budget, dominating the election debate. Since that time, when Ronald Reagan was the US President, the Iron Curtain has fallen and China has embraced capitalism. But, when it comes to personnel at least, little has changed in the Irish political 'Big House'.

Paddy Machiavelli might, like Adam in the Garden of Eden, be tempted by the claims, generally by a bored media, that Ireland needs a youthful politician who will embrace an innovative radical agenda. One glimpse at his electorate should convince Paddy Mac that such notions are fool's gold. Instead, that Chinese school of yogic patience where, if you sit by the riverside for a sufficiently long period of time, you see the bodies of all your enemies float by is the surest route to the great prize for our man.

Mr Noonan of course is not the only case study in the virtues of endurance. The current Dear Leader, Enda, is younger in years than Mr Noonan. But when Enda first skipped onto the national stage, Gerald Ford was the President of the US, Harold Wilson had just defeated Ted Heath and had become Prime Minister of the UK, Margaret Thatcher was the new leader of the Tories, and the final ashes of the Vietnam War were still smoking. So, while Mr Noonan certainly looks older, Mr Kenny has displayed an even greater capacity for endurance; mind you, many would say this was facilitated by the fact that Mr Kenny was 'lightly raced' for the first three of his five decades in the Dáil.

Paddy Machiavelli would be wise to note that one little-observed example of Enda's capacity for endurance was his decision to remain as leader of FG after 2007. While Pat Rabbitte might have left the leadership of Labour as swiftly as decorum allowed, Enda, on the other hand, after four decades of peripherality, was not for turning. Intriguingly, Enda's resilience is a trait that is shared by very different leaders. This example was set by the bon viveur Mr Haughey, who spent years on the chicken-and-chips circuit, rebuilding his career after the Arms Trial. Similarly, Enda, throughout his time in opposition, spent night after night in places like the tiny Laois hamlet of Clonygowan, staying up until three in the morning four nights a week, rebuilding a shattered party brick by brick.

We know Enda has the sort of resilience that is only rivalled by the capacity of a troop of scrap-iron merchants who have moved into a designated heritage area of outstanding scenic beauty to refuse all pleas to move on, please. But, whilst resilience can be easily mocked, Paddy Mac would be wise to avoid the common error of underrating the importance of that quality. Mr Kenny now spends his nights in far grander locations than Clonygowan, but it was the training provided by nights in such hamlets which honed the character traits that serve him so well in Washington or Europe. Paddy Machiavelli might not send Enda out to compete on 'Mastermind', but few politicians possess the utter determination, the will to power and the capacity for adversity that allowed him to engage in the apparently fruitless pursuit of a Bertie who was still the most popular Irish politician since Daniel O'Connell.

In recalling the task that Kenny faced, we should not forget that he was taking on an economic visionary and a peace-making statesman who had the ear of US presidents and British prime ministers. Indeed, had Bertie wanted a small bauble called the Presidency of Europe it was also his, but, such was his power and his greatness, Bertie turned it down as casually as a waiter might refuse a five-cent tip. In the end though, success in politics and life is often, if not always, down to issues of character. Enda is no intellectual, but, in his case, endurance was the outward symptom of an inner fortitude that allowed him to continue the fight even when every other sane person concluded that the war was lost. Indeed, Enda will continue the fight even when Enda himself does not quite know what the war is, why he is fighting it or what side he should be on.

So, endurance, resilience and some luck mean that Paddy Mac is almost there. But, the moment when it becomes clear that the current Dear Leader is sick — perhaps to the point of political death — is the time of clearest danger for Paddy Machiavelli. Politicians may be instinctive sole traders, but the one occasion that they flock together is when the fine carrion scent of change is in the air. At such times, they gather in small flocks, beside the stricken leader, watching with inquiring, bright, acquisitive, indifferent eyes as the broken form, lying on its knees, moos softly as it struggles to lift its head. Before he gets too content with himself, Paddy Mac should note, however, that the lead-up to the death of the Dear Leader contains all sorts of hidden traps. This is particularly the case should he choose to force the issue, for it may be that the Dear Leader is not half as sick as the ambitious plotters hope he is.

It is unfortunate if this is only uncovered when the plot to behead him fails. And, in this regard, the most critical thing our Aspirant Prince must understand is that should he attempt to take out a Dear Leader against his will, he is playing with a rigged deck of cards. The great advantage that the Dear Leader holds is the hard currency of power called patronage. It is not just that he has ministries, junior ministries, committee chairs and vice chairs. More important still, he has the invisible power to promise to confer future grace and favour on those who do not currently possess such delights. In contrast, those who would challenge the leader have nothing other than the thin gruel of idealism to offer. What can any over-ambitious Aspirant Prince offer the beneficiaries of the existing Dear Leader's regime except the holding of what they already have? And even that is undermined by the reality that if Paddy Machiavelli is to gather sufficient support to challenge the current scrawny lion king, he can only offer those who do not have office the 'possibility' of securing the posts held by those already in office.

This strategic advantage is not merely applicable to heads of government. The happy success of Enda Kenny shows the invisible strength of power, even when it is of the diluted sort retained by an opposition leader. In looking at the failed *coup d'état* of the innocents in 2010, it is, in retrospect, clear that the first fundamental error occurred when, in an attempt to destroy the Dear Leader's confidence, 10 of Enda's frontbench resigned. The innocents might have thought that this would see Dear Leader Enda collapse in a heap. But this move actually strengthened his hand, for apart from showing Dear Leader Enda the full hand of his enemy, suddenly, ten vacancies existed. And, at that moment, 20 of the stupidest FG TDs

realised that whatever chance they might have of securing jobs were
Enda to win, why on earth would they support the side who would
immediately return to those frontbench seats if they won?

Despite his best intentions, there are times where Paddy Mac
must at least touch the fingers of treason. This is most likely when
the nation is flirting with the sort of bankruptcy where the middle
classes are storing guns up in the attic, or planning to vote for
Labour. For Paddy Mac, the moment when it is clear that the king
is not in the best of shape is signified by the arrival of a gathering
of new friends. The wise Aspirant Prince must play an utterly cold
game with such 'allies', for few are more faithless and fickle than
those who would attempt to seduce you with the proposition that
you might take a dagger to the Dear Leader. Paddy Mac therefore
must treat these 'friends' with the utmost circumspection, for
when they attempt to whet his beak for digging, they are thinking
only of dipping their own beaks. Paddy Machiavelli will note, if
he is wise, that the greatest flaw in the late Brian Lenihan was that
he was too patient and too open with the plotters who wished to
take poor Biffo out. It is doubtful that the finance minister ever
really planned to shank Brian Cowen, for his disposition was
ultimately too gentle for such affairs. And, besides, he was rather
too busy to engage in courtly power games. But the same pleasant
disposition — that desire to agree and to sympathise and to send
everyone away happy — meant that he at least gave the appearance
of acquiescence to the designs of desperate and, in some few cases,
driven men.

The problem is that, just as pleasant generals send men out
to be executed, those who privately acquiesce with plotters and
then publicly denounce them are never forgiven. This again is
epitomised by the fate of Mr Lenihan, for when Biffo went, despite
Lenihan's status as the living ghost of Michael Collins, he could not
win the support of even one-third of his own party. It represented
some change for a party which six months earlier was waiting with
the tongues hanging out of them for Lenihan to declare and save
their skins. In fairness, Lenihan was not the only *ingénue* in such
affairs. During the run-up to the leadership race of 1979, Haughey

confidently predicted that he would win by a country mile. It took one of his rougher backbenchers to inform the aspirant Dear Leader that 'Jaysus, boss, you're the worst judge of fucking men I ever knew.'

But, whilst the Aspirant Prince should never talk treason unless he is determined to commit it, that is not to say he should walk away from all disloyal talk. After all, there is no harm in attempting, as a loyal cabinet member, to gauge the mood of the party. Paddy Mac, though, should not speak during such discussions. He must instead look sad and empathetic, but also vaguely distant. If he is to speak, the words should consist of gnomic riddles about the pointlessness of throwing sticks at an apple that is ready to fall, lest someone accidentally get hurt. There is no need to say anything more, though, for simply by meeting and tolerating bad company, the dangerous dance of mutual desire has begun.

In seeking to remove a Dear Leader it is equally important not to show too little desire once the move has been made. Richard 'the lesser' Bruton provides our Aspirant Prince with a critical example of this. One of the more intriguing features of the leadership challenge of 2010 was the ongoing spectacle where Bruton giggled like a nervous schoolgirl whenever the prospect of victory was raised. It was, to put it mildly, unconvincing. For some in FG, it was enough to swing the vote and, in truth, when in the wake of Kenny's victory he was ushered back onto the Dear Leader's frontbench under Enda's protective wing, Richard almost appeared to be relieved by his defeat.

By now Paddy Mac must be wondering just how the successful Irish *coup d'état* where you actually dispose of the Dear Leader is secured? The first and most critical element of the successful Irish *coup d'état* is that it is not attempted. Paddy Machiavelli should forget feverish plots, stirring speeches and all that romantic rot. The truth of the matter is that Irish Dear Leaders die in their beds surrounded by sorrowing political colleagues whose assiduousness in testing the Dear Leader's pulse is informed by their own, as distinct from the Dear Leader's, interests. Waiting for the Dear Leader to finally let go can be frustrating, but when it comes to the departure, Paddy Mac would be wise to note — as with so many other issues — that the electorate make the decision for you. That is particularly the case in Fine Gael and Labour, whose leaders tend to be somewhat lacking in the desire to stay in power. The voters finished off Garret and Liam Cosgrave directly, and did for Alan Dukes, courtesy of the Trojan horse of Austin Currie. Dick Spring resigned after the Adi Roche Presidential election campaign that, frankly, would have probably persuaded Churchill that the jig was up. Ruairí Quinn left because he, understandably, was simply sick at heart after battling with a Bertie who was in his pomp for five years. It was too long a sentence for any man, as Pat Rabbitte found to his own cost after five more years of playing handball against a haystack with the somewhat more degraded version. Albert was a casualty of the execrable fates, and even Reynolds, days after resigning, was already pining for the leadership that had been nipped away from his temporarily insensible form by that perky young fox Bertie.

If Paddy Machiavelli is still seeking to try his luck, he should note that the perfect template was set by Albert Reynolds. Albert and good timing were normally mutually exclusive. However, on this occasion, Albert timed his challenge to that point where Mr Haughey was still strong enough to defeat Albert the first time, but not strong enough to withstand a second assault on the citadel. More important still, Mr Haughey knew this to be the truth. All he wanted was to go out with dignity ... as if that ever happens to deposed Dear Leaders! Reynolds and everyone else knew well that this was the case, but Albert, by drawing the sword first, proved that not all political clichés are right. He who wields the dagger does sometimes get to wear the crown. Timing was everything, for Albert was waving happily at the people within a year. Call it wrong, as the poor doleful knights in Fine Gael are finding out, and you may be out in the cold for a decade. Micheál Martin curiously enough pulled off a similar trick with poor Biffo, though in truth there wasn't too much of the FF estate left by the time nice Micheál took his courage in his politically manicured hands.

Outside of the success of Albert, the Haughey endgame does, however, provide Paddy Mac with the perfect template for the fall of Dear Leaders. Mr Haughey's unparalleled Tony Soprano-style capacity to inspire the sort of fear that provoked grown senators to walk into doors and apologise for damaging the varnish, meant the power and grace of this Renaissance prince — where wealth mingled with intellect — intrigued an entire society. It has to be said that when it comes to this latter-day Irish Medici's record in the art of war, Haughey was blessed in enemies like David Andrews and somewhat more unlucky in friends like Pee Flynn. But, aided by the mansion, the island and the yacht, when he had to frighten enemies he did it well. Then, in the final months, it all fell away in the manner that a suit no longer fits an old man. Suddenly, like an old scarecrow, the Sun King of FF was being bowled over by every summer zephyr. The cruelty of the world you see is that whilst power arrives upon the Dear Leader almost invisibly, it departs in the ghostly manner of some forgotten nightmare. So it was that when Haughey became a political scarecrow, he was doing far less wrong than when he was in his pomp. But, just like 'honest' Jack, when the magic fled, it did not matter. The world he lived in had outpaced the Prince, his friends were no longer loyal and, when that occurred, the Dear Leader himself, half knowing it was time to go, was almost relieved by his execution.

The fate of Haughey should not seduce our cunning Aspirant Prince into taking the Albert approach. Far from being that spectre tapping his scythe, whispering, 'Are you ready to be going yet?' Paddy Mac should instead become the Dear Leader's comforter in old age. Apart from anything else, such a decision will enhance Paddy Machiavelli's reputation for loyalty. So, he will become that ever-available arm that is placed around the shoulders of the doting old king and a private source of assurance that all, ultimately, is well with the mutinous crew. Paddy Mac will then wait patiently until the point where all support for the Dear Leader has been eroded; he will place a gentle arm around his shoulders and then tell him — as his most trusted consigliere — that it is time 'to protect your legacy'.

Ironically, the perfect transfer of power, as it is practised in Irish politics, occurred between Bertie and Biffo, for by the time the exchange occurred, the ward boss had been hollowed out to a husk. The ease of the transfer was undoubtedly facilitated by Bertie's belief that there was no way that Biffo was in any way a match for the great shapeshifter. Given that Mr Cowen dawdled towards the great opportunity with all the enthusiasm of Shakespeare's slothful schoolboy, Mr Ahern was undoubtedly right in suspecting that poor Biffo would not take too much of the sheen off the ward boss's valedictory lustre. Indeed, he was accurate by a margin that even Bertie somewhat regrets.

It might seem strange that when it comes to securing the succession, Paddy Mac should set his trajectory to be elected at a time of difficulty. But, should he become leader whilst his party is in government, Paddy Mac will always walk in the shadow of the man he replaces. Taking the helm at a time of trouble is a different matter, for he should, hopefully, shine against the backdrop of the Augean stable he has inherited. The decision to seize the crown at this point also proves that he is a noble soul. Far from being personally ambitious, he has decided to take on a great burden. It will also help that the lazily ambitious will not be too keen to take Paddy Mac on at this point, in the hope that he might be an interim leader. Paddy Machiavelli should do little to disabuse them of such a notion, for if they want to fall victim to the common fallacy that it is easy to remove a leader, they are welcome to it. He knows that, having finally shifted one, nothing could be further from the truth.

At this final stage, Paddy Mac must clearly indicate what kind of leader he plans to be. We have noted earlier on that if a Dear Leader is nice in his treatment of coalition partners, it sends out positive signals about his genuine kindliness. It also does Paddy Mac no harm to assure his party that he intends to be a chairman rather than a chief, for up to the moment he becomes the Dear Leader, all his colleagues will still believe they are his equal. Such innocents must, therefore, be seduced by the prospect of parity and respect, whereby both he and they will discuss the affairs of the nation long into the night, with their advice being taken, of course. This, it must be said, will immediately cease when he becomes leader, for in politics, as in life, men prefer to abdicate responsibility. Consequently, from the moment the mantle of office falls upon Paddy Mac's shoulders, he is on his own.

So, now Paddy Machiavelli is prepared to make the final leap. Mind you, by this stage, given his aged condition, 'leap' is a tad excessive. Instead, the leader-in-waiting often bears a closer resemblance to the aged priests in Father Ted's over-75s soccer tournament. But this actually means that Paddy Machiavelli is perfect, for he is alive enough to do the job and wise enough to pose a threat to no one. However, as the cheering ends and he steps into the place of isolation that every Dear Leader must enter, the interior monologue will begin:

Who are you?

How did you get here?

And why on earth do you want to be here anyway?

So, what are you to do next, Paddy Mac? Well, that is where we leave the stage, but don't worry. The grinning mandarins gliding towards you with those rustling sheaves of paper will tell you that.

Epilogue ～

THE FAULT, DEAR CITIZEN, LIES NOT IN THE STARS (OR OUR POLITICIANS), BUT IN US

If military virtue were exhausted, this has happened because the old order of things was not good, and none of us have known how to find a new one.

It is popular in Irish life — particularly amongst people whose motives are often ambivalent — to claim that politics is pointless: they are all the same and there is no point in trying to change 'them'. The journey and the compromises necessary to secure power, as described in *Paddy Machiavelli*, certainly go a long way towards justifying such anomie. However, when the republic dreamed of by Pearse, and secured by force of arms by Michael Collins, ends up sleeping in a fiscal gutter beneath a starless sky, the embrace of existential indifference is surely not a sufficient response to our woes. It is important to note in this regard that, despite their flaws, the basically good-natured Irish politicians are often redeemable. Another key lesson we should learn from *Paddy Machiavelli* is that Irish politicians are not generically corrupt. Instead, at worst, they are ideological tricksters who trade on the gullibility of our greedy electorate. That said, politics in Ireland is suffering from a second cousin of corruption. Unlike the florid age of Haughey, we do not have the *faux* Gatsby efflorescence of horses, yachts, islands, artistic pretensions, mistresses, Gandon mansions, jewel-encrusted daggers and a cast of political clowns. Instead, the subtle flaw that has broken the Republic is a strain of opportunistic political cowardice, which, though not classically corrupt, contains in its appeasing DNA all the same devastating consequences.

Such a statement of claim may appear harsh. But for those who do not believe the warp of Irish politics is crooked to some degree, the proof of the pudding lies in the sawdust we are now eating. One of the iron laws of corruption is that it inevitably leads to the destruction of the state. Be it fascist Germany or Berlusconi's Italy, corruption is the wound in the stomach that bleeds until the state falls, apparently apropos of nothing. This is why progressive countries react strongly against malfeasance, for they are informed by the impetus to protect themselves. In contrast, there is something amiss in a 'democracy' that can celebrate a Lowry and exile a McDowell.

This reality means it is genuinely important that we realise it is not because of the malice of the fates or some German-inspired 'stab in the back' that Ireland has become an Ophelia decked out in the tattered wedding dress of the Tiger years. Those who are tempted by such fairy tales should remember this was an independent state which could still make its own decisions right up to our great fall. Once this argument is accepted, then the pathos where a state which up to a decade ago was a sophisticated functioning democracy ended up being a satrap of the Troika is the proof that our forms of governance are, at some fundamental level, flawed.

Our current debacle is all the more tragic because Paddy Mac does want to do good things. Rather like Rousseau's belief that all men are born free but are everywhere in chains, the great puzzle is why so often he ends up in a very different place. In other times, when we were too poor to become bankrupt, the susceptibility of our dreamy politicians to vice — and more often to simple foolishness — did not matter so much. However, Ireland is swimming in much deeper waters than the bucolic era of 'Hall's Pictorial Weekly'. Such indeed is the depth of the waters we now move in that the last episode of the politics of Ballymagash shorted poor Paddy the taxpayer for €63 billion.

If Ireland is ever to have a future beyond debt slavery, we and Paddy Mac need to examine our flaws more closely. In particular, we should ask if we set ourselves up to fail via the 'wink and elbow language of delight' in Irish politics, where the seduction of the voters is secured at the expense of the good governance of the State. Such a flaw is not just Paddy Mac's fault, for whilst Paddy the voter might not like to hear it, the politicians we choose tell us a great deal about ourselves. And if we look coldly at what has happened to this State, it has to be said that the Irish people are not as innocent as their statement of claim suggests. Fairness dictates that in this regard we are no different from others, for, across the world, people look to their own self-interest and then, in a classic triumph of the id, are shocked when everyone else behaves as they do. But our politicians identify, groom, seduce and prey upon these traits to a far greater extent than is the case among our Nordic neighbours, and we are the ones who let them do it.

Ironically, this is not always a safe course of action for our politicians since, like all libertines, when we wake up after the party, Paddy often does not like to see himself as he really is. This normally dormant trait, where the id sees its real face and revolts, was the critical factor in the uniquely vehement nature of our destruction of FF. That harrowing event where, like Dorian Gray stabbing his own portrait, the electorate sacrificed FF to expiate our sins suggests that there is a more complex relationship at play between the voters and their leaders than the conventional servants-and-master approach where, like a political version of *Fifty Shades of Grey*, the outwardly submissive voter is the secret master.

When it comes to the Irish fall, as in *Lord of the Flies*, evil circumstances, allied to flaws in the character of politicians and the people, bore us all on a course we could not resist, until we finally made a sacrifice out of a poor Biffo, just as the civilised Troika landed, scratching their disapproving heads. We are, of course, now trying to be good. But, like the dry alcoholic, Paddy retains a hankering for the livid taste of badness. Some will say that the best way to definitively change Paddy's flawed nature is by reforms such as compulsory voting, the list system or the abolition of the PR system. But, if the tales of Paddy Mac should teach us anything, it is that the only way our State can be reformed is if the Irish people themselves decide they want to be governed in a better way. Given that half a millennium after Machiavelli's eloquent plea for change Italy still hankers for a Berlusconi, the odds are not good.

They are, however, not impossible either, for we do sometimes elect a Lemass or a Garret or a Donogh O'Malley. Too often, though, they are the creatures of accident rather than design. Intriguingly, when it comes to these strange political creatures, often the citizenry are happier under their austere rule. However, in the long run, a system that is not at ease with aspiration does not appear to know how to keep the idealistic politician. We are instead too quick to slip back into our old slapdash indolence where, to paraphrase John A Kelly, the height of our ambition is to keep the constitutional bodywork we inherited from the Empire ticking over. Of course, when the crisis returns, we abandon our Berlusconis, but it is always a little too late. In this regard, perhaps the central lesson of our tale about the rise of Paddy Machiavelli is that whilst the old way of doing things is comfortable enough and often entertaining too, it is gone past time to develop different political traits and characteristics if we are to build a better country for our children.

Bill Federer
U.S. U.S. Author.
Historian.